"What goes on inside a primary classroom will not remain a mystery to parents if they read this vivid report of one year in the life of a teacher of four- and five-year-old children. The author's love for all the children shines through as she describes their learning successes—and some failures."
—*Los Angeles Times*

"A realistic and thought-provoking tour of a highly successful teacher's year-long journey and inner conversation. Montessori is her methodology; her love is practicing exactly how she believes it should be."
—Virginia McHugh, Executive Director, Association Montessori International

"Lillard is a talented and open diarist and educator. Her account is rich, filled with insights, beliefs, and misgivings."
—*The Review of Education*

"A highly readable and instructive look at how one teaches academic and social skills to four- and five-year-olds."
—*Washington Post*

"An engaging book . . . written in a style which reflects the depth of emotion a teacher experiences while trying to help a group of children reach their academic and social potential."
—*Curriculum Review*

"This is not just a slice of classroom life; not just another vindication of Montessori principles at work. It is a chronicle of dedication, a neo-realist drama unfolding the self-sustaining optimism of a good teacher who will aid the developmental challenges she finds in others and herself."

—*North American Montessori Teachers Association Quarterly*

"Lillard is an inspiring master teacher, a true rarity. Her book should be read by every teacher and every teacher-in-training. It should be on the shelf of every college of education in the country."

—Dr. Sylvia O. Richardson, Distinguished Professor of Communication Sciences and Emeritus Professor of Pediatrics, University of South Florida

"I always use this wonderful book in my courses for student teachers. It helps them understand what it is to be a reflective teacher and provides a model for adapting curriculum to the individual needs and interests of children."

—Martha B. Bronson, Boston College School of Education

Montessori
in the Classroom

PAULA

POLK

LILLARD

Montessori in the Classroom

**A Teacher's Account
of How Children Really Learn**

Foreword by JEROME BRUNER
With a new introduction by the author

SCHOCKEN BOOKS   NEW YORK

Introduction copyright © 1997 by Paula Polk Lillard
Copyright © 1980 by Schocken Books Inc.

Originally published in hardcover by Schocken Books Inc.,
New York, as *Children Learning* in 1980.

Library of Congress Cataloging-in-Publication Data

Lillard, Paula Polk.
    Montessori in the classroom : a teacher's account of how
children really learn/Paula Polk Lillard; foreword by
Jerome Bruner ; with a new introduction by the author.
      p.   cm.
    Rev. ed. of: Children learning. 1980.
    Includes index.
    ISBN 0-8052-1087-3 (pbk.)
    1. Kindergarten—United States.   2. Child develop-
ment—United States.   3. Teacher-student relationships—
United States.   4. Lillard, Paula Polk—Diaries.
5. Teachers—United States—Diaries.   6. Montessori
method of education—United States.   I. Lillard, Paula
Polk. Children Learning.   II. Title.
  LB1205.L55   1997
  372. 1102—dc21   97-3290
                                                      CIP

For the protection of the children, names have been altered.
Throughout the text "he" is often used to refer to children of
both genders. This usage reflects the rules of style at the time
of original publication and is not meant to be discriminatory.

Random House Web Address: http://www.randomhouse.com

Book design by M. Kristen Bearse
Illustrations by Lynn Lillard

Printed in the United States of America

Revised Edition
9 8 7 6 5

To
"my" children
and their parents

Contents

Introduction

Re-reading these journal entries almost two decades after writing them has had a humbling effect on me. I am in awe of the children's learning and the resilience, courage, and intuition with which they direct their own formation. As I revisit my experiences as a younger teacher, I am better able to identify my strengths and weaknesses—a feat of self-knowledge so much easier to accomplish in retrospect.

Reflecting on that long-ago classroom experience is especially meaningful to me now, as I retired from active teaching last year to become principal of a Montessori school with a student body of approximately one hundred and seventy children. I lead a parent-infant class once a week, and I am often in classrooms either observing, temporarily teaching a class, or taking visitors on a tour of the school. My sense of purpose and dedication to the children is renewed as I greet them in the hallway each morning, their faces glowing with eagerness and anticipation of a new day. I love and feel responsible for each one.

This is not, however, the same as being a classroom teacher. There is a depth of intimacy and trust in the ongoing daily relationship between teacher and child that I miss deeply. I may also be experiencing nostalgia for my younger years and missing the joy and rejuvenation of doing what I had come to do best in my life.

In its place there is a new challenge before me and with it the uncertainty, even fear, of the unknown. Part of me wants to retreat before this new demand in my life and go back to the classroom, to the known and the comfortable where the challenges are familiar, and therefore less stressful.

That time is past, however, and I know that life has led me to the place where I now belong. I am grateful that I am still an essential part of children's lives, contributing to them now from a different perspective. I am a school principal today because, shortly after setting down the journal entries that make up this book, I left the independent day school depicted in it. Together with one of my daughters, who is a Montessori teacher, and another teaching colleague from the school discussed in this book, I co-founded a Montessori preschool. Having proven to myself that Montessori principles can be applied successfully to a kindergarten setting within the regular school system, I wanted to see what the benefits would be when Montessori education was given to preschool children in its complete form: in other words, in a setting where it would be possible to follow Montessori's specific guidelines in their entirety.

The first few years in my own Montessori school were challenging ones. Developing an authentic Montessori primary class of twenty-five children ages three to six years is a very different experience from teaching twenty children ages five and six (which is the kindergarten classroom described in this book). Montessori is not a remedial form of education. It is based on meeting the needs of children for their best development from their earliest years, preferably from birth but certainly by their third or fourth year. Therefore, originating a new Montessori class ideally entails beginning with approximately eight three- and four-year-old children, and adding eight new three-year-olds each year until a full class of twenty-five children, ages three to six years, is established. But when this gradual process is followed, there are no older, experienced children during the first two years who can set the routines of the class and serve as models for the younger children. Three-year-olds learn primarily by example, not by direct verbal instruction; that is, they learn by watching the six year olds. This means that starting a new Montessori class is always a difficult task for the teacher, and the results are not immediate.

I often despaired during those early years. My disappointment was not with Montessori. I knew that this educational approach worked because I had witnessed many successfully functioning Montessori classrooms. I was discouraged with myself. What I remember most vividly is that too often the children did not use their freedom productively. They wasted their time in aimless activity or "busy work." Worse, they bothered other children who were productively occupied. I was not getting the concentration, focused work, and repetition that my training courses had emphasized and that I myself had seen in established Montessori classrooms. I struggled with the nagging doubt that I was not capable of becoming a good Montessori teacher.

Fortunately, my daughter Lynn had received wise counsel from several experienced Montessori teachers in her first years of teaching. After observing my classroom for several days, she outlined a plan that gave freedom to individual children very gradually. This carefully thought-out granting of freedom was based solely on the children's ability to control their actions and behave responsibly. Lynn's plan involved keeping the majority of the children close to me in directed group activity. Only those few children who had demonstrated their ability to work independently were allowed the freedom of the room and a choice from among those materials that I had previously presented to them. Gradually, over the weeks and months, the circle of children who had to remain with me grew smaller, until eventually only one or two children needed such consistent attention.

After three years had passed, I noticed a significant change in the smooth functioning of my classroom. My original three-year-olds had become five- and six-year-olds, and were therefore the oldest children in the class. The youngest children, at long last, had mature, responsible class leaders to follow. It made all the difference.

The social development of children in an authentic Montessori classroom is truly astonishing. Freed from the forced competition of classrooms where children are all the same age, the younger children accept assistance from the older ones and the older children help the younger ones in a natural, matter-of-fact manner. In a three-year period children go from being the youngest in the class to being the oldest. They therefore have the opportunity to experience alternating roles of giving to others and receiving from them.

Equally important, children and teachers are never forced to accomplish certain academic tasks in a one-year time frame. Children have an ample three-year period in which to explore and discover all the materials of the environment that aid in their development. There is sufficient time for a particular child's slower development in one area to catch up to his or her faster development in other areas: for example, for handwriting skills to match numerical understanding, or for the ability to combine sound with symbol to equal visual memory of map puzzle pieces. Given this relaxed time frame, virtually all the children reach levels of academic achievement beyond those expected in even first and second grade classrooms.

This unusual progress is due to the indirect preparation for future learning that takes place in the Montessori classroom. Three year olds develop organizational and motor-planning skills by carrying out, in an orderly manner, adult activities. These activities are based on those that children witness in their homes and society, and that they intuitively wish to copy: washing, ironing, polishing, sweeping, mopping, plant care, flower arranging, food preparation, baking, etc. This indirect preparation enables three year olds in a well-functioning Montessori classroom to develop the hand control and knowledge of letter formation that make it possible for them to write in cursive letters by age four without having to undergo a laborious practice period. Because they learn cursive letters, they do not experience the frustration of the constant letter reversals mentioned in my kindergarten journal entries.

When Montessori children use each Montessori material at the age-appropriate time, they use the same materials over and over again, in spontaneous repetition. In this way, they gradually build an in-depth understanding of the underlying principles that the materials represent. With these inner "keys to knowledge," they are able to explore and make their own discoveries in the environment to a far greater degree than the kindergarten children described in the following pages. In fact, not just one or two unusually talented children, but most of my Montessori students every year, react to the classroom with the same high level of independence and personal initiative as Lee, the "gifted" child described here, in the last half of Chapter 5.

Whereas Lee stood out as "different" in my kindergarten class, children whose intellectual capabilities were equally extraordinary in my Montessori classroom did not. They blended in with the other children in a natural way. Similarly, children like Timmy (see the first half of Chapter 5), who were developing learning patterns that do not readily discover the sound-to-symbol relationship required in our literacy-based culture, also fit into the classroom without special notice. I just had to make certain that these slower-developing children used the Sandpaper Letters and other preparatory materials for written language with me, or with an older child, on a daily basis. In other words, these children required more directed help in their area of weakness. They were, however, using the same "hands-on" materials as the other children, and they seldom appeared aware, or concerned, that they had to work harder to reach a sufficient level of understanding.

After witnessing the success of Montessori education for three- to six-year-old children, my co-founders and I began to wonder what would happen if we implemented Montessori's entire comprehensive plan for the development of the child. As early as the 1930s, Maria Montessori had begun to extend her work, principally at her school in Laren, Holland, to include elementary age children. Subsequently (when she returned to Europe after being interned in India as an Italian national for the duration of World War II), she also focused her attention on the child's first years of life: from birth to age three. What if we began our school with parent-infant classes, starting with two-month-old infants, and established Young Children's Communities for eighteen-month-old to almost three-year-old children, as Montessori's discoveries suggested? What if we also continued with Montessori's plan for older childhood, the years from six to twelve, by starting elementary classes for six- to nine-year-olds, and nine- to twelve-year-olds? In the years that followed, we did indeed follow this course, establishing classrooms for both younger and older children.

In our weekly one-hour parent-infant classes, we suggest to parents effective ways of "educating" their infants. All children strive from birth to develop themselves in four main areas: coordinated movement, independence, language (the basis for human thought as well as communication), and will (the ability to control and discipline one's actions). When Montessori applied her unusual powers of observation and insight to the self-formation of infants, she discovered ways of aiding them in these developmental goals that were equally as powerful as those that she had established for older children. Our experience is that parents who apply her guidelines in their homes find that their children not only develop their capabilities in unique ways, but they also appear far happier, are less demanding, and are easier to live with than their peers who have not had similar assistance in their development.

When I take visitors to our early childhood classrooms, they are usually reluctant to leave them and move on to the older children. I believe that this is because adults are unaccustomed to seeing such little children—barely out of diapers, some speaking only a few words—with such peaceful and purposeful demeanors, moving with care and concentration, and accomplishing tasks far beyond our adult expectations of them. The sight of a twenty-two-month-old spreading biscuit dough with a rolling pin, using a cutter to form the shapes, and putting the biscuits into a hot toaster oven for baking, all without assistance or an untoward incident, is a scene that is not soon forgotten. The look of pride and self-satisfaction on the child's face after such an accomplishment is a clear indication that inner development is taking place. At the same time, there is a renewed energy within the child. He or she continues spontaneously to make new discoveries and to explore the environment, whether to look at a book in the library corner, to work on a puzzle, or to paint a picture. (Yes, twenty-month-olds can paint "pictures" independently—putting on their own aprons, gathering their materials, carefully holding the brush, making a painting that pleases them, and attaching it with a clothespin to the drying rack—all with minimal need for assistance.)

Just as surprising to adults, these very young children spontaneously clean up for each other when accidents happen, learn to wait their turn, walk around each other without bumping, and share the attention of the adult. At the end of the morning, the children greet their parents or caregivers with the same eagerness and enthusiasm they had earlier shown their peers and teacher when entering the classroom at the beginning of the morning.

Visitors to our elementary levels are also surprised by the behavior and activities of the six- to twelve-year-old children. Invariably, they comment first on the peace and lack of pressure in these classrooms. The children are industrious and energetic as they go about their research projects together, most often in groups of two, three, or four. Yet their manner is unhurried and relaxed. Though constantly conversing about what they are doing, their voices are moderate and they are concentrating. The level of their written work, whether solving problems in cube root, completing a time-line on the ways in which human beings throughout the ages have met their fundamental needs for food, or completing a science experiment, is unusual for elementary students. They write in beautifully formed cursive letters: a consequence of their Metal Inset work and tracing of Sandpaper Letters as three-year-olds. More often than not, the elementary children's reports and stories are accompanied by lovely illustrations. They can accomplish all this because of earlier activities that developed their hand control and because they enjoyed, from their earliest years, free access to art materials at all times and in every classroom.

Although their academic rigor is notable, what may be even more impressive is the degree of responsibility that the elementary children develop for their own learning. The students keep journals with them in their classroom throughout the day. They record their daily activities immediately after they have occurred, for example, "9:00 worked on my presidents' report with Tom and Jane, 10:30 presentation on the Tilt of the Axis of the Earth with Mrs. Bianca, 11:00 finished the song I composed with Betty on the Tone Bars." Once a week each child has an individual meeting with the teacher in which they review his or her journal along with completed written work and work-in-progress. Teacher and child discuss the student's use of time, any behavior issues that might need addressing, and other matters. The goal is not simply academic accomplishments, but the further development of the student as a complete human being. Because the teacher is with each student for a three-year period, a deep level of trust and commitment develops between them. The resulting opportunity for beneficial adult-to-child mentoring is unique.

Several years ago, we extended our school even further. We established a secondary level for twelve- to fourteen-year-old students. In response to the changes that take place within children themselves, Montessori education varies greatly at each developmental level of childhood. When young people reach the beginning of adult-formation, at approximately age twelve, they undergo yet another radical transformation. The child who was so confident and strong in later childhood becomes a self-conscious, vulnerable young person who is often filled with self-doubt, has difficulty concentrating, and lacks direction. It is a period reminiscent of the first year of life, when the infant's well-being is tenuous and he or she requires consistent adult attention.

The goal of the young person in this beginning stage of adulthood is to develop himself or herself as an individual ready to take a responsible place in adult society. To achieve this, Montessori believed that young people require several new educational approaches. As in the first period of life, they must have the full attention of adults. This time, however, parents alone cannot fulfill their children's needs. Students on the brink of adulthood must have a much closer and more constant relationship with an adult mentor who is not of their immediate family, one who can guide and serve them in their developmental aims. Whereas Montessori wanted to have large numbers of students in her elementary classes, even as many as thirty-five or more children to one teacher, at this level the ratio is more profitably as low as ten to fifteen students to each teacher.

Additionally, the student needs a smaller and more intimate peer group. This peer group must be completely trustworthy and supportive in order to give optimal help to the student in his or her self-formation as an adult.

The ideal educational environment for students who are beginning their adult-formation provides direct contact with the
working society of adults. Montessori wanted this working experience to cover many areas of production and commerce, and
specifically to include agriculture because of its pivotal role in
the establishment of human civilization. By experiencing first-
hand contact with working society, Montessori felt that young
people would better understand the problems that have developed in modern life and how to solve them, particularly the responsibility of human beings toward the natural environment
and the increase of human power through technology. At the
same time, the students are to receive thorough academic preparation. This will ensure that they have a sufficient foundation not
only for any career that they may choose for the immediate future but, in this world where more than one career is probable,
for a lifetime of further learning as well. Self-expression in the
arts and physical challenge in the out-of-doors help students of
this age, who are so doubtful of their own abilities, to develop
self-knowledge and build confidence in their uniqueness. Finally, Montessori believed that spending time in solitude and in
nature is vital for young people in the early years of their adult-
formation.

Montessori herself did not work extensively with adolescents
or university-age students. Because of this lack of consistent personal involvement, her ideas for a plan of education for the
planes of adulthood—the periods from twelve to eighteen years
and eighteen to twenty-four years—were never developed in the
detail with which she established her preschool and elementary
programs. She did, however, create an outline for aiding young
people in their adult self-formation based on the principles described above. We followed this outline, insofar as our resources
and circumstances allowed, in developing our own secondary
program, and the results have exceeded our expectations.

To date, graduates of our school have gone on to both public and private high schools, where they have maintained outstanding records not only in academic achievement but also in contributions to the overall life of their new schools. The attributes mentioned most often in connection with our students are an interest in learning, the ability to concentrate and persevere, the ability to get along well with others in team effort, and the capacity to think creatively, expressing thoughts clearly and logically when both writing and speaking.

Many of us were prepared well in kindergarten for elementary school, in elementary school for high school, and in high school for college. Academic achievement alone, however, did not prepare us for life. Montessori education, when properly implemented, does prepare students for life, and specifically life in the twenty-first century. How did Montessori, a physician who was born before the twentieth century began and died in the middle of it, develop an educational approach that prepares young people for the twenty-first century? The answer is elegant in its simplicity. She observed children, seeking to identify positive human behaviors in their interaction with their environment. These behaviors are universal tendencies that human beings have exhibited from our earliest days and through which we have built all human civilization.

Montessori designed educational environments, redesigning and refining them throughout her long life, to encourage these positive human behaviors. All classrooms where these human tendencies are stimulated could rightly be called "Montessori" environments, whether they have specific Montessori educational materials or not. Conversely, schools that have a full array of Montessori materials but in which these universal human behaviors are not understood are Montessori schools in name only.

When I first began working in education in the late 1960s, few people in the United States had heard of Montessori. By the 1980s, however, Montessori was a well-known form of preschool education and was increasingly being extended to the elementary school years. By the early 1990s, Montessori was established as a successful, innovative approach to education that includes both preschool and elementary children. Today, the new expansion in Montessori is taking place in the middle and high school years, and in both private and public school settings.

Montessori's unique focus on the development of each person as a complete human being from birth to maturity, a concept that by definition encompasses academic achievement, helps to explain its rapid recent growth. Throughout the twentieth century, education in the United States fluctuated between an emphasis on two seemingly polar opposites: personal development versus academic rigor. Montessori discovered the compatibility consistent in both approaches. She succeeded where others had failed because she did not develop her educational ideas and philosophy through abstract thinking alone. Instead, she observed young people of all ages and in different cultures throughout the world. She sought to understand what it was that they were seeking to accomplish in their self-formation. And then she devised methods and materials to assist them in their developmental goals.

In the journal entries that follow, you will find an honest account of my commitment to bringing Montessori's approach to children into a kindergarten classroom. You will be able to learn as I was learning, to witness good days and bad ones, and to see how children thrive in a Montessori world. In many ways this volume marks the beginning of my Montessori journey—one that continues still and to which I am more committed than ever. It is my hope that you will find both guidance and inspiration within these pages.

Paula Polk Lillard
February 1997

Foreword

This is a moving book, a deeply honest one. Paula Polk Lillard brings a compassionate intelligence to her task. Her care and curiosity shine on every page and inform the observations of the four- and five-year-olds in her charge. I thought as I read that if I could sense what constituted such caring intelligence, perhaps I could get a better sense of what makes a dedicated teacher. Perhaps, I thought, if I could look at the author of these diary entries as a figure in fiction, it would be a bit easier to describe what it was that made her as she is. How would one delineate a figure in a novel who spoke lines of the kind the author set down in her diary? After all, those lines were all I had. I have never seen Mrs. Lillard teach. What can one say then?

The first and most important thing about the entries is the sense they give of the delicate balance of the human condition and Paula Lillard's appreciation of human vulnerability, including her own, "I am totally exhausted, but feel I was helpful and things are back on the track. It is amazing how much chance seems to operate. . . ." She sees her teaching as a continuation of life, not as separate from it or privileged by right and tradition.

But then one soon realizes that the entries show an extraordinary confidence, even faith, in the children she is teaching. She never doubts their curiosity, their will to learn and to master, although she is often puzzled by the tactics needed to tap these sources of energy. A mathematical consultant tells her that five-year-olds cannot understand quantities in the thousands, and she blazes her indignation into a diary entry, noting that the games her children play give them a better intuitive grasp of quantity than the consultant could ever guess. (And her pedagogical games are indeed superb!)

She also believes that people, children included, like to work hard, even to the point of exhaustion at something that they feel they are mastering. One day her teacher-daughter, observing her mother's class, tells her that a certain lesson is not demanding as much of the children as they are capable of delivering. She raises the stakes so that they may feel the challenge of full-scale effort and delights when the children boast about how hard the job was that they completed.

Somehow, the writer of these diaries never seems to lose her sense of wonder or her capacity to be surprised. She has the art of sharing this with her pupils, of keeping things current and edged with possibility. Jack one day torments some other children in the class. She asks him in their presence, with genuine curiosity, why he is acting that way—wanting and expecting an answer that will satisfy her genuine curiosity. And he tells her: they disturb and distract him when they sit right next to him when he is trying to figure something out. And she says to the other children that they should be mindful of this and to Jack she offers the advice that it might be better if he made his own wishes clearer to the others rather than tormenting them. The diary entries recounting such events are without defensiveness, without self-justification, almost naked in their vulnerability.

Paula Lillard believes in the classroom as a community governed by mutual aid in support of individual effort. Sometimes it fails and you are the fool or the knave, but you can recover and get back on the track. She believes in goals and that harmonious pursuit of them is not always possible, but that the effort to get children working together is worth it. She really has an almost mystical belief in the energy that is released by working and playing hard—"the revitalizing fuel that makes development possible." And she sees it as her job to spark that fuel. "I am responsible for sparking that interest by introducing materials to which the children can respond." But there cannot be such "internal" discipline without there also being respect for others in the group. And the diary entries are replete with her triumphs and failures and her "I get very weary with this."

About learning itself, she has an interesting point to make.

> The development of language provides a good analogy. We don't wait to speak to babies in full sentences. We surround them with fully developed language from birth on. We are not concerned that they do not understand everything we say to them. It is enough that they appear interested and give us their full attention. Somehow, through this indirect preparation of being surrounded by fully developed language, children develop language for themselves. The same can be said about learning the concepts of space and time. . . . It is not necessary to wait until the children's understanding of space is fully developed to make maps of the world, any more than it is necessary to speak to them in sentences until they themselves can speak in sentences.

And so she tempts then on, almost like a Pied Piper with the aim of bringing her children to their full powers.

Finally, here is an entry that gives some sense of the humanity, tenderness, and toughness of this extraordinary diarist.

> Early in the morning, Joan had come to tell me that Jesse was "wound up like a tight spring," lashing out at everybody. Just as I was thinking "What a civilized scene," I saw Jesse reach over and start to scribble with a black marker on Ed's wooden

clay-board. "Is that the way you treat your school, Jesse?" I asked. He looked chagrined and shook his head, but we both knew it wouldn't be his last impulsive moment of the morning.

This is a book of a strong, wise, and sensitive teacher. It is a joy.

Jerome Bruner
Cambridge, Massachusetts
July 1980

Preface

This book is based on diaries kept over a period of three years. In these diaries I have attempted to take the reader inside the classroom and tell him what occurred there. Each day I took short notes on events as they happened. I made a special effort to transcribe the children's exact words when I considered them unusually revealing. After class I developed my daily notes into journal form. My purpose was to understand the developmental needs of children through detailed observation of them.

Diary entries from the last of these three years are presented here in Chapters 2–6. As background for these diary chapters, I have included an introductory chapter that relates my ideas on education.

The diaries describe a kindergarten class in which reading and mathematics, geography, and science are introduced successfully to four- and five-year-olds. Until very recently the main focus of traditional kindergartens was a program of socialized play and reading readiness. Today most children have one to two years of preschool experience before attending kindergarten. There is a growing conviction on the part of many parents and educators that children are ready for more intellectual stimulation than the historical approach provides.

My class is part of an independent day school with a population of approximately five hundred children. The school is based on educational goals of academic excellence and concern for each child's development. Each class within the school has set curriculum goals which the children are expected to meet before being passed on to the next grade.

The children described in the diary entries were not preselected for the classroom. The balance of applications and places available in these years enabled the school to accept all of the children who applied. For the most part the children are of average intelligence, although some are gifted and some have learning disabilities. Some of the children are from affluent homes, some are children of parents in the professions, and some are from families with minimal educational and financial background. The children are from varied cultural and religious backgrounds. Class size ranges from eighteen to twenty-one children, with the ideal size being twenty.

There was an assistant in the class described. This is not a requirement for the success of the program. However, it is particularly helpful to have another adult in the class in the beginning weeks of the school when the routines of class life are being established. In other years of teaching I have asked parent volunteers to serve in this capacity, and have found this to be a satisfactory solution.

Paula Folk Lillard

Acknowledgments

I wish to express my gratitude to my editor, Eva Glaser, herself a teacher, for her encouragement and support in this endeavor. Her wisdom and insight regarding children and their education have been invaluable to me both in my teaching and in my writing.

I thank my teaching colleagues for sharing with me the insight, courage, frustration, and joy that comprise the teaching experience.

I could not have completed the manuscript for this book in these summer months without the faith and support of my family and the generous help with manuscript reading and organization of my two daughters, Angel and Lynn.

I am grateful to Marge Melgaard, Library Director, Chicago Historical Society, for her expert help with manuscript preparation and typing.

"Childhood is unknown. Starting from the false idea one has of it, the farther one goes, the more one loses one's way. The wisest men concentrate on what it is important for men to know without considering what children are in a condition to learn. They are always seeking the man in the child without thinking of what he is before being a man. . . . Begin, then, by studying your pupils better. For most assuredly you do not know them at all."

Rousseau, *Emile*

Montessori
in the Classroom

ONE

On Education

What impresses me most about five-year-olds is their drive for development. The intensity of this drive continues to amaze me, no matter how often I observe it. It seems to come from nowhere, and gives even to four- and five-year-old children an incredible curiosity, energy, and ability to concentrate. This drive is most apparent in the children's curiosity about the world around them. They want to know all about everything. No matter what topic of the world I introduce in the classroom, the children show an initial interest in it. They take the new information and spontaneously make discoveries and connections with previous knowledge. This has tremendous implications for the teacher. The questions that five-year-olds ask in their quest for knowledge of the world can be traced to the age-old questions of mankind: Who am I? Where am I? Where am I going? The young child is a natural philosopher.

The children whom I have taught express their feelings about their internal world with the same intensity with which they explore their external world. This expression is not as easy to discern, however, for in the literal sense that I am using it, self-expression means expression *for* the self. The children do not necessarily seek to share their self-expression with others.

Self-expression seems to complete the circle of the children's contact with the world. No knowledge or experience of the world appears to be their own until they internalize it and reexpress it in their own way. This phenomenon is most apparent in the classroom in the pictures, stories, and reproductions in clay that the children spontaneously make. The young child is a natural artist.

It is apparent to me that independence is a necessity if the child's drive to develop is to be realized. It is equally apparent that children are striving for this independence. In the classroom, it is not unusual for a child to spend hours practicing with a Bow Frame in order to learn to tie his own shoes, or a Zipper Frame so that he can zip his own coat. However, in many of my five-year-olds the desire for independence has already been driven underground by discouraging adults or an alien environment. So far, I have taught no five-year-olds in whom it could not be reawakened, although in one instance (recounted in Chapter 2) it took as long as three months. Clearly, independence is the child's most fundamental need. His whole future development, and therefore his ability to contribute to his society as an adult, depends upon its fulfillment. Unfortunately, it is the need which our present culture gives the young child the least help in meeting.

Equally important are the children's desire and opportunity to exercise their wills in the classroom through choice of activity. Children want to choose their activities for themselves. It is through exercising their wills in the classroom that they gradually develop self-discipline and the ability to concentrate there. When they have developed discipline and concentration through giving their attention to things of their own choice, they are ready and able to concentrate on materials that I choose for them.

The most amazing phenomenon of all in the classroom is the children's response to work. The word "work" brings connotations to the adult mind that have no place in the lives of children.

For the child, work and play are two sides of one coin. They flow one through the other, and coexist in every process of his activities. The energy that the child releases in work-play is the revitalizing fuel that makes development possible.

When I speak of work, then, I mean the child's work: the work of his self-development. It is an ongoing process and includes what adults mean when they use the word "play." It is important to remember that from the child's point of view, work involves no end product, as the adult's work does—unless we consider the child's own development an end product.

The children's response to work in the classroom is startling. First of all, they obviously enjoy work. They seek it out, do it for hours on end, sometimes repeating the same work over and over. These spontaneous repetitions are startling. When an exact connection is made between the child's outer work and his inner development, the child may repeat the use of one material for an entire morning. It is the best evidence I know of that the child's interest in work lies in his own self-construction, not in transforming the environment. Children pace themselves in their work and alternate their choices of work. The benefit of their work is obvious to the children. When they are finished, they appear to have been in touch with their innermost selves. They are calmer, more relaxed, and more contented than before.

An inner source seems to guide each child's development. It is watching this inner response to the environment on the part of each individual child that makes teaching such an interesting experience for me. For all of their similarities in the drive for development—the pursuit of independence, the desire to choose, the response to work—each one of my children responds to the environment in a unique way. It appears that each child's inner guide is the source of this uniqueness. I can best observe the inner guide working in gifted children. They take to the environment like ducks to water. Except for creating the environment and introducing materials into it, I often feel extraneous to these children's development. Although this is less true with children of average intelligence, I can still see the inner guide operating in their response to the classroom. I feel that I am a secondary partner in the task of their development. The child's primary partner is his inner guide.

The children's inner guides are positive forces in their development. Children in my classroom spontaneously help each other in cleaning up after accidents, give sympathy when others are unhappy, choose to work with others and to help others with their work, enjoy serving others and sharing in conversation and ideas. They readily adopt the routines of community life, taking only the first weeks of school to establish them: putting materials back where they were found and in the condition in which they were found, not disturbing the work of others, quietly pushing in their chairs, closing the door gently, keeping their voice levels moderate, and so on.

If the children's inner guides automatically guided them at all times, my role in their lives would be much simpler. They do not. There are times when the children are aggressive, competitive, and teasing with each other. Their drive for social development deteriorates into socializing for socializing's sake. They seek to depend on a charismatic leader among their peers, instead of developing genuine friendships that demand more of them than hero worship. They regress to dependence on adults and attempted manipulation of them. Their vast energies are displayed in keyed-up behavior, overexcitement, and hyperactivity.

This negative behavior becomes less and less prevalent as the year goes on. Indeed, visitors invariably remark on the children's independence, calmness, and energy as well as their kindness to each other. The negative behavior does not disappear entirely, however. It recurs most frequently on the playground. The playground is an unstructured environment where my influence is at a minimum. This gives a clue to my role as an adult in the children's lives. Clearly I am needed to structure an environment and maintain my influence over the children within it. In spite of their growing self-discipline, they are at a stage where external discipline is necessary. Because there is so much confusion about the question of discipline in education today, I want to share my ideas concerning it before going on to a discussion of the structured environment.

As a teacher I am responsible for developing two kinds of discipline in my classroom. The first is internal discipline. This discipline is developed through repeated work based on interest. I am responsible for sparking that interest by introducing materials to which the children can respond. An individual child can respond to a certain material because it meets his developmental needs. There are three stages in the path to a fully developed self-discipline. In the first, the child has no idea of selecting and limiting his actions. In the second, he knows what he would like to do, but he cannot always do it. In the third, he knows and is able to follow his chosen path. As a teacher, I must be aware of which stage my children are operating in at any given moment.

The second kind of discipline I must establish in my classroom is external discipline. When a child's disorderly action springs from a good motive, I do not always feel that I have to interfere. When it does not spring from a good motive, I must always intervene. The key word is "always." The children positively must know that I will stop any such behavior immediately and consistently. Sometimes I get very weary with this, as the diary entries indicate, but I persevere nonetheless. Just as important, I always try to anticipate disorder and avoid situations in which it is likely to develop. I must be organized and remain undistracted in order to accomplish this. It is one reason why I prefer a classroom atmosphere of reflection and observation, and why I ask the children not to interrupt me but to wait quietly next to me until I can give them my attention.

Our present culture is somewhat timid and unsure in its approach to the discipline of young children. For my own part, I consider the limits I establish in my classroom to be rules, not prohibitions. Like traffic lights, they are necessary regulators in community life. By viewing them as safeguards against chaos, I gain the confidence and energy I need to be persistent about them.

In considering the structured environment that I seek to develop for the children, it is helpful to remember the purpose of the child's development. Man is a social being. I believe that the child's drive for development is fueled not by narcissistic or self-centered energies, but by his unconscious desire to fulfill his destiny in society. The dependence of man upon man, and in turn the interdependence between man and his universe, are the framework within which I want my classroom to come to life.

The goal of my kindergarten classroom is the capitalization on and extension of the child's natural interest in the world about him. I want to build this interest into a permanent response to life. If a child ends his education with his formal schooling, he will never reach full development. The purpose of formal education is to produce not temporary students, but lifelong learners.

To fulfill this goal, the structured environment has to reflect the outside world. In so far as possible, I present all of life in miniature to the children within the classroom. This means the environment is rich, varied, and beautiful. Civilization's most important advances are presented there: the arts, history, geography, science and the natural world, reading and writing, and the mathematical concepts of the decimal system and the four mathematical operations. The continuum of human life through birth and death is reflected on.

This is much more information than is usually presented in a kindergarten classroom. However, children are more ready for these experiences than might be supposed. Children today are more sophisticated than anyone would have believed possible just twenty-five years ago. Television has indeed transformed the world into a global village. I was shocked by the details my children knew of the Guyana tragedy (discussed in Chapter 2), for example. My children are taking in information I want them to have, as well as information that I don't want them to have. It is important even in a classroom of five-year-olds for the children to have an opportunity to express their thoughts and clarify their knowledge of the world's events. For good or for bad, a childhood protected from the world's struggles and involvements no longer exists.

There is a problem in presenting the world in miniature to the children in the classroom. The concepts of time and space are not fully developed in young children. The use of maps and calendars, references to historical periods, the development of evolution, all require an awareness of time and space for full understanding. In order to deal with this complexity, it is necessary to understand the principle of indirect preparation in human development. How does the child develop concepts of time and space? Is the degree to which he can express outwardly his understanding of these concepts a true indication of the degree of his development of them? These are hidden processes that cannot be observed directly. A clue to the internal state of the child's development and what will aid that development is his outward interest and attention.

The development of language provides a good analogy. We don't wait to speak to babies in full sentences. We surround them with fully developed language from their birth on. We are not concerned that they do not understand everything we say to them. It is enough that they appear interested and give us their full attention. Somehow, through this indirect preparation of being surrounded by fully developed language, young children develop language for themselves.

The same can be said about learning the concepts of time and space. My five-year-olds are tremendously interested in maps of the world. I know that only gradually will they begin to make the connection that the maps of the world which they are making represent vast distances. In the meantime, they are learning the names of continents and their shapes, and that different peoples live on these continents, peoples with different ways of dressing and housing themselves, with different languages and customs. This knowledge is a framework within which the children eventually will operate with understanding of space and time itself. It is not necessary to wait until the children's understanding of space is fully developed to make maps of the world, any more than it is necessary to wait to speak to them in sentences until they themselves can speak in sentences or to limit vocabulary used to words the children already understand.

I follow the same reasoning in introducing written language into the environment. Again, the children's interest is the key. They are fascinated with letters and letter sounds. Children appear to reach their most intense interest in learning to read and write at ages four and five. This innate interest in written language parallels their intense interest and development in oral language from birth to age three. In my opinion, there is no other explanation for the way the children devour written language in my classroom. If I am correct, schools are making an error in not introducing written language until the first grade. By then the child typically has reached age six, and his instinctive urge and capability for written language may have already peaked. If reading is to be introduced to five-year-olds, it is *essential* not to use methods that were devised for six-year-olds. I outline an approach that is successful with four- and five-year-olds in Chapter 3.

Presenting the world to children within a structured environment has an artificial aspect to it. Therefore, it is important to guard against viewing the classroom as a permanent exhibit or museum. In order to reflect life, the classroom has to have changes within it daily: a new picture on the wall, a new book in the library, a new record being played, a new math or language material on the shelves, a new slide in the microscope. In this way, too, the children's alertness to their environment is developed further, as they come to expect and look for these changes. A few such changes every several days are enough to maintain the children's interest, without overwhelming them with too much variation and complexity.

The curriculum for the environment consists of three kinds of materials: materials through which the children can develop their skills for independence and academic knowledge, art materials (including writing tools) for their expression of self, and materials for the maintenance of the room so that they can develop pride in and responsibility for their own environment. Each of these materials is organized down to the smallest detail so that the children can use them independently.

The mathematics, language, and geography materials in my classroom are largely Montessori materials or extensions of them.

These materials were developed by Maria Montessori at the turn of the century. As a medical doctor, Montessori worked with the children in insane asylums and, later, the slums of Rome. She devised a method of education which was extraordinarily successful in reaching these children. She gradually developed her ideas into a total philosophical approach to human development. The schools that she and her followers eventually established for children from varied backgrounds exist throughout the world.

These materials lend themselves well to the kindergarten environment that meets the developmental needs of five-year-olds. I could use other materials, however, if they followed similar principles in design: simplicity, durability, beauty, possibility for creative use and discovery, the presentation of one new concept at a time, a progressive relationship between materials so that one material leads naturally to the next, and, insofar as possible, the opportunity for the children to correct their own mistakes.

I introduce the materials to individual children, to a small group of children, or occasionally to the group as a whole. After this introduction, the children are free to choose that material for use whenever they like. With few exceptions, there is only one of each material in the room. This guarantees a variety of materials in use in the room at any given time, and helps to diversify each child's selection. It also helps the children to develop discipline and acceptance of reality in a world where it is not possible always to have what one wants.

The environment is arranged carefully so that five-year-olds can function in it as independently of the teacher as possible. Each set of materials is arranged in its own area of the room so that there is a section each for math, geography, language, room care, art, and science materials. Each material has a specific place on its own shelf so that the children know exactly where to find it and where to return it. The materials and shelves are not marked with coding devices such as numbers. Such crutches are unnecessary and hinder the development of the child's ability to memorize and build a mental picture of his environment.

One of the most important aspects of any classroom environment is its atmosphere. The tone of a classroom reflects the personality of the teacher and is in this sense always individual. Difference in noise level is an example. I like an active class with a steady hum to it, but one with an atmosphere that is conducive to reflection and concentration. In a partylike atmosphere or one with a great deal of bustle and confusion, the children respond to the materials on a superficial level only. In my experience, young children respond best to a calm and relaxed classroom atmosphere.

I do not break the schedule of the day into small time segments. The children demonstrate over and over again their preference for an uninterrupted work period of two and a half to three hours. Free choice of materials during this time is a major factor in the development of the children's discipline and love of learning. They do not tire, because they pace themselves, alternating their choices of work between easier and more difficult activities and between art, room care, and academic materials. Occasionally, they "take a break," as they call it. They leave their work temporarily to walk about the room looking at the science shelf, a book in the library, or other children at work.

At some time each day it is important for the class to come together as a whole. I refer to this time in the diaries as "line time" because typically we sit around an elliptical line of tape on the floor (which the children also use to practice walking and balancing on). We gather each day at 10:15 or 10:30, or at 11:15 just before going home. This is the time when we talk about our cultural studies in art, music, literature, and science, and the children share their work, reading their own stories and showing their maps, booklets of insets, or equation booklets to the rest of the class.

Besides the physical environment and schedule, there is another element of the classroom environment that is equally important in each child's development: the other children. These other children are like nineteen models for a child to learn from and be inspired by. Children are learning constantly by observation. The more they observe others, the more they absorb for themselves. This is why it is better to have a full class of twenty children than a smaller one of sixteen or seventeen. Having more children guarantees a greater variety of materials in use in the room at any given time and more ways of experiencing and responding to those materials. A variety of talents and abilities in the classroom also gives the children greater perspective in their understanding of other children. Still another advantage is that the teacher is not as readily available. The children therefore develop more independence.

Of the many characteristics that I try to develop in order to teach well in the environment that I have described, I will mention only the four that I consider the most important. I try to remain intellectually alive. This is important for any teacher, but I think it is essential in teaching five-year-olds. A person who has no knowledge of man's history and achievements, or whose interest in them has died, cannot present the world to children and keep alive their interest in it. I am certainly not a specialist in any field. Nor do I believe this is necessary. It is intellectual curiosity, and the children's awareness that I am learning even as they are learning, that are important.

I try to develop my intuition. I need the capacity to sense what others are feeling and an awareness of the subtleties of their behavior.

Being sensitive to others means being sensitive to oneself. An interest in and capacity for self-knowledge is essential when teaching young children. It is only through self-knowledge that humility and an acceptance of human limitation becomes possible. Ease with and confidence in self are sensed immediately by small children. To a person who has these qualities they will give a place of legitimate authority in their lives. I need to occupy this place in the lives of the children in order for them to trust me to set limits for them and to choose a direction of knowledge for them to follow.

I try to develop flexibility. A rigid, controlling person cannot lead the children to independence and self-disciplined responses to life. The children need their freedom in order to develop these responses. I need flexibility in giving that freedom to the children and in setting limits on it.

The framework of the teaching relationship which I try to develop is one of teamwork. If I am to follow the children's inner guide in directing their development, the children and I have to operate as partners. Following the inner guide is not an easy task, as my diary entries clearly indicate. The decision of when to direct and when to stand back and allow the children to direct themselves must be made continually.

To develop sensitivity to the children's inner guide, I need to have the opportunity to observe them. This means that in spite of being absorbed in any one situation. I must maintain my awareness of the room as a whole. This is an important reason for having a fairly small room, as well as a limited number of children within it. I also need an opportunity for one-to-one relating with each child. This is made possible by the introduction of most materials on an individual basis and the informal atmosphere of the classroom, which allows for constant exchanges between the children and between the children and myself.

Teamwork between the teacher and the children is only possible in an atmosphere of trust. I develop the children's trust by seeking constantly to understand and meet their needs. I take care never to humiliate them. When discipline is necessary, I find it effective to ask a child to remain with me wherever I am in the room and with whomever I am working with at the time. This is a temporary restraint on his freedom. As soon as he appears ready, I give him his freedom back, usually with a redirection to work of either his choosing or mine. I try diligently to prepare the children for whatever is expected of them. That requires foresight and organization of detail on my part. The diary entries show that I am not always successful. Above all, I maintain my high standards for the children's behavior and remain consistent in my expectations of them.

The children develop my trust in them, too, by the consistency with which they seek their own best development and knowledge of the world and themselves. To teach young children is to have one's faith in human nature constantly rekindled.

TWO | # Class Life

I have emphasized the beginning weeks of class life because they are the essential ones. The entire year will stand or fall on how well I manage them. At first they appear to be deceptively easy. The children are in awe of their new experience and are anxious to discover what is expected of them. However, this first period of grace is followed by a testing time in which the children try out their new relationships with each other, with me, and with the environment. This is the most demanding time of the year for me. Most of the children have not yet discovered their capacity and desire for work, nor developed their ability to be independent. I must help them work toward independence by guiding them to materials in the environment which will enhance their self-mastery and self-knowledge. I have to be firm in my expectations of the children's social behavior. In a real sense, I must substitute whatever self-confidence, wisdom, and discipline that I possess, for that of the unformed children's.

This period can last from one to three months, depending on the class, but it usually will be no more than two (as was the case in the class described here). The children's early hesitant manner and later testing behavior are transformed into an eager and self-confident response to the environment. A social community is formed in which each child is a responsible member of the whole. From this point on, the children's development is rapid.

The second section of this chapter, entitled "The Children Develop," deals with the remainder of the school year. I have concentrated on the spring, however, with only minimal references to the winter months. This was necessary in order to relate the children's progress by the end of the year.

The reader will notice that I have included few entries on the language and mathematical development of the children in this chapter. I considered them so important that I have devoted separate chapters to them. Nor have I attempted to describe the classroom materials in this chapter, feeling it would be cumbersome to the reader if I did so. Instead, I have listed the materials with a brief description of their design, purpose, and use in Appendix B. The language and mathematical materials are also discussed in the chapters which deal specifically with those areas.

It was difficult to choose less than one-fourth of my diary to represent the life of the class a whole. I tried to select entries that would give a sense of what I was working toward in the children's development.

their gradual independence
their development as social beings
their response to work
their ability to pace themselves
their confidence through gradually developing skills

I tried also to show the extent to which the children learned from each other.

Finally, I attempted to portray my role as the teacher in preparing the classroom environment, in setting limits for the children's behavior, and in guiding their learning. The last goal was achieved at times by directing the children to specific materials and at other times by giving them freedom to direct themselves.

BEGINNING . . .

September 6   I don't think I ever will get accustomed to the empty look of the room after I have prepared it for the first day of school. Actually, it isn't completely empty. There is a round green rug in the library corner with a rocking chair, several brightly colored floor pillows, a Renoir print on the wall, and a large orange tree plant next to it.

There are other plants around the room, on countertops and shelves, and there is a toy or art material at nine individual places on two large tables. There is an elliptical line of yellow tape on the floor at one end of the room. It is both for the children to walk on, practicing their balance as all young children love to do, and to sit on for "line time," our time each day for group discussions and instruction. In the middle of the line is a cardboard box full of puzzles, toys, and activities that the children are familiar with in their own homes.

It is the bare shelves in the room that make it appear so empty. I felt apprehensive as I looked about it today. What will the parents think when they bring their children tomorrow? There won't be time to explain to them that I want to start everything very slowly in the room. In this way four- and five-year-olds will be able to comprehend and cope with their new environment. I want to talk to the children about books first, for example, and show them how we are going to care for them and use them here, before giving them any to handle. I want to introduce each material, showing the children not only how it is used but just where it goes on the shelves so that they will always find it in one place. It is unusual to give this much thought and to be this patient in presenting experiences to children in our culture, particularly in introducing them to manners, which I also will be doing. It will be different for the parents and for the children. I know from experience with what relief the children will greet this slower-paced, thoughtful approach in which they are carefully prepared for what will be expected of them. I also know that it will cause anxiety in some of the parents.

It is not for the children that it is necessary to begin with empty shelves, however. It is wise for me, too, to begin the year slowly. I need time to get ready for full action, just as the children do. I need to look at the room with fresh eyes. Is what I am putting there for the children only, or am I fulfilling some vanity of my own? Am I trying to impress parents or visitors or other teachers? It is simple enough, beautiful enough, meaningful enough? Will it last through many usages? Is it carefully organized and maintained for child usage? Does it represent the best in life? Does it help to enhance the highest values in life? One of my grown daughters came to look at the room as I was leaving today. "Mom," she said, "there's a lot in this room. It depends on your values. It's like a sanctuary. It's a reflection of you and what you think about life." That helped me to feel less apprehensive.

I have typed up a schedule* to follow the first four days. If anything, I want the mornings overplanned, so I have broken the schedule into five- and ten-minute segments. A more general plan might leave me with awkward gaps in activities. If some activities last longer than planned, others can be skipped. The activities on the schedule involve acquainting the children with the room, a short individual work time, group activities such as singing, juice time, and reading a story, and outside time.

The room introduction lessons are a key part of these first few days. I will show the children where the folder box is (a box with a folder for each child to put his own papers), the bathroom and its sign to turn over to show when it is in use, where the tissues are, how to get a drink of water, etc. I will show the children how to come into the room in the morning, shaking hands first with

*See Appendix A.

me and then with Joan, my assistant. I will show them how to hang their coats on hangers and take them to the hall, how to sit on the line with a space between them, how to raise their hand when they want to speak during group discussions, how to unroll a rug to work on and then to reroll it, how to walk carefully around the rug so that the child working there will not be disturbed, how to carry a chair, how to push in their chairs when they put their work away, how to close a door quietly, etc. Each day the schedule will vary, adding a few more items, until the children know how to function with ease in their room. The secret of success in keeping the children's attention during these lessons will be to keep them brief, do them as dramatically as possible, and involve one or more of the children in each one.

The sessions will be split the first two mornings. Half the class will come for the first hour and a half, and the other half will come for the second part of the morning. The third day all the children will come together, but only for two and a half hours. Next Monday, our fourth day, will be the first day with all the children coming at 8:10 and leaving at 11:30. By that time I should not need such precise planning, and can ease into a more flexible schedule. There will be less and less time spent in group activity, and more and more in individual work time.

The latter will be centered on choices from the toy box at first. They will be extended gradually to materials on the shelves. I will be introducing these two or three at a time each day, first the art and room care materials, then the academic ones: mathematics, language, geography, and science materials. As I introduce each material, I will be careful to show the children the section of the room and the shelf where it belongs. One section of the room has all the art materials, another the room care, another the math materials, and so on. Arranging the room in this way gives it the order and structure which young children need in order to function independently.

The toy box has a special purpose in the room. It is to provide activities with which the children are already familiar and comfortable. In this sense it serves as a bridge with their home environment. When they feel more at ease in their school environment, they will no longer need this bridge with home. They will indicate their readiness to do without it by no longer choosing from the toy box during work period. When this happens, I will take it out of the room. (Interestingly, the children never seem to notice when it is gone.)

I feel nervous about tomorrow. It is not unique to feel this way, I know. Teachers who have taught for forty years have told me that they always feel this way before a new class begins. As one teacher expressed it, "It is a performance and you want to do well." There is a concern for the unknown as well. It will be several weeks before I begin to know the children well as individuals and can estimate how much work I have cut out for me. I have never had a group that I couldn't get to function well. Still, if too many of the more difficult children that I have taught had happened to end up all in one class, how would things have turned out then?

First Day   It was obvious that the children were feeling mostly apprehension as they came to the door with their mothers this morning. They had all been to preschool, but this was a new school for most, and very few had ever seen me before. The nine children for the first session came in one at a time over a twenty-minute period. It gave me a chance to lead each child individually to the two tables with activities, and kneel down next to each one, talking to him or her alone for just a moment.

Even though I've come to expect more or less angelic behavior on the first mornings, I felt this first group of children was really outdoing itself. It gave me an unreal feeling to have everything happen so flawlessly. I kept thinking, "This is going much too easily." Because the children were so quiet, they heard me at once when I called them to the line. I showed them how to sit Indian style and to leave a space between them. I walked in and out among them, tiptoeing so it would be more like a game to them. It also helped to set a quiet atmosphere for listening to me. "Can you hear a sound?" I whispered, as I walked.

I had my schedule on the floor in front of me, and followed it pretty much as I had set it down. Originally, I felt somewhat silly dramatizing the procedures that I was showing the children. Now they seemed almost natural. It is the children's response to them that helps me to be less self-conscious. They are completely attentive and caught up in the scene anytime I go through actions deliberately, almost in slow motion. These are actions, of course, that they know they are going to want or need to do themselves. It may be this aspect that mesmerizes them, as much as my way of doing them.

I asked the children, "Whose room is this?" There was the usual consternation of other years as they tried to guess. Finally, I said, "I'll give you a hint. It doesn't belong to adults." "It belongs to kids?" they said incredulously, exchanging looks of disbelief. This is a special moment in the beginning of each class for me. The children's faces and tones clearly show that I am presenting them with a new experience in their lives. It makes all the effort worthwhile. Sandy, the youngest in the class, finally blurted out triumphantly, "Ours!" "Yes," I said, "it is yours. It is yours to work in and yours to take care of. You will have to know all about your room then, won't you? I will have to show you how to take care of it. I will show you how to take care of the plants, how to sweep the floor, how to wash the tables and shelves, how to mop the floors, how to dust and polish the materials you will work with, how to clean up after accidents. Today I put the flowers in the glass vases on the tables, but tomorrow I will show you how to."

Next I asked different children to go and stand next to various items in the room—the door, the box of tissues, etc. I asked each child to go as quietly as possible to his destination. "Can you walk so we don't hear a sound, Jesse? Good for you!" The children remained quiet and attentive. Next we talked about the empty shelves in the room. Strangely, this aspect of the room that always worries me ahead of time is never noticed by the children. It is a good lesson in not assuming too much similarity between adult and child. "Why would the shelves be empty in your room?" I asked. "If it is your room, then you need to know where everything goes. If everything in all those cupboards was already on your shelves, it would be too much to remember, wouldn't it?" The children all nodded their heads. "I will put two new things out on the shelves each day, and that way you can remember where they belong." At one point the children got slightly noisy in their responses. I lowered my voice to a stage whisper. They followed my lead and lowered their voices, too.

"Now we are going to choose from the toy box," I said. "You may work with your toy either at a table or on a rug. In your room, no one may touch your work, and you may not touch anyone else's work. If you finish with your toy, you may put it back on the top of the toy box and exchange it for another. Close your eyes, and I will whisper each child's name. When you hear your name, tiptoe quietly to me and choose a toy." I selected two toys from the toy box for each succeeding child, so that the choice would be more manageable for them. The children worked for about fifteen minutes. It was a good beginning, and I had a chance to speak to each child individually again. Some got up and exchanged toys. It gave me an opportunity to show them how to push in their chairs first, then pick up their toy. I want to get this habit established from the beginning or we will be spending a year bumping into tables and chairs. It's a nuisance, though, and I felt the tedium of establishing these routines all over again after being accustomed to my smooth-functioning classroom last June.

Finally, we had juice, which Joan served to us. I wanted the

children to see how this was done the first time before partici-
pating in the serving with her tomorrow. I read the story of
Madeline, which I hoped would be familiar to them, and the
hour and a half was up.

I felt really tired as we prepared the class for the second group
of children. I must have been under more tension than I was
aware of in teaching the first one. The second session was all
right, but I didn't feel this group was as totally absorbed in the
moment and getting every bit out of it, as the first one was. It
may have been the makeup of the group or it may have been that
both the children and I were tired. Overall, however, I am
pleased that the first day has gone so well, and relieved that I
won't have to go through this again until next year!

Second Day   I just don't want to do anything. Partly it is the
weather: ninety-two degrees and humid. Partly it is the strain of
double sessions, even if they are short. Repeating the same procedures with two groups of children in the same morning is not
my idea of fun. I am exhausted from working my whole being
overtime. All morning I had my mental and emotional antennae
out trying to cover every direction at once, and to take in as
much information as possible about eighteen little people. All afternoon I have been arranging materials from the cupboard and
getting them organized for setting them out on the shelves in the
next weeks. There are so many details to think of. For just the
Plant Care, for example, I need a blue and white checkered plastic cloth, a blue watering can, a blue and white water spray can,
a white soap dish for the blue sponge, a white porcelain dish with
red and green paper flags on toothpicks (red means that the
plant has been watered, green that it needs watering), a paper
towel for putting dead or cut leaves on, a pair of scissors, a small
blue cloth for wiping up any spills. All of this must be arranged
carefully on a blue tray in order of use, left to right, top to bot-

tom. It takes time and energy to deal with all these details, yet I know the success or failure of the materials depends on how they are organized.

Third Day   For the first time, the general impression the children gave coming in was one of eagerness, confidence, and possibly relief. They have figured out what to do in these two days, and seemed pleased about it. In general, work time went well, and I extended it from the previous fifteen-minute periods of the first two days to thirty minutes. The children used the materials and toys with reasonable care and involvement for so early in the year. Timmy was the exception. He put his choice from the toy box back almost instantly, and then spent the whole thirty minutes wandering. He also called out loudly whenever he thought of something he wanted to say. Madan, too, kept forgetting to walk and ran across the room whenever he wanted something.

Anna asked to do the Sandpaper Letters.* She knew all their sounds, so I will get out the Movable Alphabet for three-letter word dictation with her. Lee and Jesse asked to do the letters with us, too, which pleased me. As much as possible I like to give the children a chance to choose academic work themselves. That way I worry less that I am asking them to do something that is too much for them at the moment. While I worked with these three children, Joan watched the others and helped them to follow routines: to push in their chairs, sit up straight on their chairs as they worked, walk around rugs, etc. We'll continue these roles while I get a feel for where all the children are in numbers and letters and until the routines become more or less second nature to the children. Then I may ask her to work with a specific child

*All material with names involving letters, shapes, etc., are presented in "The Three-Period Lesson of Seguin." See Appendix F.

on a material he is not mastering readily. She will be doing much of the remedial work in the classroom. I will concentrate on introducing the new materials.

I was surprised the children did so poorly remembering where materials went today. They were reasonably good about putting everything away carefully, even and straight with the shelf, but all in the wrong places! At the end of the morning we went on a "secret walk" to see what was out of place in the room. Amazingly, all they saw at first were the seven chairs that were not pushed into tables. Eventually one child saw that the markers were on the first shelf where the clay should be, another noticed the chalkboard on the second shelf where the markers should be, and still another that the clay was on the bottom shelf next to the pasting materials where nothing should be. I called on individual children to rearrange the materials. It looks as if the class will be slow to absorb the structure of the room. Each day I will have to begin line time by asking different children to stand by each material that is out, thus drawing attention to their position on the shelves to the whole class. A few children will begin to remember, and then they will be able to help the others.

One procedure that the children have picked up beautifully is holding still as statues when I ask for class attention. They stop instantly when I say, "Excuse me, please." They really enjoy seeing what difficult positions they can hold for a minute. They must have played Red Light, Green Light. In any case, it is so much more pleasant and interesting than ringing a bell to bring the class together.

Fourth Day   I was very pleased this morning because the children worked with enough involvement for me to keep work period going for a full hour. The specials have begun as well. Each morning four children will go to art from 8:30 to 9:30. That means every child will go once a week. On Mondays and Fridays half of the children will go to drama at 10:35 and half will remain in the classroom. On Tuesday and Thursday everyone will go to music together at this time. On Fridays half the class will go to the library at 10:30 so that each child will go once every two weeks. Our scheduled gym time is 11:00 each day. This leaves almost two and a half hours each day from 8:10 to 10:35 for individual work time and group lessons.

Fifth Day   Wonderful! Work period was from 8:45 to 10:00 and the children were still working very quietly and with no underlying restlessness when we stopped. Joan again watched routines while I worked with individual children on academic materials. I missed quite a bit of detail this way, as it was necessary for me to get very involved with the few children I was working with. However, I still could keep a good feel for the room in general, and I was pleased with the way it was working. Plant Care and the Cutting Exercise are favorites, and also the Collage Tray and Painting Tray. For the first time, two children wanted the same work at the same time and hadn't resolved it on their own. The two children, Linda and Susie, both seem accustomed to being catered to. "What will we do?" I asked. "There is only one Painting Tray in your room." Susie said, "I asked Sam if I could have it when he finished." "Oh, then, Linda, you must ask Susie if she will tell you when she is finished before she puts it away so you can go to the shelf and be ready to take it next," I said. Linda accepted this solution, and I was relieved. I had visions of tears and a tantrum. Other children at the table were aware of all this and learned from it, I hope.

Sixth Day   The children came in with a bustle today after last night's big rainstorm. They went busily to work after they hung up their raincoats. When I stopped them at 8:30, everyone had work out from the shelves. I introduced the Silver Polish and Cleanser Tray at opening line time. (We have a silver candlestick in the room which the children polish. When it is a child's birth-day, he carries a blue tray with the candlestick and a lighted can-dle in it and walks along the yellow line while we all sing "Happy Birthday.") My introduction of the Silver Polish was a classic ex-ample of inadequacy. I have gotten careless about practicing a material before introduction, and so in my setup I forgot: first, the acrylic tray to work on, second, a sponge for wiping up, and third, a paper towel for a final polishing of the candlestick. The children loved it, of course. I kept saying, "Oh, I forgot!" as I got up each time to retrieve the missing items from the cupboards. I didn't wash the polish out of the toothbrush either while clean-ing up. One of the children said, "You forgot to wash out the toothbrush!" It was a good example of how quickly the children begin to pick up the idea of these exercises! "In your school, what do you want? Shall we wash out the toothbrush or do you think it is all right this way?" I asked. Truthfully, I was going to leave this step out. "Wash it out," the children said.

There was a good range of materials in use all morning from room care to academic to art work. I have covered about two-thirds of the class now in assessing letter sounds and number skills. The energetic boys of the class were really going at the room care materials. At one point, I looked over to see Jack do-ing the Silver Polish. He was concentrating so hard while screw-ing the top on the eye dropper bottle containing silver polish that he was biting his tongue. Robbie was at the next table, carefully polishing the mirror. Sam was next to Robbie doing the Plant Care with equal precision and concentration.

The children are beginning to catch on to the routines and to help each other with them at last. For the first time Susie did not tap, tap on my shoulder but waited for attention. When Sandy put the Painting Tray down turned the wrong direction on the table, Emily told her. "Your chair is on the wrong side!"

About 9:30 there was a general restlessness in the room, and several children were bothering others. This kind of phenomenon occurs daily to a minor degree midway through the work period, but sometime during midweek, usually Wednesday or Thursday, it is more of a disruption than other days. This has happened through the years in all the classes that I have taught. It must be part of the children's natural rhythm in a class of this kind. Sam was bothering Robbie, who was painting. I told Sam that he must stay at the rug where I was working with Linda and Madan. After a few minutes, I said to Sam, "I have told you that there is no touching of another person's work. Tell me what work you want to choose now." "Collage Tray," he said and off he went to get it. I kept Timmy with me for a while, too, and several others. By 9:45 all were quiet and industriously at work again. It was like the rising of a wave, then its breaking and settling down again. The quiet afterward felt like that after a short storm. It had an entirely different quality than the quiet earlier in the morning.

My approach is the opposite of the one in which such a pitch of noise and activity is dealt with by turning the children loose on the playground to run off steam. My experience has been that they come back from such episodes either exhausted or more keyed up than ever. Rechanneling their energy by keeping a few of the more restless children with me, and then sending them off to work of their own choice, often result in the most productive work of the morning. Best of all, the children appear calmer and more contented with themselves afterward.

I didn't think to demonstrate to the children ahead of time how they were to pass in and out the door when getting their raincoats to go home. There was a good deal of bumping into each other, much of it quite rough. I ended up feeling like a nagger and a scolder. "Be careful, Madan. You pushed, Karen. Watch out, Jesse." I showed the children afterward how to pass each other in the door politely. I felt bad that I had not had more foresight and been more thoughtful of them.

Seventh Day   I do get tired of insisting on the routines. It was a nuisance to have to get up from working with Jack and Robbie on letters to go over to Emily across the room. "Emily, remember to speak only to the children at your own table. You are disturbing Jack and Robbie and me, and we are working way over there," I told her. She forgot again and the second time, I asked her to come and sit with us on our rug for a few minutes. The children handle this correcting better than I do. They are quite matter-of-fact and patient about it. I am bored with it, and eager to get on to the next stage when it won't be so prevalent.

Occasionally, a child tests me. Today Karen was twisting the mirror Emily was polishing. I got up from my writing with Lee, and told her to come and sit with us. In a few minutes I told her that she could go back to her work. She pouted instead. I simply said, "Fine, you may stay here as long as you like." I continued my work with Lee. She sat for a few more minutes before going back to work.

The children are getting very good at caring for the room. It was quite a scene late in the morning with Madan carefully sweeping dust into the dust pan, Jack using the dust mop, and Robbie the floor mop. He even mopped over a chair that some-how was covered with spots of silver polish. Susie came by and said to me, "They really take care of their room!" Today I shut my eyes on the line and sent them off tiptoeing to straighten anything amiss in the room. When they were all back on the line, they told me to open my eyes. I went on the "secret walk" alone then, and the room was perfect. Someone had even straightened the folders in the folder box!

I am finished with the materials that I like to introduce at a beginning line time, and the children seem ready to try a longer work period. That means that Monday we can come in and go right to work without breaking for an 8:30 line time. I'll intro-duce Bach tomorrow so that we can have music as the children come in the room each morning. Then I will feel that the year has really begun.

September 18   I omitted the first line time as I had planned to do. It was the children's first taste of freedom from interruption during the entire two-hour work period, and they obviously relished it. After last Friday, I felt that I knew the children well enough at last to mark down on a note pad a few things to do daily with each child. I will tie this pad to my skirt for handy reference. At the end of each day, I will use my note pad to mark down each child's activities on a master chart. In this way, I can be certain that each child is moving ahead in both language and math, and that he is using a variety of other materials.

What I like best about the class so far is the independence that already is established, the interest in work, and the readily adopted routines. I loved Anna's coming in from art today and saying to Linda, "The Pasting is here, and it's supposed to be there. How do you like that!" (The pasting materials were where the markers should have been.)

September 20   After class Joan said that she was pleased with the variety of the children's work choices and their independence in choosing them. There are a few children whom I don't always feel this way about. I think of Jesse today, for example; he was wandering from child to child. I thought that sooner or later he would get into trouble, so I asked him to stay with me until he could choose his work. He couldn't choose, though, and sat with me for a long time. At one point, he said, "Why am I in school?" We did the Sandpaper Letters together eventually. Afterward he said, "I think I'll do the Clay now," and he was off.

Today I brought in the *National Geographic* for September with a story in it on a solo assault on the North Pole. I use the *National Geographic* as a basis for a social studies program. I bring it in each month, telling about one story in it, and we find the spot where it has taken place on one of the children's maps. (The children have been making maps of the world by tracing pieces of a wooden puzzle map of the world.) I leave the magazine in the library then so that the children can browse through it. Often they bring it to me, wanting to know about a particular picture. I want to build a habit in the children of looking at such magazines in their homes and bookstores, so that a bridge is built with the adult world of their parents.

September 25   I had taken the toy box out Saturday, and as in other years no one even missed it. It was the first day that we have had individual snack time, too. Joan asked Linda if she would set up the pitcher, cups, napkins, and crackers on a table. After Linda had it all ready, she went about the room, telling each child, "Snack is ready." Some children came right away. Others worked a while longer. Joan stayed close by the table while each child got his napkin and cracker first, then came back to pour his milk. I put on a Bach record as I always do during this time each morning.

I stayed after school to get materials out for Parents' Night tonight.

I had three ideas that I wanted to get across to the parents: the idea of partnership, the goals of the year, and the development that would take place in their children during this year. I told them that we felt privileged to be in partnership with them for their children's development over the next nine months. They, however, were the senior and more important partners in the relationship. We would be relying on them to keep in close touch with us and to tell us how things were going at home. I asked them to call us immediately if they had any concerns or information that would be helpful to us during the year.

I mentioned our two goals for the year. The first involved the basic skills. We wanted to take their children just as far as they could go in language and mathematics. The second was just as important to us. We were interested in the quality of life in the classroom for the children: the things that make life interesting, meaningful, and worthwhile. That was why we would be concentrating on the social life of the class as well as introducing the children to the arts and sciences. We would be playing the music of Bach, Mozart, and Beethoven, and learning about Rembrandt, Renoir, and Picasso. We would be studying the beginnings of the universe, the evolvement of life on earth, and finally, the world of men and their accomplishments. We would cover these areas with broad brushstrokes. We would not attempt to instill detailed knowledge in the children, but would try instead to capture their imaginations and keep alive in them the instinctive curiosity children have about all aspects of their lives: how the world began, where people came from, what else is in the world. Our goal would be to provide them with a framework within which they could put the detailed and specific knowledge that they would gain in later years. Last I showed the parents the work of the children from other years so that they might get a glimpse of how much their own children would accomplish this year.

I don't know if my sales pitch worked for the parents, but it worked for me. I came home feeling inspired.

September 26   The children's pride and pleasure in their independence at snack time was obvious today. They found their own places, chose whom they wanted to sit with, and set their own snack. Madan said, "I'm going to sing the prayer to myself," and he did.

Sandy and Robbie were working side by side both using the world map. Robbie was very patiently showing Sandy how to place the map pieces correctly, and helping her hold them while she traced them. It was a beautiful example of an older child helping a younger one with the materials.

September 28   I am not happy with the way outside time is going. There is definitely a rough element in this class. Jack is the ring leader. He is not hostile but he is aggressive. I can keep his energy channeled in positive directions in the classroom, but outside I have left the children pretty much on their own. Jack likes to organize teams, and several times children have fallen down while chasing each other on the blacktop. When we came back in today, Anna said, "They [Jack, Robbie, and Ed] were looking at our underpants." "Mine, too," Emily said. "Not yours," Jack said. "You've got pants on!"

September 29   Jeff, our Lower School headmaster, came by to tell me that Carmen's mother had called him. She told him that Carmen was very unhappy at playground time. She was afraid of the other children and that no one would play with her. I felt terrible that Carmen's mother hadn't called me herself. I tried playing Duck Duck Goose with the children during outside time, hoping that organized games might help matters. When Lee got caught, he went off and stood by the building and cried. I thought it was best to leave him alone and not make too much of it. In a minute, Sam did the same thing. The children weren't being very helpful, saying "Ha, ha! You got caught. You're in the soup!" Still, I was surprised that both boys reacted this way. Linda did go in the soup when she was caught, but she said, "So!" in such a pouty way. I do have my work cut out for me with this group!

October 2   I'm amazed at how much the children gather from just being in class and observing each other. I showed Jesse how to make a map today. I say "showed" him how, but actually he already knew! He had memorized every step of the process from watching others. He knew exactly how to carry the continent pieces over to the paper, pinching the knob in the middle with his thumb and index fingers, not twisting them even slightly, getting them exactly in position on the paper to trace, and exactly in the right order, too. (I have discovered that the easiest way for the children to get the continents in the right places is to begin with North America, then South America, calling attention to the exact spot where they join. Asia and Africa are next, again calling attention to where they join, then Europe, and finally Australia.) Jesse worked on his map so intently and with obvious pleasure and pride. Once he came up while I was doing the Sandpaper Letters with Tommy. I looked up to see if he wanted me. "I'm just walking around. I'm taking a little break. I'm not finished yet," he said. He worked for two hours in all, and still has some ocean left to color tomorrow. His coloring is so carefully done with even, light strokes.

I have brought to class a small salamander which I found in the basement. Many children took the science basket with the *Golden Guide* book on reptiles to a table to look it up. Linda brought a twig with berries and a leaf on it, and she found it in the Golden Book on trees. We have science baskets and books for moths and butterflies, insects, spiders and their kin, flowers, trees, reptiles, and amphibians now. Science always makes the classroom come to life. It is as important to me as it is to the children. I need to learn something intellectually rewarding every day, too.

October 3   Jesse went right to work on his map. That was definitely the right connection to make for him at this point. I wonder why he hadn't asked me to do one earlier. It's that intuition of when and where and what to be ready with for a particular child that makes a class go, or not go. I know when I am right. There have to be hundreds of times when I am missing opportunities, and am totally unaware of it.

Today when I was doing the Movable Alphabet with Edith, I dictated the word "fox" to her. Jack was across the room doing the Cutting Exercise and Robbie was next to him using the markers to color a picture. As they worked, I heard them both saying to themselves, "*k-s, k-s,*" for the sound of *x,* then the whole word, "f-o-k-s." It reconfirmed my faith in this indirect approach to teaching.

I felt the routines finally were automatic when Linda skipped over a rug today, then turned around and went back, and carefully walked around it again all on her own. It always seems such a monumental task at the beginning of the year to get a class going. Yet we are only three and a half weeks into the year, and it is already done. I can feel a definite change in the class as they move out of this first stage of routine setting. They're more relaxed and look more confident.

October 5   The children are beginning to bring in more of the things they find. Edith brought a butterfly, Carmen a caterpillar, and Jesse some oak leaves. I brought in a terrarium with a little toad in it a few days ago, and Sam brought in some earthworms. There was some bustle in the room today as I showed the children how to catch flies in the room for the toad. (We use a plastic cup and piece of cardboard.) When someone caught one, others would get up from their work to watch the toad in hopes of seeing him eat it.

I have put papers out in an open file box so that the children can practice their numbers and letters when they wish. The letter writing paper is a special paper with a single blue line above, a middle solid blue section (for the main body of a letter such as *a*), and a single blue line below. The lines above and below the solid section indicate where ascenders go above the lines as in *d* and descenders below the line as in *g.* Paper for writing numbers is marked off into squares. This enables the children to write their numbers in uniform size. Carmen practiced *g* over and over again, and several children practiced and practiced their numbers on the number paper. It was the kind of repetitious drill that would be cruel for a teacher to ask a child to do. By simply having the papers available, the children have begun to do them spontaneously. Explosions of repetition of this duration and quality have convinced me that I get more work out of the children (and they get more out of their work, too) when they have an opportunity to choose these activities for themselves.

October 6   I forgot my individualized notes today, and I felt a little lost all morning. When I checked with them at home, I realized that I had covered much of what I had planned. The difference was that I felt hesitant all morning. It took an extra moment of thought each time that I looked up ready to work with another child, or saw one without work who I thought needed direction from me. It made me realize how crucial my daily hour of recording and planning material introductions is to my ease and confidence in the classroom.

The transition period is definitely here. The awe the children felt at the beginning of the year is gone completely. They no longer wonder what they are to do here, or what will come next. They appear somewhat unsettled; in fact their adjustment to date has been on a superficial level. Their seeming unrest actually is progress for them. They will be less tentative and more open now. Their relationship with me and with each other will be more open, too. I think it is the realness of this stage that I like so much better.

The children have learned all the continents now. Each time a child finishes a map, I go over the names with him. At line time I hold up all the maps completed for that day, and we go over them again. Today Madan said, "Did you know Australia is famous? I saw it on a TV commercial. They have koala bears there." Linda had found our monarch butterfly in the *Golden Guide,* so I showed the children the insects' migration pattern on the map. I also pointed out where Pompeii was. Jack had seen the Pompeii Exhibit at the Art Institute, and went on nonstop about it for fifteen minutes. Even though children of this age cannot really comprehend distances and sizes in the way required to understand a map of the world, they are fascinated when we associate what we are talking about with the maps in this way. I think that it is similar to their fascination with history even though they have an undeveloped sense of time. They are amazed by the way people dressed in Bach's day, how they went about, what kinds of houses that they lived in, etc. I think it is important to feed their curiosity about these things at five so that later, when they do have the more sophisticated understanding of time sequence, they will have a store of facts ready to put into historical perspective.

October 12   I asked Jesse to work with me when he came in today. He said, "Do I have to? I wanted to do the Collage." "All right, Jesse, come and get me when you are done," I said. But he didn't. He spent all morning on his collage. It was magnificent: a little city with stoplights (plastic discs on a string), bridges (loops of colored paper), and a trench made of toothpicks. "The water goes in here," he said, pointing to the trench. At ten o'clock I asked him to put it away. "I'm not finished," he said. "You can finish it tomorrow, Jesse. Now we have to do the Movable Alphabet," I answered.

It is definitely a major decision each time a situation like this comes up. Should I insist that the child work with me or not? In general, I try to find a time when the child feels more ready. Today, for example, I didn't insist that Madan work with me when I first asked him. He was having a happy morning but really wasn't doing much of anything. Mostly he was talking to other children as they did their work. Toward the end of the morning, he looked more receptive. I asked him to do the Phonetic Objects with me. He seemed quite happy to do them, and was proud of his work afterward. Should I have insisted that he work with me the first time I asked him? Would it have been a more productive day for him in all? There is no way to be certain.

Emily has had the hardest time accepting what "goes" here. She tries each day to take her coat off and hang it up in the hall, instead of bringing it into the room and using a table to put it on the hanger and zip it up as we have shown her. Joan has to watch for her each morning so that she can be certain that she does it correctly. Emily came bouncing up to me this morning with her little pixie face and twinkling eyes to shake hands. She was humming to herself, and was quite keyed up. "Now, Emily, you are in school now. You must slow down," I said. I asked her if she wanted to work with me when I was with Sam. "No, I want to do another map," she said. That helped to settle her down a bit. Later Ed came up to tell me that there were three people in the library. (We have limited it to two because of the small space involved.) Emily and Sandy were the ones who had come in last, each insisting that she was there before the other one. I couldn't be certain if either one was telling me the truth, so there was nothing to do but ask them both to leave. I was not satisfied with the solution, and neither was Emily. She seems to view school as a sort of constant entertainment for her benefit. She was proud of her map, however, and it showed a good deal of improvement over yesterday's.

October 13   Jesse came in and asked me to show him something new right off this morning. Perhaps he felt inspired from our work with the Movable Alphabet yesterday. In any case, I am glad that I hadn't pushed him earlier yesterday, but let him spend most of the morning on his collage. I introduced him to Phonetic Objects, and he did a fine job with them. Later in the morning (after he had finished the collage from yesterday), he came to me again and asked me to show him the Constructive Triangle Box Two. That is just how I want the children to feel, that I have interesting things to show them and all they have to do is come and ask me.

October 13   I read the children a book called *The Dead Tree* at line time. It started a discussion about death. Some of the children talked about grandparents who had died. Carmen said that her grandfather has "a tumor in his head" and that "he is going to die in six weeks." It was so explicit a statement for a five-year-old that I wonder if it could be true.

October 16   There are more and more days that I really feel good about now. This was a typical good day. When the children came in, they seemed to take a while to choose their work. I was tempted to intervene. What is it in our culture that makes us feel uneasy if we are not constantly busy and teaching our children to be constantly busy as well? Why shouldn't the children take a while to make their choice of work in the morning? I really don't trust yet that they will be able to make a choice eventually.

They did settle themselves quite nicely, however. When I looked at the clock, it was only 8:20. Jack and Timmy were doing the Decimal Numeral Layout together, Jesse the Binomial Cube, Ed a map, Robbie was writing numbers on a number paper, Lee was doing the Strip Board, Emily and Madan both were making lovely inset books. I think it was the most careful work Madan has done yet. He still tends to forget to put work away and to push in his chair much of the time. Emily had the best day that she has had, and I feel encouraged about her. After her inset book, she finished two continent booklets. Then she said, "You can show me something." She sounded as if she were doing me a favor! Susie polished all the Geometric Solids. I have all of them out now: an ellipsoid, rectangular prism, sphere, etc. The children learned all of their names from my presentations of them one at a time at line time. I'm pleased that I thought of suggesting the polishing for the Solids. The children are past the height of sensorial interest in learning by touching. Polishing the Solids gives them a new interest in handling them. Carmen was the only child who couldn't get herself started today. She came up to me right away, saying, "I can't find anything to do." I introduced her to the Trinomial Cube and then she read the three-letter Phonetic Word Cards to me. I didn't notice her after that, so she must have managed by herself the rest of the morning. This just wasn't the day to get Jack into any work of my choosing. He had an "I don't feel like working" look. After he came back from art, he used the Markers, Cutting, and Painting.

Madan and Robbie, and later Jesse and Sam, each read the board together. I had written, "This is Monday, October 16, 1978. It is a sunny day." They took turns using the wooden pointer to point to the words as the others read. There are many reasons why the children might be choosing to read the board message, but I think at least one of them is their fascination with using the pointer itself. It is adding these "points of interest" to the work in the environment that seems to rouse the children's response to it.

October 17   I worked with Madan on forming and writing addition equations with the Small Numerical Rods and Numerals. He tends to dawdle in his work but he is certainly capable. I felt that he was trying to get more attention from me throughout the morning. He kept coming up to me for extraneous reasons, and I was irritated with him. He just hasn't settled in yet. He is trying, though. He came to sit next to me at juice time. When he got up, he said to himself, "Chair first!" Then he pushed it in, and went to throw his cup away.

While I was showing Carmen how to count the Hundred Chain, Jesse, then Susie and Robbie, all came to watch. That gives three other children a preview of the Hundred Chain. The children's voluntary interest at such times always thrills me. I am convinced not only that they are really learning because they have given their attention spontaneously, but also that they are developing an interest in learning itself. If I can help the children develop that, I'll feel that it has been a year well spent.

October 18   Madan is irritating me. He finds ways to keep me working with him. I realized after the morning was over that I had worked with him nonstop for over an hour (although there were other children working with us as well). Joan told me later that he had told her at the end of the morning, "I wish Mrs. Lillard would work with me more. Just me." I'm not just imagining that he is hanging around me!

Carmen does worry me. She looked so unhappy at about 8:20. She was just standing by the sink, looking lost. Later she went over to Joan and listened while she read something to Timmy in the *Golden Guide* about salamanders. She went to art then, and when she came back she started a map. She was happier, but she hasn't connected on a deeper level with either the work or the other children yet.

At 10:00 it was really noisy, and I asked for quiet. "I can't even hear Susie counting right next to me," I said with irritation in my voice. They sensed it and were quiet then. I felt uncomfortable about it, though. It was an outer control that I had exerted. I had "put the lid on" rather than help the children to settle themselves through their work choices.

I stopped the children for line time at 10:10, a few minutes early. Jack had been particularly jumpy earlier, and I simply had kept him with me as I did the Sandpaper Letters with Timmy. I had told Jack that the next time he felt jumpy, he should do the Cleanser, Polishing, Plant Care, and so on down the list of room care materials. At line time I talked to the whole class about what to do when they are feeling restless. Jack raised his hand. In a very serious, confident voice he repeated the list verbatim: "You should do the Plant Care or you could do the Polishing or you could mop the floor," etc.

October 19   I feel like I'm going through the storm season and today the threatening rains finally hit. It's the first time this year that I have felt that my approach to the children had lost out. They simply could not handle their freedom today. I stopped them once to ask for quiet, but in a minute the atmosphere was right back to where it had been. There was a definite undercurrent of unrest and rebellion in the air. It was like a tide rising higher and higher as the morning went on, and this time there was no possibility of riding it out.

Everything has hit at once, of course. Most important is the tension, excitement, and fear that Halloween stirs in children. Second, it is the shakedown period for the children's acceptance of the classroom community that I've outlined for them. Third, it is the midweek peak. Fourth, this group of children appears to be more accustomed to constant adult attention and direction than classes that I've had before. I felt today as if they were on strike as a class against the responsibilities that they were being asked to handle: responsibility for themselves and for their environment.

Jesse, Madan, Emily, Karen, and Lee (who was a surprise) were among the worst. Lee got silly two times during the morning. He was sitting next to Madan, who began it, I suppose. He ruined a very nice Strip Board paper of the Addition Tables of Three by scribbling on it. That incident got the message through to me more than anything else that today everything had combined into just too much for the children to handle. Jesse was very tense all morning, and was close to tears on the occasions when I spoke to him about slowing down. Eventually, he tried a map, but he wasn't pleased with it. It was a day that he should have spent with the room care materials. Even art was too much for him. He announced, "I'm going to make a skyscraper!" He got the Collage Tray and began. He became even more frustrated. He was just too keyed up to set his standards for a five-year-old's work. He was in the land of Superman and Star Wars.

Toward the end of work time, he enjoyed doing the Hundred Chain with me. Only this kind of one-to-one steadying seemed to help him. In music he kept losing control completely. Alice (the music teacher) was teaching the children a song about tigers "roaring," and had them stalking about on their hands and knees. It was obviously not a good choice for the day, but how was Alice to know?

By 9:40 I felt irritated with the whole situation. Only Madan angered me in a consciously personal way, however. He button-holed Joan right off when he came into the room by asking her to do the Sandpaper Letters with him. It was an obvious (and successful) attempt to have her to himself, as he knows this work backward and forward. He went to art then. When he was back at snack time, he was singing grace with silly words, and beginning to carry the other children at his table off with him. After this he was laughing loudly and being silly with Lee. I stopped the whole class this time, as I was trying to do the Bank Game with Karen, Emily, Sam, and Timmy. Before this Madan's tendency to silliness and lack of interest in work had been relatively harmless to the life of the class. Today the children were up for grabs, however. I suppose it was the negative influence that he was having on the other children that angered me so much. They needed all the help from each other that they could get today.

There were some standouts in progress, however, even on a day like this. Anna and Susie made maps of the world with great care, and then labeled both the continents and the oceans. Susie also found in the *Golden Guide* the milkweed pod which Joan had brought to class yesterday. Sandy worked long and hard on a Continent booklet and was very proud if it. She has been much less abrasive with the other children this week. I was particularly pleased with Timmy. He got the Wood Polishing out and polished the rectangular prism in the Geometric Solids, and did the Mirror Polish for the first time. Jack really tried hard all morning. He started the morning wandering a bit, first looking at the National Geographic relief globe which I brought in today. It shows the topography of the ocean floor as well as the continents. Then he looked at a magazine in the library. Finally, he got up and went through the whole list of activities that we talked about yesterday. He polished Geometric Solids, scrubbed the door with the Cleanser, and polished the silver candlestick. It was a classic scene. At 8:50 he settled down to a map. He worked on it very carefully. When he finished, he labeled both oceans and continents. Though he had tried so hard all morning, he couldn't keep himself from erupting a bit about 9:50. He ended work time by sitting with me and Jesse as we did the Hundred Chain.

I stopped work time early, but probably not as early as I should have. The most obvious sign of the children's state of mind today was the disorder with which they left the room when I called them to line time. We went on a "secret walk" to rearrange it, but mostly I had given up.

After our unsuccessful music class, we came back in the room to find the photographer there to take the class picture. It meant that we didn't get to take the walk in the woods to find a home for our salamander as I had planned. That had been my last hope of salvaging any joy from this morning. Many days like this and teaching would be an unbearable frustration.

October 23   It really wasn't a bad day, but it wasn't the usual golden Monday either. It makes me wonder what the week will bring. There was a general undercurrent of restlessness in so many of the children. Jack, Robbie, and Ed all came in rather excited. They chose Markers, Cutting, and Clay, but only Robbie went on to harder work later. He labeled a map including the oceans, and wrote equations to ten with the Small Numerical Rods and Numerals. Karen wandered around after Joan, and couldn't choose for herself. Madan's silliness was just on the brink of erupting all morning. He did get the Flower Arranging out, and filled every vase in the room, but I felt that he could have let go any minute. I worked with Jesse on the Strip Board as soon as he came in. That helped him, but he was another one who was barely in control today. I also did the Movable Alphabet with a number of children, which kept them in closer contact with me and that steadied them.

Carmen doesn't seem very happy to me. She was wandering until 8:30, then practiced writing. Later in the morning, I heard Jack say to her, "Would you get out of here! It's *my* work!" He clenched his fist at her. It's the first time that he has responded with such aggressive energy in the classroom. I was surprised. Carmen was soon busy mopping the floor, cleaning the door with the Cleanser Tray, and taking care of the plants. She is fine on individual work, but she's having a hard time finding her niche in the group as a whole.

Susie had her first pouty day in a long time. She sat on the line with her hand on her chin, looking miserable and hoping that she was having a similar effect on me, I suspect. She had fallen down over the weekend and bruised her nose and mouth. It did look pretty awful, but the other children did not mention it. Susie insisted to me, however, that "the children are making fun of me." I tried to walk a tightrope between being sympathetic and not letting her get locked into her pattern of manipulative behavior. I was busy with other children for a while, then I asked her to work with me. She went up and down all morning, but I was pleased with the way that she handled herself in general. It was certainly a big improvement over the beginning of the year.

October 24   It wasn't as bad today as I expected. I think it was because I really worked hard at directing children all morning. Some I never really "let go of." Emily was one. She came in all keyed up. As soon as her coat was off, I saw her pushing her stomach against Sandy's and pulling a toy truck out of her pocket. I told her that I would keep the truck until school was over. I asked her to get the Clay and sit next to me. This calmed her a bit, but I told her that I wanted her to tell me what work she was choosing all morning. Later in the morning she made a mess on the Painting Tray. She cleaned it up haphazardly afterward. I sent her back three times to do it more thoroughly. Finally, she got serious about it and cleaned it superbly. She was quite proud of it afterward. It takes so much energy on my part to persevere at such times. I really need my rest these days to be certain that I am up to the challenge.

Jack had a good day in the classroom but he was a disappointment on the playground. Joan said that she had spoken to him twice because he had been too rough with other children. Finally, he pushed Ed at the top of the slide, and it could have been really dangerous. Ed came in to me crying.

Madan was on the edge of erupting all day. He began with the Room Labeling Game, which I introduced yesterday. Sam did it with him once, and then Ed. I had to keep a close watch on them. Madan would try to think of silly things to do, such as putting the sink label inside the sink so the children couldn't use it. Later he had the Clay and was being silly with it, putting it on his eyes, etc. I spoke crossly to him then. "Madan, we can be in a fight all year, or you can control yourself. There is *no* silly behavior in this school."

Karen and Linda had superb mornings. They both labeled their first maps and were so proud of them. I was really pleased with Karen. I think it was her first deeply involved, enthusiastic work of the year.

October 25 These days I feel as if I'm sitting on a volcano. I've kept the class together except for last Thursday, but it's an uncomfortable feeling, knowing it could disintegrate at any time. I don't enjoy teaching at times like these. It's only the belief that things will begin to improve after Halloween that gives me the will to keep going with this kind of program.

On the plus side for the morning, the Bank Game went the best yet. Robbie, Ed, Madan, and Karen all did it together. They were very enthusiastic and wanted to keep repeating it. We did it four times in all.

Emily cleaned her paint tray superbly today. That extra effort with her yesterday did pay off!

Edith started everyone cheering for each other in gym today as each child tried to climb the rope. That's at least a beginning in their caring about each other's success.

October 26   Having the children shake hands with me first in the mornings really works out well. I like the one-to-one closeness with each child that it gives me, but it is important in receiving the "signals" right off, too. Karen today, for example, looked unhappy when she shook hands with me. "Karen, you look very unhappy. What is it?" I asked. She just pointed to her throat. "Sore throat?" I asked again. She nodded her head. Then I showed her the I Spy word game. She can read the labels easily after matching them with the pictures, when I hold them up independently from the cards. She did a map later, but in the middle of the morning I saw her in the library reading in the rocking chair. She didn't look at all well. I felt her head, and I was certain that she had a temperature. Joan took her to the nurse. It was 101 degrees.

I'm certain that Madan is quite capable of handling this environment on his own, but he is refusing to do so. Joan says that she feels he is constantly testing us. He was shadowing me this morning, and it irritated me. Unlike Timmy, who I am convinced now is in the process of finding himself, Madan is unproductive in his floating. I think that it is disturbing the whole class. He is like a sore thumb in our midst. Today I decided that for a while I will give him a choice of two materials each time I see him. Even though he has manipulated me into this, there is a chance that he will decide that freedom is more pleasant than constant direction after all. Perhaps also the work itself will eventually take hold for him. I don't feel very hopeful, however. Nine months is just not long enough to have an impact on patterns five years in the building and undoubtedly being reinforced at home.

I got Jesse started on equations to ten with the Small Numerical Rods, then he went on to nine and eight on his own before he ran out of steam. Joan got him started on the plants then, and it really took hold. It was a classic example of work settling a child. He washed every leaf of every plant in the room, sprayed them, clipped dead leaves, and watered them. It took him one hour.

Susie, Robbie, and Linda all found prints in the Renoir book that they have in their homes. No wonder this is always such a successful part of the curriculum. Susie said, "I've seen that one in the hallway on the way to music!" I've been waiting since the first day of school for the children to notice that the print of *In the Meadow* by Renoir is in our library corner and in the school hallway as well. This class has taken longer to make the connection than any I can remember. I believe in waiting for the children to make their own discoveries. However, I almost had given in to the temptation to mention this print to the class. I'm so glad that I didn't.

October 27   Madan thinks of any excuse to ask my attention. "What should I do with my paper?" he asked this morning. "What do you think that you should do with it?" I asked. "Put it in my folder," he answered. "Right," I said. "May I get my snack now?" he asked next. "Emily has told you snack is ready, hasn't she?" I asked. "Yes," he said. "Do you need to ask me, then?" I asked. "No," he answered. Is it possible to free him from this kind of relating to adults? I'm wondering if it is even desirable to do this. In Madan's case I can tell that his parents tend to encourage this type of dependency in their children. Maybe I will only confuse him.

I chose two things for him to do today: the Addition Tables of Two with the Strip Board and the Phonetic Object Box Three. He went off willingly, but unenthusiastically. He had a neutral, passive look about him. He dawdled over both pieces of work all morning, but he looked as though he felt secure, sitting there with work in front of him. It was hardly the involved concentrated effort and interest that I am after!

I was giving a short group lesson to the children whose turn it was to stay in the room, while the others went to library time. I was teaching the vowel sounds, both long and short. Their responses showed that they really are absorbing the total environment: For long *o*, they said "oval," and for long *a*, they said "Asia." Carmen was playing with her shoelaces and not paying attention. "Carmen, you must pay attention," I said several times. I got what I deserved: a four-year-old puffed up with dignity, arms folded in front of her, saying with a pouty toss of her head, "I ain't gonna do it!"

October 30   It was a good morning, and I have a feeling that things will begin to come together now. Robbie greeted me by saying, "Lucky, it is almost Halloween." Yet there was less tension in the class today. Perhaps they are relieved that the waiting is almost over.

The children do start off with confidence in the mornings now, all except Madan. Is it too late for him? He is bored and dependent at age five. Achievement is no problem for him, but there is no spark of independent response to the environment. Nothing is sadder to me than a life lived like that. He wandered off from following me about, and the inevitable happened. He picked up the cone at the Geometric Solids and pretended to lick it for the benefit of Ed, who also was standing there. "Where is your work, Madan? That is the problem," I said. He got the Clay then, but later he was hanging around Joan.

October 31   Madan was hanging about. "What do you want, Madan?" I asked. "I don't want nothing," he answered. Later he tried to buttonhole Joan with the Sandpaper Letters again. I stepped in then and told him to do the Tables of Three with the Strip Board. He got it out willingly, but in a minute he was standing watching me do the Twenty-five Chain with Jack and Susie. "I want to watch," he said. "No, go and do your own work, Madan," I said, feeling that he was simply avoiding doing something on his own. He did the Tables of Three nicely then, and I told him to go on to the fours. He did them well and was so proud of them, but it's like pulling teeth to get him off the ground.

Susie said, "I love those little things!" We were doing the Twenty-five Chain. It is the minute size and pretty color of the glass beads that appeals so much to the children, I think. It really makes a difference, having materials to work with that children respond to so totally.

I feel elated. I'm pretty certain that the tense period is behind us. From now on things should begin to roll. No wonder I dislike starting over each fall so much. This has been hard work. Most of all, there is always the tension over whether this way of teaching will work just one more time, or could those other successful years have been happy accidents, not to be repeated again?

Another reason for my present elation is that I can feel a deep affection developing in me for individual children. This doesn't happen overnight, any more than the children's independent response to the classroom can happen instantly. Both take time to develop. In the beginning, I wonder if I really will feel as deeply for these children as I have for the others before them. It doesn't seem possible when we are first starting out, and even less so when the "testing period" is in full swing.

November 1   It was a good Wednesday with perhaps a little higher noise peak around ten than I would have ordinarily expected.

Madan is, I'm afraid, driving me crazy. His first interruption was to tell me that his throat was dry. The second one was not to tell me anything. I said that he must choose work. "Can I do that work over there?" he asked. "I have shown that to you, haven't I?" I said. "Yes," he said. "What does that mean?" I asked. "That I can do it," he answered. "Right," I said. He got his work then, but when he was putting it away afterward, he deliberately stepped right in the middle of the rug. There was the most obvious testing look on his face as he looked up and our eyes met. I took hold of his arm, and spoke crossly to him. He looked at me with a contrite, soulful expression. A little later he was standing over Karen as she made a calendar. I told him that people don't like others standing over them when they work. He chose the Collage Tray to use then. How can I get him to use himself? I looked over at Lee, busily counting away on the Twenty-five Chain, which I had introduced to him yesterday. What a study in opposites! I asked Madan to set snack for me, hoping that might give him some time with me without its interfering with the idea that I want to get across to him, if it takes me all year; he *must* learn to be his own "motor." About ten he came to me again. "When is it going to be line time?" he asked. "Madan, that makes me very angry," I said. "I am busy helping Robbie make equations to ten with the Small Numerical Rods, something that I have already shown to you. Now it is his turn. I told all the children at the beginning of the year that I don't have time to answer questions like that." When will it end? *Will* it end?

November 2   Madan came in with the greeting "I have a cough." "Too bad to come to school, Madan?" I asked. "Yes," he answered. "But you came anyway," I said. "My daddy sent me," he explained. Next he announced, "I'm going to do the Strip Board." That surprised me. He needed the Tables of One and Five to complete the pages for a booklet. He went to art, then came back and finished the fives with a consistent effort. He was so pleased with his booklet that he asked for it back after I had put it with the work to take home. "I want to look at it," he said. It was a sign of hope, but later in the morning he came to me. "Did you know that I'm five and a half now?"

A child had been scribbling with a pencil on the white shelf close to the pencil basket. No child had cleaned it up spontaneously, so this morning I asked Edith if she would like to clean off the marks with the Cleanser. She really scrubbed and scrubbed. The shelf finally looked spotless. Later Joan pointed out to me that a child had scribbled an inch square of pencil marks right back in the same spot on the shelf. Madan came to my mind, but perhaps I was being unfair. I asked the children to line up and walk carefully past the pencil basket. Edith's eyes got as big as saucers when she saw her shelf. When the children went back to their seats, I told them that Edith had just cleaned the shelf this morning. Now someone was ruining it for all of them for the second time. I told Joan after class not to say anything more about the marks on the shelf but to wait and see if anyone would take care of it spontaneously tomorrow.

November 3   Madan came in very early. He went straight to get the Cleanser Tray and cleaned off the pencil marks on the shelf. I guess that I wasn't wrong on that one!

November 7   I am so pleased with Emily. She is taking everything seriously now. She comes in with her twinkling eyes as before, but now she goes right after the work instead of looking for a "party." She made a Continent booklet first, then looked up the dead baby mouse which Carmen brought in Friday. She found it in the *Golden Guide* on mammals, so we read about field mice and talked about mammals generally at line time. She counted the Hundred Chain with me next. She was much better this time, but she needs a good deal of practice.

Madan asked to do the North American map as soon as he

came in. We worked with it sensorially first. I was so pleased! He worked consistently and with good concentration when he began making his map. It was quite a good one, and he did well with the names of the countries, too. He knows all the larger ones and seemed to enjoy pronouncing the smaller ones: Guatemala, Nicaragua, etc.

Jack and Robbie were deliberately leaving Sam out of their play at outside time. This just doesn't seem to be a group of children who can play well together. It is Jack, of course. All goes fine when he stays out of it. What is it about him? I'm afraid that he could grow up to be a bully if he doesn't learn to deal with this part of himself successfully.

November 8   Marvelous! Emily greeted me with "I'm going to 'mabel' my map today." She had insisted that she didn't want to label any of her earlier maps. I am so glad that I didn't push her to try this sooner. It is a good example of listening to the children and not being rigid with them. I never would have guessed a month ago that Emily was going to develop into a self-starter like this.

Madan began labeling his North American map, and needed only a little encouragement to keep going. "Panama. That's the canal one," he said. "I've heard about that on the news." Emily talked about having lived in Spain when she finished making her world map. I feel deeply that making maps should be part of a kindergarten curriculum. They are a beginning in helping the children orient themselves in their world. "Who am I? Where am I?" These are major concerns for them.

November 9   Jack started off with the Cutting Exercise, an excellent choice for his small-muscle control, which needs developing. "Would you like me to show you something new when you are finished cutting, Jack?" I asked. He hesitated slightly as he thought it over. "Yes," he answered. In a few minutes, I showed him how to subtract with the Small Numerical Rods and Numerals. After he made the equations subtracting from ten, he said, "Now we do the nines, right?" He yawned and looked tired for a moment. "Would you rather put this away now?" I asked. "Yes," he said. However, in a few minutes he came up to me in another part of the room. "I think I'll do another one," he said. He continued this all morning until he had made a whole booklet. When he had just finished the eights, he said, "You sure get us into hard work." "Would you rather I didn't do that, Jack?" I asked. "Nope. I want to learn things," he said matter-of-factly.

I have been feeling better about Carmen in class, but problems developed on the playground again today. She came up to tell me, "Robbie is being mean to me." I thought that was unlikely, but I simply told her perhaps she should play with someone else. Later I saw her sitting in a pile of leaves all by herself. I called over to her, "What is the matter, Carmen?" "I'm just an old rag!" she pouted. Linda heard her and went to talk to her. She came back to me a few minutes later. "I *tried* to help her," she said. Carmen continued to pout. Linda went off to play with Susie and Karen. This is the second time in three days that I've been aware of Carmen's refusing rescue from the other children. How long will they keep trying to help her?

November 13   I feel terrible about Carmen. She came in this morning looking as if she were going to cry. She said that she had been in Wisconsin to see her grandfather. He was in the hospital, and very sick with a brain tumor. "He couldn't talk to me. He just squeezed my hand," she said. So that has been the problem. It really was true that her grandfather was so ill. Why in the world hasn't her mother told me? Surely she is aware of the impact of illness and death on children. I kept a close watch on Carmen all morning, and asked her several times if she would like to work with me. Outwardly, she appeared to want to be left alone.

However, I think that she is close to a state of depression and needs active help from me.

Everyone else was into a heavy work day. There were superb maps done. Emily and Sandy were working next to each other. I heard Emily say something about "hard work" to Sandy. Her voice was full of pride. They both labeled the oceans and continents when their maps were finished, and Sandy labeled the seas, too!

Even Madan had a good day. "I'm choosing my work from that shelf over there!" he announced, and he got the Trinomial Cube.

I have parent conferences tonight and tomorrow night. I'm eager to learn how the children are responding to school at home. I never feel as if the year has begun in earnest until the first conferences are over. I need the confidence that comes from knowing that we are all working together, children, teachers, and parents—both parents. Every year I come as close as I possibly can to insisting that fathers attend at least this first conference.

Parent Conferences   It was gratifying to hear about the children's responses at home concerning school. The parents seemed surprised by the children's pride in their work.

Madan was the biggest surprise to us, however. His mother said that he feels that he is our favorite! Occasionally he asks her why we like him so much better than the other children!

I could see one reason at least why Carmen's mother hadn't told me of her father's illness. Her eyes welled up with tears as she talked about his struggle since last April. He was given six months to live. (Hence Carmen's six weeks.) Apparently, Carmen had gained all her knowledge of the illness and imminent death, even the size of the tumor, from overhearing phone conversations. Her mother hadn't told her anything directly.

Jack's parents expressed their concern over his intolerance toward others. He dislikes "imperfections," they said. He has mentioned that others are short, clumsy, wear glasses, etc. Parents are generally so on target about their own child. When they don't feel threatened, they will communicate their feelings, both positive and negative. I always pay close attention to what they have to say, particularly if it is contrary to my own impressions.

November 14   Carmen smiled as she came in today. I asked her if she wanted me to show her how to make a North American map, and she was off on that all morning, complete with perfect labeling. I will never get over how much more children can and want to do than I expect them to. I had removed the labels that Joan had made for Alaska, Cuba, the Dominican Republic, and Haiti since they are not on the control map. I had told Carmen their names, however, when we were using the map sensorially during the introduction and she insisted on labeling them, too! I got them back out of the cupboard for her. How can human beings sense what others feel for them? I know that Carmen can tell that I understand what she is feeling at last. She is still close to a state of depression, but I know it is going to be all right at school now.

Madan, of course, had to be right next to me when I was working with Carmen. "What are you going to do with Carmen?" he asked. "Madan, I was with you a good deal yesterday. Now it is Carmen's turn," I answered. He finished the Continent booklet then and started on a Cuisinaire booklet of equations. He is definitely improving. He let go in music later, however, and I sat next to him to help him to control himself. Is that why he imagines that he's a "favorite"?

THE CHILDREN DEVELOP

November 15   It is a humming class now. Everything has fallen into place at once: "testing time" is over, conferences are finished, the environment is developed, a depth of feeling has been established between the children and myself, and the children themselves have shown tremendous development in just two months.

Madan got his Cuisinaire booklet out. Aside from insisting on showing me each page as he finished, he was reasonably independent all morning. He does consistently forget to put away his work, however.

Carmen had a much better day. What a difference it makes knowing what is wrong in her life. She went to art. Afterward she cracked nuts. I had set them out for the children to prepare for a Thanksgiving party that we've planned with the other kindergarten class. Best of all, the girls played in the leaves together at outside time. Carmen was in the midst of them all.

I had put carrots out for the children to fix for tomorrow. A number of children washed and cut them. How they do love food preparation! I probably should have something out for them every day. It's not only the process that is important but the self-confidence that preparing their own food gives them.

November 17   Sometimes I wonder if I'm pushing the independence aspect of the class too much. Then something happens to reinforce my original ideas about it. Ed asked me to tie his shoelace this morning. "Let's practice with the Bow frame, Ed, and then you can tie it yourself," I said. He worked on the frame with intermittent help from me for ten minutes or so. Soon I had completely forgotten his shoe as I was busy helping other children. He came up to me later with a pleased smile, and pointed down to his now tied shoelace.

November 21   The whole morning was a huge success from preparation and work period to the party beginning at 10:30. It was interesting to see how individual children dealt with their excitement. Some chose regular work. Others concentrated on

party preparations. Madan, Jesse, and Ed were chief party pre-
parers. They spread peanut butter on celery, cut cheese for
crackers, cracked more walnuts, arranged the flowers, scrubbed
the tables, opened and counted paper cups, plates, and napkins.
I had set up each of these activities for individual use at separate
tables. After a child finished doing as much as he wished, he
straightened his place for the next child.

At 9:45 I called the children to the line. Each child had chosen one child from the other class to be his guest. We were to be
the Pilgrims, the other class the Indians. We rehearsed how the
children were to greet their guests at the door, lead them to
the buffet table and then to a preselected seat, and finally go to
the cider table and pour glasses for themselves and their guests.
We talked about manners during a party and how they were to
clean up after their guests before telling Joan or me that they
were ready to go outside.

By 10:30 we were all seated on the line again, each child wearing a Pilgrim hat that he had made in art. Bach's music was playing. The buffet table was arranged with a linen tablecloth, two
lighted candles in silver candlesticks, and baskets and bowls of
prepared food. I stood at the door and called each child up to
greet his guest individually. The expressions on their faces as
they met each other was one of the best moments of the morning. I hadn't realized how intense their friendships were. Some
children had been together in preschool, but others had become
friends from playing together during our outside times. They
had a good time at the party, chatting away with each other, and
going back for seconds and thirds.

I think that it was the individualizing into pairs, as well as the
careful organizing and rehearsing of details, that made it possible for thirty-six five-year-olds to have a party together with very
little adult interference. I only had to speak to several children
during the entire thirty minutes about "party manners."

I overheard some marvelous comments. "This is just like a

dinner party!" "You just keep eating and eating." "We sure have some terrific Pilgrims in here!"

A few children were wound up when they came back in from outside—Ed, Jack, Karen. They were easy to calm down, however. It makes such a difference knowing each child well now. I know just how far they will go, and how and when to bring them back.

November 22   Madan showed great strides in independence all morning. Since I hadn't worked with him individually for several days, I asked him if he wanted to do the Phonetic Cards with me. "No, I'll go and choose my work," he said. He did a nice collage. I asked him again about the cards. "Not yet," he said. He chose the Pouring Exercise next. Eventually, he did the cards with me, and then went on to the Marker Paper.*

The children were excited about vacation. This was particularly obvious in the number of accidents that occurred. Susie knocked over a vase of flowers, and Anna broke a small bowl with paper clips in it. Anna looked somewhat distraught over the broken bowl. "All it is, is a mistake," said Karen, looking up from her work. She got up to help Anna clean it up.

Jack and Robbie made North American maps, then labeled them. Jack said, "I can't find this one." When I told him it said "Dominican Republic," he knew exactly where it went! How do they learn so much? He put some labels on Robbie's map by mistake. "Hey, that's my map," Robbie said. "Thanks for those!" They do get along so well. It's too bad that this isn't true of Jack and the other boys. I think that it is because they hang around Jack so much, especially when there is excitement like today. Jesse and Ed were the worst. They really provoked Jack. Joan thinks that they hope some of the "hero halo" will rub off on them if they are near Jack. This morning Jack said, "All the kids

*See Chapter 3, page 111f.

like me too much. I don't expect it." It is a burden for him all right.

November 27   When we were naming Susie's world map on the line, I asked the children if they had heard about the people dying in Guyana (the mass suicide of hundreds of members of the cult religion led by Jim Jones). I showed them where it was on the map. I was stunned by the amount of detailed information they knew. Carmen said, "Do you know how many people died? Nine hundred and ten!" Sam said, "I saw the boxes. They flew the bodies back on airplanes." Anna talked about poison being forced down the children's throats. "They sprayed it in," she said. Robbie said, "The man in the glasses killed everyone, and then someone shot *him!*" What an incredible impact exposure to television is having on their lives and development.

November 28   Robbie was heading for a map, but I suggested that he finish counting the chains that he started yesterday. He seemed to enjoy doing them, but I was uncertain if I should have steered him away from his original choice of a map. In fact, I had a nagging feeling that I was pressuring the children all day. I had the flu and felt terrible. I was pressuring myself just to be in the school at all.

I started Jack on the chains yesterday, too. When he saw Robbie working on them, he got his own paper out. (They were writing the multiplication equations with them: $10 \times 10 = 100$, $9 \times 9 = 81$, etc.) Joan had to help Jack. He would call the numeral tag 21 twelve, and begin counting the next unit bead thirteen instead of 22. I'll have to re-present the Tens Board, which shows how these numbers are constructed. Jack insisted on finishing his chains, however. At the end he said, "I worked harder than Robbie, didn't I?" What drives him to compare himself with others constantly? Does he feel threatened because his talent appears to be average, or is he worried because he's shorter than average in physical size, as his parents are?

November 30   It was a productive, smooth-running morning until music. I had to speak to Madan, Jesse, Jack, and Lee at different times. The children in this class are more ready to "let go" than others that I have had. I think it is because there are so many strong individual personalities in this class. They seem to be all chiefs and no Indians. They are a fairly cohesive group in the classroom now, but their individuality works against them in a situation like music where they don't have a secure environment of interesting work to hold them together.

December 1   Jack finished his December calendar. He walked past Robbie, who was working on his. "I've already finished my calendar," Jack said in a put-down tone. Robbie simply said, "Well, I'm working on mine now."

At snack time Linda looked at me very quizzically and said, "That music is different." It was the first time that I hadn't played Bach. I had played Handel's *Messiah* instead.

December 5   The Christmas buildup has begun all right. The children were at loose ends when they came in. They were quickly into a rash of room care activities: Jack the Cleanser, Madan the Dust Mop, Timmy Sweeping, Robbie the Floor Scrubbing. It seemed a little frenzied, but it had its effect. By 8:40 Jack was calmly at work with the Marker Paper, Madan with the Hundred Chain, Timmy with a December calendar, Robbie with Number Writing Paper—all without my redirecting them in any way.

Ed was walking on the line balancing a basket on his head. He was trying his best to keep himself under control, but his impish look was too tempting for Karen. She was making a map close to the line. She stuck her hand out to stop him and giggled, "Ticket, please." It was just enough to set off Jesse, who was making a North American map at the other end of the line. When Ed got to him, Jesse began to imitate Karen. Our eyes met then, and he put his hand down.

December 6   Excitement was in the air again, particularly because Susie is having a birthday party this afternoon for the whole class. She had a hard time getting going this morning, but eventually she began reading a story in the library with Linda. At the end of the morning she told me, "I got excited. Then I read a book, and calmed down."

Jesse is so wound up. He even forgets now and runs across the room when he wants something. "This isn't a running school, Jesse," I said each time. Jack looked up at me and said, "It's a working school, right?"

Jesse and Ed teamed up to make North American maps. It wasn't the best combination, but they managed better than I expected. Jesse finished the day making a Marker Paper booklet. If all the days before Christmas go this well for him, I'll feel that he's developed a good deal since September.

December 7   Jesse came in quite excited this morning. "You know what!" he said. "I went to Lakehurst [a shopping center] and I saw *The Two Circus Girls!*" (We have this Renoir print on our library wall now.)

December 8   The children are reacting more each day to their excitement. Early in the morning Sam looked as if he was going to cry. "What's wrong, Sam?" I asked. "Jack called me a slowpoke and I can't help it if my mother was late this morning," he said. At snack time Jack and Robbie were having an argument with Jesse because he threw part of his cookie away. "You should have kept it for home," Jack said. Ed came up to tell me, "There were seven spills today!" It was true, too. Timmy came to me and said, "Please tell Jack not to be mean to me." "What did he do, Timmy?" I asked. "He said that I think that I'm so great. Will you tell him?" he said. I took Jack out of the room then, to talk to him alone. "Jack, you are hurting people's feelings," I said. His eyes filled with tears. How am I going to help him?

Just as I was thinking, "What is wrong with this class?" the children surprised me by playing beautifully outside together. The slide was covered with ice and the minihills around it were perfect for sliding, too. The children giggled and laughed as they slid about. "Hey, I love it!" Susie called. Carmen waved happily to me. It is wonderful to see her so much more a part of things now. She is even trying to climb the rope in the gym each day, something that she had refused to do in the first months.

December 12   What an incredible work day. There was no way that we could break for line at 10:15. I reluctantly stopped everyone at 10:30. We would have been late to music if I had waited any longer. It was quite a sight after snack: a room full of so much energy and so much work and so much spirit. Karen was lying on her stomach, coloring Africa on her map. Her head was resting on her arm and her red-stockinged feet were swaying in the air, keeping time to the *Messiah*. Linda was looking at a book of Bible stories in the library. I was sitting next to Ed, who was writing a story and talking to himself as he wrote: "A good *o*, a good *f*," etc.

December 13   I was helping Sam and Ed, who were practicing writing letters. They were off on a regular binge. "This is fun. I'm going to do a booklet of these," Ed said. "I'm making from *a* to *z*," Sam said. "Which way does *a* go? I know, I can get the Sandpaper Letters." We all had snack together. "This is a better school than my last one," Ed said. I had started Anna on a subtraction booklet with the Cuisinaire Rods at our table, too.

"Me, too," she said. "There's much more things to do here."
"Back to work!" Ed said after snack, and he started in on his letters again.

When Jack and Robbie were putting their maps away, I saw
Robbie push against Jack's chest with his hand. When it was time
to go home, Jack said to Robbie, "Know who my best friend is?
It isn't you!" Oh, dear, Jack. Not Robbie, too.

December 14   Much of the children's conversation with each
other as they work is about the TV Christmas specials. "That long-
eared donkey was weird," Robbie said. "Did you cry?" Jack asked
him. "No, of course not!" Robbie said. "But poor Nestor's mother,
she suffocated," Jack insisted. Underneath all the bravado is a
sensitive little boy who isn't afraid to be open about his feelings.

I've been giving the children and myself a vacation the last
few days. I have hardly directed any work from my daily notes.
The children have done very well on their own. Their self-
chosen curriculum has consisted mostly of maps and labeling,
Marker Paper and Story Marker Papers, art work, and room care
materials. This limited choice of materials makes my role in the
classroom clear at this point. I am needed to get a wider variety
of materials in use in the environment and to challenge the children with new materials when they are ready. They can manage
without my more direct participation for a while, but I'm certain
that the room eventually would lose its lively, forward-moving
quality if I kept up our mutual "break" too long.

December 15   Robbie and Madan asked me to come watch
our toad, Fred, "take a bath." He was plunked in his drinking
dish, half of him falling out on all sides. He did look comical. He
is like a silent representative of all the unseen life with which we
share our planet, reminding us that we are responsible for pro-
tecting that life as well as our own. I think that it is essential for
the children's development to have at least one living creature in

the classroom. When this creature is an amphibian, there is the added advantage of helping to develop the children's feelings and awareness for the lower forms of life.

During the morning Linda came to tell me "Jack hates Edith." Earlier Anna had brought me a very carefully done North American map. Unfortunately, there was a black crayon mark in the middle of the Atlantic Ocean. "What happened here, Anna?" I asked. "Jack did that," she said. During snack I saw Jesse go up to Jack. Jack said, "Shake," and squeezed Jesse's hand until he winced with pain. Timmy came up next to sit down at the table, and Jack did the same thing to him. Timmy was upset and bumped into Lee, who was carrying his milk to the table. "Now see what you made me do!" he cried, close to tears, as the milk went in all directions. I stopped the whole class then. "Jack, please apologize to Jesse and Timmy for hurting their hands. Then help Lee clean up his spill."

"What is it, Jack?" I asked him later alone. "What about Edith?" "She bothers me," he said. "I am at this table, not a private table,* then she comes and sits next to me. It just bothers me." I had seen Anna put her rug across from Jack's to make her map, so I knew what the answer was there. At line time I said, "Jack, would you tell the children how you feel when they always sit next to you?" He was a little embarrassed but managed to explain, "Well, I'm doing hard work. It just bothers me that everyone is always talking to me." We talked about it for a while. At the end I said, "I think we can leave Jack alone with his work, don't you? And Jack, you could go to a private table or you could say, 'I like you very much but I want to work now,' couldn't you?"

December 18   It was a smooth and industrious day, although there was an undercurrent of excitement in the air with

---

*We have four tables in the room that are for one child only. This enables children to work by themselves when they wish.

the tree trimming to take place at 10:30 and the party that the children are going to give for their mothers to plan for tomorrow. The children often react by working even harder than usual at such times. It reminded me not to make the mistake of planning more excitement for them on these days: a group project or any other unnecessary change in routine. It is their work, not extra entertainment, which steadies them.

I have hardly been conscious of how Madan has gradually established his independence from Joan and me. He wasn't choosing his work earlier in the morning, so I asked him, "Would you like me to choose something for you, Madan?" "No," he said. He kept walking along the shelves and looking a little longer. Then he chose the Gift Wrapping Exercise, working at it with good success for quite a while. Afterward he cracked nuts, cut carrots, and made a world map. How could I have had so little faith in him a month ago?

Jack, Sam, and Robbie were having juice together at one of the small tables. I saw Jesse go up to them several times to talk. The next thing I knew, Jesse and Jack were shoving each other in earnest. "Jack started it! He kicked me!" Jesse cried, close to tears. I knelt down next to the table, eye level with Jesse. "Jesse, what did we talk about on Friday?" Ed said quickly, "Don't hang around Jack." "Both apologize to each other, then Jesse, go back to your work," I said. Jesse went back to his Continent booklet, but he looked wistfully at Jack's table a few times while they finished their snack. You could almost see him thinking, "That's easy for you to say, Ed! You're with Jack already!"

The children were very good at the tree trimming ceremony. In fact, they now handle all special occasions with very good discipline.

December 19   Timmy and Madan were standing and looking at Emily's Nativity Set, which she brought in to share. "This year I'm just going to celebrate Christmas. I celebrated both that one time." "What's the name of that one?" Timmy asked. "Di-wali?" Madan (who is Hindu) asked hopefully. "No, I'm Christ-ian and Jewish," Timmy said. "Oh, that's your guy that got hanged up on the cross," Madan said. "I don't have him."

The children were dressed in their best clothes for the party. Many started right off helping with party preparations. Carmen cracked nuts, Susie put peanut butter in the celery slices, Sam cut cheese for the crackers, Timmy cut carrots. Anna fixed flow-ers. Madan polished silver bowls and the candlesticks. "We're all elves in here!" Anna said as she went past me carrying a vase of red and white carnations.

Early in the morning Joan had come to tell me that Jesse was "wound up like a tight spring, lashing out at everyone." Just as I was thinking, "What a civilized scene," I saw Jesse reach over and start to scribble with a black marker on Ed's wooden clay board. "Is that the way you treat your school, Jesse?" I asked. He looked chagrined and shook his head, but we both knew it wouldn't be his last impulsive moment of the morning.

During all this preparation and work time, the conversations had been lively and full of anticipation. I could sense the inten-sity of the children's feelings for their mothers. Karen said to Emily working next to her, "I'm not going to play with you." Emily's face fell. "Because I'm playing with my mother!" Karen finished. Emily looked relieved. "Oh, yeah, that's what I'm doing, playing with my mother!" Emily said enthusiastically. Jack and Robbie were working on maps in a secluded corner. "So what if your mom has gray hair," Jack said in a consoling voice. "She's only forty," Robbie said. Jack was determined to help. "The bad-ness is, if it's gray, you know some people laugh at gray-haired people. But so what? It doesn't make any difference. So what if you're bald? My uncle's bald. He's got hair on the sides and in the back and no hair on the top. So what! It doesn't make any difference."

We came to the line and began our rehearsal in much the

same way as we had for Thanksgiving. This time we practiced taking the mothers' purses and pushing in their chairs for them. The party itself went beautifully. The children were so proud to be waiting on their mothers. The mothers seemed both pleased and surprised. After the party was over, I told the children that they could look about the room with their mothers and whenever they were ready, they could go home. They all began to get work out! They were still going strong at 12:00, a half-hour past dismissal time.

December 20   This was the last day before vacation. The children started off so quietly, industriously, and confidently. I was quite impressed. Ed made an intricate design by superimposing the trapezoid inset in several different directions. "You could spend all morning just filling in each little section, Ed," I said when he showed it to me. Linda came up to me at the end of the morning. "You know what? I believe Ed, he's made a grown-up inset!"

"Where's the tray, because I haven't practiced yet," Carmen asked. It was her fifth birthday today. She practiced for quite a while with the tray and unlighted candle, walking carefully heel to toe on the line. Later, when we sang to her at line time, she was perfect. The tray and lighted candle never dipped even slightly and not a single step went off the line. I don't think any other child has done it nearly as well. Her mother told me later that Carmen had been worried about doing this and had practiced at home with her. It's times like these that the pressure of being both a perfectionist and young is revealed.

Anna was really into work all morning—first a whole Strip Board booklet, then a North American map. Jesse worked with the Collage Tray almost all morning. He made a Christmas card with inlays inside of Jesus and the stable. It was intriguing. He finally got to be with Jack at the very end of the morning. They were doing the Phonogram Object boxes, and for once Jack didn't seem irritated by Jesse's jumpiness. Jack had only a fair morning overall. He had started out finishing his world map, but at juice time the giggles started at a table with Ed, Robbie, and Edith. The only conversation I heard was Ed saying something about "boobies." I called him over to sit with me. Jack got the chalkboard and wrote numbers then. He ended the morning with his old standby, Cutting. I felt he was using it more for a tonic than work. Ed and I did the Gift Wrapping together. Next he watered the plants. "That azalea took a real drink!" he announced. (I teach the children the exact name for everything in the room. Knowing it's an azalea, not just a plant, adds interest and contributes to the children's sense of ownership and self-confidence in their room.)

What a wonderful, sensitive, and enthusiastic assistant Joan has been. She certainly has the right spirit for this kind of teaching. She has written on her Christmas card, "Thank you for the experience of working with you. I just love to wake up in the morning to see what will happen next!"

January 8   I was disappointed this morning. The atmosphere wasn't as calm and industrious as before vacation, although it settled considerably after juice time. I think that I expected too much. I had forgotten that the children always lose touch slightly with the routines of the class over a vacation period. This particular class lost ground with the communal feelings that they were developing, too.

Karen bounced into class and with a happy, pleased smile on her face, went right after the new Canada map. Madan only waved sadly to me, instead of shaking hands. "We didn't even get to put up our Christmas tree," he said. "My grandfather died."

We have a new boy, Nick, in the class. His parents have brought him to our school because he "wasn't being challenged enough" in the public kindergarten. I felt overwhelmed by all the procedures and routines to go through all over again in introducing him to the room. There is a fully functioning class to help this time, however, and that will make all the difference.

After juice, Jack began to do the Phonogram Objects, then Jesse and Robbie started on them, too. They got quite involved and the morning generally began to roll. Linda, Carmen, Edith, Sandy, and Anna all were writing stories. Linda's is four pages and she's not finished yet!

At line time I told everyone that Madan's grandfather had died in India. Carmen looked up and said quietly, "My grandfather died, too, my mother's father." She was solemn and sad, but I sensed that she felt relief that it was over, too. I read a book about the death of a great-grandmother to the children. It glossed over sorrow and grief too much to help the children. I feel that children are crying out for us to be more honest and open with them about death. I tried this morning, but I feel inadequate. Partly, I am afraid of parent reaction. Death, religious belief, birth, and its relationship to sexual life—every teacher knows that these are areas where she has to tread lightly.

January 9   It was a much better day. My expectations were too high yesterday. I had put out a number of new materials and I was needed in too many places at once.

Ed was wound up but worked hard on the new Pouring Exercise, then wrote a fine story. Jesse was keyed up also but kept himself working. He wrote a story, too.

January 11   I have taped our old calendars together (September through December) and rolled them up in a scroll. It is to help the children develop the concept of continuity in the months and, eventually, that the twelve months of the year form a complete cycle. It stretched a fourth of the way across the room when we unrolled it and was half as tall as the children. All the children stopped to watch.

January 12   I got to many of the children whom I really hadn't seen all week, and that was probably the best thing about this morning. I was feeling out of touch with many of them since vacation. I worked with Karen, Sandy, Susie, and Carmen on the Geometric Solids. I was disappointed at how much they had forgotten in the month or so since they used them last. It was a good reminder of the amount of repetition over time that is necessary before children can make knowledge their own.

January 18   It was such a relief to be back today. Before I knew it, I had forgotten both the past four days of being snowed in and having school canceled and the weather forecast this morning. It is supposed to snow four or more inches again tonight, followed by freezing rain tomorrow, and another major storm by Sunday.

It was a very smooth day, but no wonder—Jesse and Ed weren't here. It makes all the difference for Jack. He had a truly perfect day. He knows what he wants to do if he is only left alone to do it.

January 22   The children definitely are getting the idea of how the calendar works. Today Robbie said, "That's too early. You got mixed up." I had written January 15 on the board.

I began the introduction to the creation of the universe and evolution today. It is a good time for it. The class is together and well grooved, ready to concentrate on something new and stimulating. Their eyes were wide when I talked about the Big Bang and hydrogen flying out in all directions. I brought out the Collage Tray, which I had set up with various cellophane papers, colored strips, tissue paper, etc. Each child could make two "Big Bangs" with it, one to take home and one for our new shelf display. The latter will start with creation and follow through all the stages of the earth's formation and the beginning of life to man himself. I had made a model of the Big Bang for them. However, I told them that they would have to imagine how they might make one, since it was all a mystery. Jesse said, "I'm going to make little circles for the dust." He does have a wonderfully creative way with art materials. I have added a basket with colored papers with a paper punch for his "dust."

January 23   The idea of the Big Bang has so caught the children's imagination. Anna, Linda, and Robbie all spontaneously made pictures of it with the Markers, then labeled them. A two-hour work period isn't long enough. So many times the children are just warming up to their most intensive effort of the morning, and I have to stop them. This morning, for example, Jack had settled down to count all the Chains and write the multiplication equation for each one. He had just finished the Eighty-one Chain. Susie was completely involved in finishing her North American map. Karen was finishing a Canada map. Robbie was practicing letters. Ed and I were doing a Phonogram booklet together. Nick and Emily were doing the Phonetic Objects next to us.

At line time we talked about the hydrogen dust forming into clouds. I said that the dust did this because matter has a "kind of love for itself" called gravity. We talked about Isaac Newton then. I had set up a tray with an apple on it, a label that read "gravity," and a card with "Isaac Newton 1665" written on it. I showed Newton's picture in the National Geographic book *The Amazing Universe*, which I use for much of the information on the universe.

January 25   I worked with Anna, Sandy, and Carmen on the Geometric Solids. We matched them to their bases as well as reviewing their shapes and names. They know them well now. "That's an ellipse in there," Anna said, pointing to the red felt pad in the bottom of the basket. How many times a day must the children be making these connections, and I am totally unaware of it?

January 26   I told Linda that she could make her Big Bang. Before she could get started, Joan came to tell her it was her art day. She was annoyed that she had to go. "Which is more important after all," she said, her arms folded defiantly in front of her, "art or the Big Bang!"

January 29   I told Ed that I noticed that he had an unfinished Strip Board booklet in his folder. "Oops! Thanks for remembering me," he said. He finished it then, and had a great morning generally.

At 10:15 Sandy wanted to make a calendar, Edith and Madan wanted to do the Stamp Game, Susie had done a magnificent inset and it had inspired a run on them for Emily, Karen, and Anna. I hated to stop work and didn't until we had absolutely no choice at 10:30.

We talked about the birth and death of stars at line time. The children were excited about the stars expanding into red giants and finally ending up as white dwarfs.

February 5   Susie was sitting by the maps and taking a long time to take her coat off. She appeared to be daydreaming, and I was tempted to urge her to get going. She came up to me a few minutes later. "I want to show you something," she said. She pointed to the Canadian and North American maps. "This is this, and this is this," she said as she pointed from Greenland on one map to Greenland on the other, the United States on one, then the other, doing so with ease in spite of the differences in scale and color coding. I never know how or when the discoveries and connections will come!

February 8   The children have eased out of relating to Jack as the hero leader in an almost imperceptible way. I think that it is the result of the other children's closing the gap in development. As the oldest in the class, Jack must have appeared especially competent and confident to the other children at the beginning of the year. Now the other children have developed similar confidence and independence in their manner, as they have learned to write and read and handle the rest of the curriculum with competence.

February 20   The children and I were rested after the holiday yesterday. It was a smooth-running, happy first day of the week. Ed said, "Can I do this map?" I had just put the map of the United States out this morning. I introduced it to him in the usual way, having him use the control map first, then making the complete map without it before starting to trace any pieces. I was amazed that he had no trouble with it at all. When I named both Georgia and Wisconsin, his face lit up. "We went to Georgia! We went to Wisconsin!" Anna labeled her world map. "I don't even need the map to tell me where the labels are," she said proudly. "I just sounded out Antarctica and Australia." I had brought in some daisies, and Anna filled every vase. They do make the room look cheerier on these snowy days.

February 23   We have had visitors almost daily for weeks now. They are both prospective parents and teachers from other schools. The children are quite accustomed to them and usually pay no attention to them. Today, however, I felt our visitors were having a negative effect on Ed. He was keyed up for action all morning. Only by speaking to him early on and by watching him closely all morning did I manage to keep him from getting out of control. The visiting teacher was very complimentary about the class. She particularly mentioned the level of the children's writing and their relaxed attitude and kindness to each other. I was pleased because I had not felt that it was a particularly good morning.

February 27   Madan and Robbie did the Decimal Tray Two together, a reinforcement for them both as they know the breakdown well: ten units for one ten bar, ten tens for one hundred square, etc. Later Edith and Susie were doing Decimal Tray One: naming the thousand cube, the hundred square, etc. Again it was something that they already know. This spontaneous repetition of what appears to be already known is the key to the children's successful development, I'm convinced.

March 1   We've had one good day after another. There was a wonderful exuberant hum of activity all morning. The head of the school history department came to our room for a minute. "What a nice class," he said. "What I like best is their independence." I was pleased because our headmaster had talked to us about working toward developing more independence in our children at the last school faculty meeting.

I have set up the Collage Tray so that the children can make a solar system chart. There are colored papers to cut for each planet and sun, and labels for each. Edith, Sandy, Anna, and Emily all finished making theirs today.

Emily broke the glass for the Painting Tray today. I showed her how to pick up the pieces slowly (she was doing it much too quickly) to avoid cutting herself. She swept up all the smaller pieces with the yellow brush and dust pan. She seemed proud of cleaning it up so well and all by herself. I'm convinced that cleaning up on their own after accidents helps the children to have a more matter-of-fact attitude about them. It is well worth the risk of their getting a slight cut.

March 2   We've had parent conferences the last few days. I had nothing but good news to relay to the parents, so the conferences were less tiring than the fall ones. The parents were impressed with their children's reading and their interest in the beginning of the universe and the stars. I sensed in all of them an awe for their children's development this year, and a deeper enjoyment of them now that they can share more interests.

March 5   It was so busy today that I couldn't keep track of all that was going on.

Carmen, Karen, and Jesse were doing beautiful complex insets with great care next to me at the table. "School sure keeps you busy!" Carmen said to me as she traced her inset.

March 7   It was another extremely busy morning with everyone well into materials on their own steam. Carmen and Emily both brought in more newspaper pictures of Jupiter and its moon, Io. Six children watched Robbie feed mealworms to Fred. They were all being very enthusiastic but their voices and actions were disciplined and moderate. I thought, "How marvelous to have a class where almost half the children can be excited over feeding a toad and cause no disturbance to the others."

March 8   Linda read the board message at line today. I had told the children about Copernicus yesterday, so the message was about him. All the children remembered that he had realized that the planets go around the sun. We had talked about his waiting until he was about to die before he made his theories known. It was a good lead-in to discuss *Voyager I* sending back pictures of the ring around Jupiter today, and that scientists wouldn't have to suffer like Galileo and Copernicus for this discovery.

Timmy came to tell me that Jesse had hit him. Later Jesse came up to Linda, who was doing the Stamp Game with me. She was in the midst of counting, and Jesse interrupted her to talk.

"Oh, now look what you did!" she said as she lost count and had to start over. "Jesse, why did you hit Timmy?" I asked. "I wanted to tell him something. I didn't hit him hard," he answered. "Well, Jesse, it's just like with Linda right now. When other children are working hard, you have to wait until they are finished before you can talk to them. Where is your work?" I asked. He pointed over to his almost finished United States map. "If you want a break, Jesse, why not just watch what others are doing or go in the library for a while," I suggested. He went back to Timmy instead, and said, "I'm sorry, Timmy."

March 14   As soon as he came in, Lee asked. "Can I do another collage?" (of the inside of the earth). Making these collages stirs other art expressions of our science studies, too. Timmy was doing the Clay while he waited his turn with the Collage. He came over to tell me, "I made it out of clay." "What, Timmy?" I asked. "The earth, like that thing over there," he said pointing to Lee's collage. Robbie made a painting of it. I asked if he would like to write a story to go with it. It was two pages. "I went down in the earth. I saw the crust and hot lava. I saw the inner solid core and the mantle and the outer liquid core."

Sam came to tell me that Robbie and Jack were being mean to him. Class was running very smoothly and independently, so even though Joan had left the room for a meeting, I took quite a few minutes to have an in-depth conversation with them. "What's going on, boys?" I began. Silence. Finally, Jack answered rather reluctantly, "Just teasing." "What's teasing?" I asked. "Saying some bad things, mean things," Jack said. "I'm old and I really don't know what you mean by 'mean things,'" I said. "Four-eyes," Jack said. "No, you didn't call him four-eyes today," Robbie, ever the literal one, said. "He's a smart aleck," Jack answered. "That's what you said today?" I asked. "Yup, he was bothering me. He was saying, 'Hey, Jack, hey, Robbie, want to do some stuff,' and staring at us, like this," and Jack made a silly face. "Tell me next time that happens, okay? Then I can try to help Sam," I said.

Jack just couldn't stay out of any situation that arose all morning long. He hadn't been like this for weeks. Finally, I said, "Jack, will you stop trying to tell everyone what to do!" Madan and I were doing the Stamp Game, so I said that he would have to get one and do it with us. After one equation, Jack said, "Let's do a booklet." "Me, too," Madan said. Jack had a bad cough. When I mentioned it to him, he said, "I've just got a broken body today, it feels like. I've got a sore throat and it hurts here when I swallow and I've got a cough. . . ."

March 15   The children were very disciplined with their prevacation nerves. Sam poured his milk glass too full at snack time. He spilled quite a bit when he was pouring it back into the pitcher. Jack lifted the pitcher for him and Karen picked up the tray, while he was wiping up the table. "Over here," Jack said, and "Over here," Karen added. "I know," Sam answered. "And on the floor," Jack continued. "Not with that sponge!" Sam had started to use the table sponge on the floor. "I'll do it for you," said Jack, and he wiped up the floor with the mop and a bucket of water.

Vacation at last. The weather has made it an unusually long winter. I am so pleased with the children's accomplishments and development!

April 1   The children slipped back into the environment and routines with much more ease than they had after Christmas vacation. They seemed more rested and easier in their relationships with each other, too. Only Jack seemed a little testy. He said, "So what?" several times during the morning in response to other children's remarks. I wonder if he is upset because he didn't go away for vacation.

I asked Jack to do a Stamp Game with me. "I really wanted to do a Canada map," he said. "All right, but let's do one addition problem first," I answered. I can always count on Jack to be agreeable about working with me. Jesse is just the opposite. I wonder if his parents put too much pressure on him, particularly in asking for correct behavior and deference to adults. He doesn't seem to trust me. This morning he had worked on an unfinished United States map from before vacation, then drawn a very detailed picture with the Markers. He was starting for the Clay when I asked him to do a Stamp Game with me. "I wanted to do the Clay," he whined, making a face. "Only one addition problem, Jesse," I said. He was unhappy at first, but he did get in the swing of it as soon as he started to choose his number. "I'll have no hundreds," he said. After the addition problem he said, "I'm going to do another one. I'm going to do a book."

I was aware all morning that the children were happy to be back. I couldn't help thinking what a shame it is that they lose this relaxed, contented feeling about school as they grow older. Would this happen universally if the same kind of structured yet relaxed and independent learning environment could be extended to the older grades?

April 3   I brought yellow chrysanthemums today. Ed saw them right away. He had a pleased smile on his face the whole thirty minutes it took him to arrange all six vases full. Afterward he spent the whole morning on room care: pouring, polishing, etc. Linda saw Ed arranging the flowers as soon as she came in the door. "Finally, she brought some flowers!" she said to Joan. When she shook my hand, she said, "Thank you for getting the flowers!" Since Ed had arranged them all, I told her later that it would help the flowers last longer if she changed the water tomorrow and cut the stems a little.

April 4   In gym today no one chose Jack for Duck Duck Goose. "My feelings are hurt," I heard him mutter under his breath. When Edith finally chose him, he almost knocked her flat on the floor by shoving her hard against her back when he caught her. He was so intent on successfully tagging her that he was oblivious to his roughness in doing so.

"I know who wrote that symphony. Beethoven," Madan said. Beethoven's Fifth was playing. "How did you know that?" I asked. "I saw it on television," he answered. I thought that was surprising, until other children said they had seen it, too. "It's a commercial for wine," Sam said. "It took him [Beethoven] four years to write it."

April 5   Robbie was working on the book of insets that he had started yesterday, and Jack was next to him working on the Addition Strip Board. I saw Sam talking to them, and then go to Joan. She went to Robbie and asked him to apologize to Sam. I could overhear Robbie saying to Jack afterward, "I got in trouble. . . . *You're* the one. . . ." Robbie banged his fist on the table in frustration. "Every single time . . . ," he went on. They talked to each other a bit more, Robbie looking angry and annoyed with Jack, and Jack looking contrite.

In a few minutes Sam was back standing next to him. I got up and asked him to come with me. "There's a roomful of children, Sam. Why would you insist on sitting next to the only ones who don't want you there? You will have a sad day that way and think that no one likes you," I said. He made a calendar then. When he brought it to show me, he said. "Hey, there's something strange. When I sit next to Jack, he says, 'Why do you always sit next to me?' When Robbie sits next to him, he never asks him that." He shrugged his shoulders as if it were inexplicable. He did stay with other children for the rest of the morning, however.

Linda was in the rocking chair in the library, looking at the book on Beethoven. She was talking to Jack and Robbie at the table behind her. I could hear her say "Beethoven" and "Mozart." The boys kept to their work there all morning. At line time I talked again about school being the place where we are friendly with everyone and home as our place for being with special friends.

Linda recut all the flowers and put fresh water in the vases. She carried them about like a little princess, yet with a newly developed sense of humor about her. She put a vase down in the middle of the table where Madan was sitting. "Put it right here," he said, pointing to a spot closer to him where he could smell them.

April 6   I set out a pan of water with blue dye in it to represent the forming of the oceans on the science display shelf. I also added some rocks of various kinds to the volcanic rocks already there. At line time I explained to the children that minerals were released as well as water vapor in volcanic eruptions and that they added to the rock formations already begun in the crust. I also put out a labeled rock collection and guide so the children would look up and label the other rocks.

April 9   I saw Robbie's mother yesterday. She said that Robbie came home from school elated last week. "Guess who the new guy is?" he said. She thought he was talking about a new student because he was so excited. "Mr. Beethoven!" he announced. "He had trouble in school, and he could hear music in his head, and he was clumsy and spilled ink in his harpsichord. Do we have any of his records?" They found his first and third symphonies, and Robbie has been playing them at home.

April 11   "That music's different," Jesse said when he came in. "It's Beethoven's Ninth, Jesse." "Oh, boy, it's going up!" he said.

April 12   The map of Europe is out now. Anna said, "I want you to show me that!" pointing to it. Karen joined us for the pre-

sentation and then made a map, too. When I showed the girls
Greece, Anna said in a surprised voice, "That's where I come
from! My grandpa was Greek!"

The weather has suddenly turned sunny and warm—seventy
degrees. I think all the children had a touch of spring fever by
ten o'clock. They were still working but gradually with less and
less intensity. We stopped for line time a little early because we
were waiting to go outside. I wish that we had a door to the outside so that the children could take their work out on a day like
this. It's unnatural to coop them up this way.

April 13   I feel humbled. I'm afraid that it was a day that I
deserved. I was getting too smug about my wonderful class. One
day was rolling along after another; I had even wondered the
other day what I had been thinking was so difficult about this
class earlier in the year. I felt as if I had made it all up. I even had
trouble remembering which children had required so much
more attention. Today they resurrected their old selves.

The day began innocently enough. Madan was the first one in
as usual. I was writing about Jesus and Good Friday on the
board. Madan was talking as much to himself as to me, as he sat
down to finish the Thousand Chain that he has been working on
for several days. Jesse had helped him yesterday, but he had gotten silly. Finally, Madan said to him, "Don't be silly!" What a
change for Madan, I had thought. Today Madan said, "It's better
to do this work alone. Only two more trays." (He was on eight
hundred. He was referring to the coasters with the numeral tags
grouped by hundreds.)

Gradually, as more and more children came in, I felt the unrest building. Children were choosing work, but they were getting up to leave it and talk to others much of the time. It seemed
to be from sheer good spirits over the turn in the weather, and
excitement over Easter. Carmen came in looking sad again. It

has been like this each day for a week, but she soon brightens up. Today she said, "My cousins are here. Guess what? My grandma's husband died." So she still grieves.

Emily's mother came in with her. I told her that she could only stay a few minutes because we were having four teacher visitors today. I felt as if we were right back where we started with Emily last fall. Her thumb went into her mouth. She didn't want to work. She looked as if she would have merged right into her mother if she could have.

It took some doing, but things were better by 8:45. I had gotten Timmy started with the Cleanser. Anna was adding to the rock labeling collection. Emily cried when her mother left, but afterward settled down to make a map next to Karen. I got Nick settled with the Cuisinaire Rods making equations to nine. Edith was doing the Noun Article Box. Jack was finishing a map of the United States. Sam was doing the Pouring Exercise. Robbie was writing a story. Lee was practicing writing letters. Carmen was doing the Marker Papers. Linda was making a volcano with the Collage Tray. Karen and Sandy had snack together. I heard Karen say, "It's the Ninth." "It's the Ninth of Beethoven!" Sandy corrected her.

By 9:30 I sensed restlessness again. Then I knew that the day was not going to be redeemed. Ed was making noises with the animals that he had just made out of clay. He simply could not stop. Finally, I had to tell him to put the clay away. Jesse was in tears because he "made a mistake" on his picture with the Markers. Madan and Sam were getting silly, so I asked them to do a Stamp Game with me. They were so keyed up they had difficulty remembering how to do it.

We had a short line time, then I sent the children for their library period. I sent all of them, instead of just half as I was supposed to. I simply couldn't face a group lesson with those who should have remained in the room. Madan was silly in the hall.

Jesse and Nick jumped down the last steps to the library. I put all three boys at the back of the line. Then I went back to the classroom to answer the visiting teachers' questions.

They were impressed with the class and couldn't see why I felt discouraged. "Did it fall apart after I left?" one teacher asked. It was not a question of "falling apart," of course. It was a question of the degree of the children's involvement and independence and will and discipline. This morning I had to substitute my will and discipline for theirs as I had had to do last fall. The situation had a surface appearance of fairly smooth and independent functioning because I was working hard at this. It was a deceptive appearance, however.

I was completely drained by the morning, and was disheartened and irritable all afternoon. I need a week without visitors or meetings to get some rest and regain perspective.

April 16   I asked Jesse to write the alphabet with me so that I could check his letter formation. "I was going to . . ." he began. "I know, Jesse, do the Markers," I said. "No," he shook his head, "the Clay." "First you must do the letters with me," I said. Always there is the reluctance to work with me but once he gets going, he's happy. "A—there you are!" he said cheerfully as he searched through the box of Sandpaper Letters to begin.

Many children have colds. "Wow, in this class everyone's coughing," Lee said.

April 17   Another day of fantastic weather, and spring fever is definitely with us. Even children like Linda and Anna were caught up in it. I was more prepared for such a day, however, so it went much better than Friday or Monday. I am beginning to relax and feel more rested. It's supposed to be seventy degrees and sunny tomorrow. I've decided to take the children to my home to visit our pond and woods. We all need to experience the awakening going on around us, and to get away from the man-made world of indoor environments.

April 18   We stopped work at 9:30 to go on our field trip. At line time yesterday we had talked about life beginning in the oceans. Before our trip to the pond today, I told the children about photosynthesis. Then we started off. How different it was from our fall trip. There was none of the pushiness and unkindness with each other that I remembered. There were five mallards on the pond as we came down to it, and two turtles on the raft. A dragonfly was skimming over the water. The dragonfly makes a good background for next week's discussion on evolution. I had given each child a large jar for collecting. Timmy found snails for everyone. It was special to have him be the leader for a change. He was covered with muck but happy in his success. Everyone brought back algae, too. I brought back some that were bubbling nicely so that I could talk to the children about plants freeing the oxygen from carbon dioxide and making pockets of it in the water.

When we got back to class Nick dropped his jar. It broke, and muddy water and glass went all over. I helped him clean it up. I felt bad for him. He is so much less independent in his care of himself than the children who have been in the class all year. They can go right after such a mess on their own, and thus they are relaxed about their accidents. Poor Nick was very tense.

April 19   What has happened! I don't think that I've even enjoyed teaching the last five days, except for our time at the pond and isolated instances here and there. There is the same undercurrent of teasing and lack of impulse control in the class that we were dealing with all last fall. At the beginning of the morning I thought our trip yesterday had calmed the children. Everyone settled down to work in a quiet way. At nine o'clock I felt an indefinable atmospheric change. It wasn't that the noise level rose so much. It was more that the children seemed gradually to come unglued from their usual paths. A visitor had come in the room at 8:45. I told her, as I tell all visitors, that she was free to speak to the children if she wished. She was a quiet, calm person, and spoke a few minutes with each child as she went around the room. The children seemed to respond with less and less attention to their work, which was so unlike them. Soon there were little teasing exchanges going on here and there. I even had to speak to Karen, Anna, and Sandy, who on the whole have been very disciplined for months. One indication of the mood of the classroom was the number of things accidentally dropped. It seemed as if every few minutes something hit the floor: a canister of Phonetic Objects, the container for the I Spy cards, a cup with the numeral tags for the Chains. When I stood up and the cellophane tape dispenser fell on the floor, Joan looked up at me and said, "It's what you call the 'dropsies'!" It was an excellent description of the whole mood change. I should have known then that we all needed to stop, come together as a group, and get ourselves together with some group lessons, as we used to do last fall. I didn't think of it.

The children were attentive at line time, but they had trouble naming the countries and continents on some of the maps, something they haven't done in ages. I think that it was the mental equivalent of dropping objects. Off they went to music, and apparently they were really impossible. It was mostly Jesse, and—I was surprised—Jack and Robbie. When I went to get them, other children were still giggling as they lined up: especially Sandy, Madan, and Timmy. We waited for them for a time, then I told them to wait there with Joan until they were ready. "Yes, ma'am!" Jesse said. I told him that he would have to stay with me after Joan took the other children outside. We stayed in the room while I got some papers ready for the children to take home. When Jesse and I went outside, it was clear that it was a disaster there, too. Joan was comforting Sandy, and Robbie was obviously restricted to Joan's side. Jack had been having trouble, too. Susie was pouting in a corner by the building. I had no idea why. Sandy got up and started blocking the end of the slide and teasing Jack, who was trying to come down it. It was a clear indication that she had brought on her trouble with Robbie herself. Later Timmy was dumping dirt on the slide to tease the children who wanted to come down. He has been moving subtly in this teasing direction for several days now. I told Joan that I felt right back where I started from last fall.

April 20   It was a much better morning. A number of children were unsettled: Karen, Linda, Timmy, Madan, Sam, Robbie, and, of course, Jesse. However, I was prepared for it and kept myself so constantly alert to the classroom as a whole that I immediately could step into any specific situation. Perhaps the children sensed the change in my mood, too. I didn't enjoy the morning, though. I've never had a class have this kind of relapse in the spring before. It has made me doubt myself.

At one point during the morning I looked up to see Sam and Susie working across the table from each other. Sam was pulling out two points of his shirt on either side of his chest where breasts would be on a woman. I heard Susie say, "I don't have them, Sam. Not yet."

April 23   Finally, a good day again. Everyone really worked and the testing restlessness has disappeared. Joan and I stayed late after school to set out new materials and make Phonogram booklets for the children. I have only one more math material and some grammar work left in the cupboards now.

I hope the class is back on the track. The regression of the past week or so really upset me. The children have come a long way since fall, but I know they could go a lot farther in the remaining six and a half weeks.

April 24   At last—back on the track! "That's more like it," I kept thinking to myself all work period. In retrospect, I think that part of the problem was my own lack of inspiration. I haven't been as conscientious about bringing out new materials as I should have been. I think the children were ready earlier for the materials that I got out today. It was I who wasn't ready. My journal writing is taking too much of the energy that should be going into class preparation. I feel that the class's coming together again, however, has been a joint effort on the part of the children and myself. It has been going on in a subtle, behind-the-scenes manner these past ten days. The children had been trying to figure out what had gone wrong, just as much as I had. In any case, today had the feel of a rebirth.

For the first time in a long time, I felt that our daily visitors were seeing something worthwhile.

April 30   Everyone cheered when Lee got to the top of the rope today for his first time. Half the children make it now. All of these are so proud, and the others are trying so hard. What pleases me most is the way they support and cheer each other on now.

May 1   My thoughts were mostly with Jesse and Emily today. I am encouraged about Emily. Jesse discourages me. He has been choosing only art materials to work with. I'm worried that he is relying on me to direct him to academic work. Today Joan insisted that he do the Sight Word cards with her. She said that once he got going, he seemed to enjoy it and was very proud of himself for knowing so many. "Why is he this way?" she asked. Who can know the answer? I do know that at this point he has completed a great deal of academic work. I care now about nurturing his will and discipline as much as possible in the remaining weeks. This can't be done if Joan and I are constantly directing him.

Jack is shaking hands with me in a very perfunctory manner in the mornings. We did the Sight Word cards together and then he made a map of Canada. He doesn't seem to be putting much heart into his work these days.

We played a Planet Game outside today. I had marked off a long cord with large wooden beads to designate the spacing of the planets from the sun. As we unrolled the cord and came to a wooden bead, I hung the appropriate planet card on a child. That child then remained at his spot while the rest of us continued down the field unrolling the cord. We had begun with Pluto. It really startled me when all four planets, Venus, Earth, Mars, and Mercury, popped off the reel within the last few feet before the sun. Pluto was a football field away from us. The children loved it and got very excited. I had to speak firmly with many of them to keep the situation from deteriorating. Jesse had the toughest time. He actually had to hold hard to Joan's hand to keep himself from flying in all directions.

After class Joan and I spent several hours on the environment. There are so many details to look after, and details are so time-consuming! We talked about some ideas for a collage on early life in the ocean, but we were just too tired to start work on it. We have gotten to sea worms and fish developing in the ocean, and soil developing out of the rocks on the land in our line discussions.

May 2   It was a great day! At the beginning of the morning, Jesse told me, "Three new things!" I had changed the picture in the library to Picasso's *Lady Ironing*, set up a microscope with the slide of a paramecium, and filled a second tray for the shelf display. This one has several kinds of mosses and a few small plants to simulate the first fernlike trees. On the line we talked about the Diplovertedon crawling onto land and insect life beginning. After our discussion, I put some small plastic salamanders and centipedes in the "ocean" tray, and an alligator climbing onto the "land" tray. "Isn't that fun," I said to Lee, who was sitting next to me. "Yeah, it's neat," he answered with his shy smile.

Jesse was a huge success today! "Jesse, you can do any work that you want to," I said, "but when you do art work, I want you to do it at a private table. You use it for so long that the other children don't get a chance to do it, too. I think the reason is . . ." "I know, I talk," he interrupted me, nodding his head. By 8:30 he had finished using both the Clay and the Markers. He was busy all morning: working on his Phonogram booklet along with Susie, Linda, and Jack, doing Fraction Skittles with Edith, then the Sight Word cards alone, and the Verb Game with Jack, Sam, and me. Not once during the morning did he look uninvolved or insecure. Joan and I were stunned.

May 3   Jack had begun the day all right. He got out his Phonetic booklet and began to work. "It's so quiet in here," he said. "I don't like it when the whole class is here. Then there's too much noise." He sounded a little irritable, but was busy looking up words. When Jesse came in, he got his Phonetic booklet out and sat next to Jack. I heard Jack say to him, "Do you like school? I don't like school." Later Jack got the Clay and was making loud noises while using it. Linda was trying to write a story and said it was bothering her. I asked Jack to move to a table by himself. I thought then that something seemed amiss with him. By gym time, I no longer had any doubt. He had an out-and-out fight with Robbie. They were waiting their turn on the rope. Jack punched Robbie and grabbed his nose. Robbie fought hard to keep back the tears. When I asked what was going on, Robbie shrugged his shoulders. So did Jack then, of course. "Why did Jack hit you?" I asked. "I don't know. He just did," Robbie answered. Madan and Sam on either side of them confirmed that

Jack had started it. I went through the usual "children are not for hitting" routine, all the while feeling frustrated and helpless. "You will have to spend the day right by my side tomorrow, Jack," I said.

May 4   When Jack's father brought him to school, he asked to speak to me in the hall. He told me that they were shocked to learn that Jack's grandfather has a virulent, fast-killing form of cancer. So that was it. They had told Jack Wednesday night that his mother was leaving Thursday to see her father, who was "very sick." Jack's father told me that he was going to take Jack and his brother on a trip next week since they expected that his mother would not return home for at least that long.

As soon as he came in, Jack got out his Phonogram booklet.

"I'm going to sit over here," he said, going to the table by Fred's terrarium. I told him that he didn't have to stay with me all morning, but that he should come and find me if he felt that he was going to have problems like yesterday. He was unsettled and restless all day. When I asked him if anything was wrong, he said, "We're not talking about it. It's a family secret."

In no time, he had come over to me saying that Jesse had written on him with the red phonogram pen. I was doing the Twenty-five Chain with Timmy, and so I asked Jesse to stay with us. "What happened, Jesse?" I asked, after Timmy finished the chain. "I asked Jack if I could have the Markers when he was finished, and he said no—for no reason," he said. "Well, Jesse, you can't write on him in any case, can you?" I answered. It had unglued Jesse for the day, unfortunately. He punched Timmy when I had to leave them for a minute to write Lee's story for him. I had asked Ed to join us after he fed Fred the earthworms that he had brought from home. Ed had laughed at Jesse because his undershirt was showing a little below his shirt. Jesse called him "stupid." Timmy called Jesse "stupid." Jesse punched.

I said, "Boys, I am a teacher, not a policeman." I was definitely discouraged.

May 7   The weather has turned warm and glorious at last. The morning had a tumultuous beginning, particularly for a Monday. Five children were watching Fred devour the earthworms that Jesse had brought. Edith, Sandy, and Emily were at a table writing stories. They were giggling and being much too loud. I asked Emily to come sit at the table where I was introducing the Noun Adjective Box to Madan. That is all the directing that I did, however. By 8:30 the tone of the room had completely shifted, and all was quiet industry. I want to be certain that I don't jump the gun when a morning begins this way, and move in too quickly to get things going. The children are quite capable now of setting the tone of the room without interference from me.

There was a good mix of work all morning—a great many stories on the new paper, reading in the library, Cuisinaire Rods, Stamp Games, the Collage Tray. I started Anna on a Multiplication Board booklet. The moment was right, and she quickly got to the sixes before line time. We had visitors again today, and they seemed very impressed with her obvious enthusiasm and concentration. When the right connection between child and material is made, you don't have to be an "expert" to spot it—that is for certain. The child actually glows.

I have put little dinosaurs in the land tray. The whole shelf display has been a huge success, the children spending a good deal of time each day looking at it and talking about it together. "I love this little guy. He's so cute," Susie said today, pointing to the plastic salamander in the water.

The children were relaxed and played well together on the playground. Perhaps by the time Jack comes back next week, we'll all be ready to deal with him again. I suppose I feel guilty that I am so grateful for this respite from having him in class, but there is no question that it is a blessing for us all just now.

May 8   Susie greeted me with "That's Mr. Bach. I can tell." (I have been changing the music each day to see if the children can recognize the composers we have studied.)

Finally, I had a chance to begin the day with Carmen. It has been ages since we worked together. She gets herself occupied immediately each day with an excellent choice of work. It continues this way all day. I have trouble finding an appropriate opportunity to ask her to work with me. We did the four operations with the Stamp Game. "Oh, no!" she said when she got to ten units and realized that she would have to exchange. She was tired by the last problem. I hope that I didn't encourage her to keep going too long. I keep forgetting how young she is.

Jesse walked past me with a drawing done with the Markers. "I didn't do it very long," he said. "I did half, I'll do the rest tomorrow." He is carefully filling in every brick of a brick building. He did the Clay next, and then painted a picture with meticulous care. It was 9:40 by then, and he had shown no interest in academic work. He had really concentrated on his art work, however, and not gotten up to wander and talk while he was doing it. I asked him if he wanted to finish his map now or do a subtraction paper with the Cuisinaire Rods. He finished his map, working very carefully and with good concentration. It's progress, but I'd love to see him respond spontaneously to the academic materials as the other children do.

May 9   It was eighty degrees again, and the children were like wilted lettuce. They tried gamely, continually getting out ambitious work and just as continually putting it away again after ten minutes or so of effort. I missed their usual sustained energy and zest.

By 9:40 Jesse had done the Markers and the Clay. I was thinking of intervening, but I was too busy. I was glad that I hadn't had
a chance to when I looked over a little later and saw that he was
working away enthusiastically on his Phonogram booklet.

May 10   The children finally woke up! The weather was
eighty degrees again, but they apparently had adjusted to it. The
morning got off the ground quickly and gained momentum as it
went along. I hated to stop the children at 10:30. Several of them
groaned loudly, "Oh, no, do we have to?" It was as if they suddenly were intent on doing all the work that they hadn't felt up
to for the past several days.

May 11   It was another busy day of spontaneous language
work: stories, the Command Game, Room Labeling, and reading. I asked several children to do the Cuisinaire Rods and others came to join us voluntarily: Robbie, Susie, Sam and Nick. We
did subtraction equations. I want to make certain that everyone
is very confident with the rods as this is their major math requirement for the first grade. Robbie was a little unsure of them,
so we'll have to concentrate on them each day with him for a
while.

We talked more about mammals today: opossums and the babies developing after birth in their mother's pouches, what early
mammals looked like, and how later mammals developed from
them. We just touched on the Ice Age and the disappearance of
the dinosaurs.

May 14   What an industrious day! The children didn't want
to stop at 10:30. I wish there was another solution to this two-
and-a-half-hour work period. It just isn't long enough.

Jack was back. His father said that they have told Jack that his
grandfather is dying of cancer. "I'm not sure that he knows what
that means or that he accepts it," he said. Jack kept to himself at

the beginning of the morning. He did the Markers, a map of Canada, and the Clay. By the end of the day he seemed more relaxed.

Anna said, "I don't know what to do." The next time I saw her, she was helping Linda carry in the bird feeder. They did the Room Labeling together next. Anna was warmed up and going strong on a Multiplication booklet after that, and didn't want to stop at line time.

May 15   Jack was at loose ends. He started to work several times, trying to finish a Canada map, and beginning a Continent booklet, but he put them away soon.

We've discussed the Ice Age more fully now, and talked about the Age of Mammals that followed it. The Collage Tray has cotton, blue tissue paper, and stones for making the Ice Age on the display shelf.

May 16   Jesse did only art work today. He looked unhappy when I asked him to do the I Spy cards. He was sent back from drama for "acting up." I'm worried about him next year. He could be one of those children who becomes a "behavior problem" when he is faced with an environment of constant, required work in a formal setting. However, the children have taught me over and over again each year: Trust them—patience and trust. And there are four more weeks to go.

May 17   It was another active morning. I sat with Jack a good part of the morning while he worked on his yellow booklet. I felt better about him. He was more relaxed and looked happier.

Jesse spent over an hour on the Cuisinaire Rods, then devoted the rest of the morning to his art work. His paintings always cover all the paper. He is leaving them at school so that he can make a book out of them. On the way to music he said, "I saw that picture! Oh, what's its name—from the blue period." Sam saw it then, too, and said, *"The Gourmet!"* There is a large print of Picasso's *Gourmet* at the end of the hall, just to the right of where we turn to go to music. I had put a print of it in our library right after spring vacation. I have put in many other prints since then. The connections come so much later.

I introduced Sam to the Noun Adjective Box. He knew just how to do it. "How did you know that, Sam?" I asked, half expecting his answer. "Because I watch people," he said.

Linda has been such a happy soul for a number of days now. She almost always fills the bird feeder first. Today she arranged the flowers next, and then read books in the library with Anna. After juice she was walking across the room humming Beethoven's Fifth to herself.

May 18   In the middle of my notes in class this morning, I have written, "How can they do so much!" After class I was completely wrung out simply from the effort of keeping up with them. Jesse, Nick, and Sam all sat at one table doing insets all morning: beautiful insets. I was particularly pleased with Nick's and Sam's efforts because their small-muscle control needs development. Jesse's designs were unique, imaginative, and well executed. I think I have missed the boat with him all year. His sensitivity to stimuli and his underlying nervous tension may well be accompanying signs of an artistic gift. I should have been trying to reach him more through his art work all year. He should have had more diverse materials to work with. That magnificent collage last fall should have been my clue. I feel stupid and guilty.

I finally got to introduce the Noun Adjective Box to Linda. Later she wanted to borrow a green felt pen from Susie's markers for her yellow book. Susie said no. It was just crossness on her part. Moving again must be unsettling her. (I just learned a week ago that her family is moving again as soon as school is out. This will be her eleventh move in six years of life.) Later when

Susie wanted one of Linda's colors, Linda said, "Sure." What a change from my two prima donnas fighting over the Painting Tray last fall. Linda has developed such a sensible tolerance for others. No wonder the children all like her now.

When half the children went to the library, the other half kept working. That meant a three-hour work period for them, and most were still asking not to stop at eleven o'clock: Jack was doing the Multiplication Board, Emily the labeling, Jesse, Sam, Nick, and Robbie the insets. That has to be a record three hours on insets!

May 20   Jack looked a little sad when he came in. I asked him to do a Stamp Game with me, mostly because I wanted to give him support. "After this I'm going to do my Multiplication booklet," he said. He is handling his situation well. When I asked him how his grandfather was, he said, "I don't really know." After a slight pause, he went on, "It's really a case of dying." His voice was sad but accepting. His parents' openness with him has made all the difference. He may not know exactly what dying means, yet he is taking the first steps toward accepting it as a part of life.

May 21   I do hate to stop the children from working. Today Sandy had finished a story and begun a Multiplication booklet. She had been working on it for an hour when it was line time. I said, "No, you can't start another page, Sandy. It will take too long." "Can't I just try to finish *part* of another one?" she begged.

May 22   The children are supposed to wear "grubby clothes" to school this week for fingerpainting in art. Linda came in the door with a lovely clear plastic child's apron. "My mom says to give this to you. It's for me to wear to art. You see, I really don't *have* any grubby clothes. Even my blue jeans are nice!" She smiled as she said it, as if it were a good joke. She does enjoy the princess role but she handles it with humor these days—an important development since last fall.

Jack and Nick worked on their Phonogram booklets. "I just *love* working on my Phonogram booklet," Jack said. What a wonderful development is taking place in him. In fact, the sociogram of the whole class has been changing gradually, particularly since Jack was absent for a week. The other boys have developed their individual relationships to the point that they no longer hover over Jack. He seems relieved by it. He doesn't even seem to mind Robbie and Jesse pairing off to do inset work together, as they have for several days now. Joan and I both have been amazed by this spontaneous shift in relationships. We couldn't have planned it better if we had tried. This is one of the most important developments for the class this year.

May 23   Jack came right in this morning. "You know what? Boppa died this morning," he said to me. Then he went straight to Joan. "My grandfather died. We're going to leave to the funeral tonight at seven o'clock, and we won't be here tomorrow or Friday." He began a story right away. He drew a picture of a hospital bed with his grandfather in it, and his mother at one end of it and his grandmother at the other. He wrote "Boppa" and "hospital" above the bed. He dictated his story to me. "One early morning my grandfather died. My mom called. It was sad." Jack then asked, "Can I take this one home today? I'm going to give it to Grammy" (his grandmother). He had an involved and relaxed morning then, doing insets with Nick and Sam.

He read his story at line time. It was a natural starting off point for a discussion. I asked if anyone had ever been to a funeral. Anna had, and gave a good description of what it was like. She talked about the prayers and the church, and about the "box" being put in the ground. "We didn't see them put any dirt on it, though," she said. I explained that people usually didn't stay to watch that because it was sad to watch then. "I didn't even get to see the box go in the ground," Carmen said with sadness and bewilderment, and a touch of anger in her voice. "My brother and I had to stay in the car." "Who was with you?" I asked. "No one," she answered. "Was that scary?" I asked. She rolled her eyes wide. She kept staring off into space and looking sad, as we talked more.

Jack said something about the funeral being at night when it would be dark. "The funeral won't be tonight, Jack. It will be in the morning," I said. "Whew! It won't be scary! Oh, whew!" he said with genuine relief.

"Are funerals always sad?" he asked after a moment. "Not always, Jack," I answered. "Not when someone has been really sick and suffered a lot. Sometimes then people are relieved to know that the person whom they loved isn't suffering anymore." "Boppa was suffering," he said. "But we were *so* sad this morning. We *all* cried. I hope Pete's still in heaven." Jack's dog Pete had been killed several months ago. "Pete and Boppa will always be here," and he pointed to his heart. "Boppa was only sixty-two. Pete was too dumb to look where he was going," he continued.

May 29   Jack and Nick made world maps together, then Jack made a book of lovely insets. He had a normal day, but on the playground he was much quieter. "Do you want to tell us about the funeral when we go in?" I asked. "No. It just makes me sadder," he said. He sat quietly with me a long time. Finally, he said. "It was cancer. He only smoked one pack a year. He smoked one cigarette and threw the rest of the pack away. He was smart. Did you know him?"

Linda and Susie were having problems, Linda said, "I hate Susie. She thinks I'm a shrimp. She thinks she has a bigger pool than I do." "Does that matter, Linda?" I asked. "It does to me!" she said emphatically. Two steps forward, one step back.

May 31   Susie wanted to do more Strip Board booklets, but asked permission not to use the strips to get the answers. "I know them," she said. I asked her a few addition equations and she does know them! I was amazed.

Ed has developed more than anyone, I think. He brought peonies to school and arranged them all day. He also brought an encyclopedia. He had looked up Bach and Einstein.

June 4   Gradually, over the past few days I've been feeling the steam is gone from the class. They just aren't working as hard. Perhaps it's just me. The daily journal writing has put a strain on me and I'll be so glad when that is over. I'm apprehensive about starting on the book, though. I'll feel better when school is out, and I can get started on it.

June 5   I went through many children's folders to encourage them to finish work already started. Edith and Lee are the exceptions about the work involvement. They are still going strong, finding just what they want. Edith made an Earth booklet. Joan and I have put together booklets with blank pages for the children to make the story of the earth's beginnings up to now. She kept saying, "I don't want school to end." Lee practiced his numbers again. He'll have them right by first grade—left-handed or not! He did the Article Adjective Noun Box and objects next.

I had snack with Karen and Sandy. They were discussing the music that was playing. "It's Mr. Bach," Sandy said. "No, it's Mr. Beethoven," Karen said. "Mr. Bach!" "Mr. Beethoven!" etc. Finally, Sandy said, "Are we going to get into a fight?"

June 7   Surprisingly, the children came in calmly and purposefully, and went right to work. It took them until the last day to realize that this was really their last chance to do their favorite work, I think. It's as if their need to work finally surfaced again after several days of semi-vacationing.

Jack wanted to do the Asia map. "My first time," he said. Lee did the Snake Game, then the Seguin Boards, and finally Grammar Box Three. Sam did the Dot Paper Game. Jesse finished a world map, then used all the art materials. At snack time Sam was setting a place for me. Jesse asked him if he could get my milk for me. That touched me.

Madan alone wandered, his hands in his pockets, looking a little forlorn. "When will it be line time?" he asked wistfully. "I love line time." Sitting next to me later, he said, "I don't want school to end. I want school to last forever!" Susie looked sad, too. "I don't want to go," she said. No wonder. "Going" doesn't mean just leaving school. It means moving that eleventh time.

At 10:30 I asked several children to start bringing me materials to put in the cupboards. I wanted the children to have the experience of putting their room "to bed." It would complete the cycle of finding the room almost bare in the fall, gradually building it into an alive and vital environment together, and then returning it to a lifeless state again, ready for the next group of children to begin again in the fall.

Soon almost everyone had started to help. Some carried things to Joan and me, others took sponges and washed the shelves and tables. In a little over an hour the room was stripped absolutely bare. Children were standing up on the shelves washing the windows, leaving a good deal more work for the janitors, I'm afraid, because window washing had not been part of our Room Care Exercises. The children were using sponges full of cleanser. They enjoyed themselves immensely, however.

Finally, we took our terrarium outside. We sat in a circle watching Fred take his first tentative leaps to freedom, a bit bewildered after his sequestered terrarium life. And the year was over. It had been a good one.

THREE | # Language

Visitors to the classroom repeatedly ask how the children's unusual progress in reading and writing and mathematics is achieved. This chapter and the following one consist of diary entries which document these academic areas. As I have said before, early academic achievement is not necessarily helpful to young children. Indeed, it can be harmful. Only if it has taken place in an environment suited to a child's needs will it result in the deeper goals of enlightened self-image and lifelong love of learning.

My approach to reading differs significantly from the customary introduction of the subject in most classrooms. I approach reading indirectly, through writing.

In order to write, the child has to develop hand control, a knowledge of letter sounds and formation, and the ability to connect sound with symbol and to proceed left to right and top to bottom. I work on developing these skills before introducing writing and then reading.

These writing skills themselves are also approached indirectly. Each specific Room Care material is organized and used by the child in left-to-right, top-to-bottom progression. Small-muscle control is developed through polishing the silver, tying of the

Bow Frame, pouring from pitcher to glass, etc. Art materials such as the Cutting Exercise, the Clay, the Markers, and the Painting all develop hand control. Academic materials emphasize the use of the thumb and index fingers. The tiny glass beads in math, the knobs on the map puzzle (for lifting the pieces) in geography, and the tiny fragile Phonetic Objects in the language exercises, all aid the development of muscles required to hold a pencil.

The major materials for directly developing hand control are the Metal Insets. By tracing their metal shapes and carefully filling in the outlined space with continuous lines going from top to bottom and left to right, the child's hand is developing the muscles he will use to write letters. When using the Metal Insets, the child is of course unaware that he is preparing himself to write. He makes the shapes and fills them in because it gives him pleasure to do this.

In addition to the materials which lead indirectly to writing, and thence to reading, the environment overall is an indirect influence on the child's development of written language. Written language is everywhere in the environment. The children literally are surrounded with it. In the geography section of the room, they find maps with labels on them, and continent and state cards printed with the name of each. On the science shelf, they find dinosaurs to label, rocks to identify and label, and insects to look up in *Golden Guide* books and label. In the art section, they find a collage of the planets (complete with their labels) to make. With the Sensorial Materials they find cards for the Geometric Solids, "ellipsoid, ovoid, pyramid," etc. In the library they find pictures of Bach and Beethoven with their names written underneath, or a basket of Picasso prints with their titles written on the back. They also find adult magazines and books there. There are publications which they find in their own homes, such as the *National Geographic, International Wildlife,* and *The Family of Man.* In this way, their awareness of written language in their outer environment is heightened, too. When they pass the chalkboard, they find a daily message to read. There are language games going on throughout the room: a "chalkboard" label from the Noun Room Labeling game on the chalkboard, a "blue" label from the Adjective Room Labeling Game on a blue towel, etc. Children are acting out commands with the Command Card Game and verbs with the Verb Game. They see stories written and hear them read, see labels written for the Phonetic Objects and Phonogram Objects Games, hear Sight Word cards read, etc.*

Language is simply everywhere: a variety of it, and all at once. The children themselves are the key to this outcome, of course. They teach each other, directly and indirectly. I think of Anna, who taught all of the Noun Room Labels to Susie in several weeks, and Sandy's activities with Emily all year. Although at times I was concerned about Sandy's dominating Emily's personality, she nevertheless was an integral part of Emily's eventual success in beginning reading.

For this chapter I have selected diary entries which describe the language development primarily in one child, Sandy, and secondarily in three children, Linda, Ed, and Emily. Only occasionally are other children mentioned so that the reader can have some awareness of the class as a whole.

Sandy knew no letter sounds at the beginning of the year. Her progress in language development was slow at first. It picked up momentum as the year went on, however, and by the end of the year she was one of the better readers in the class. At four and a half in September, she was also the youngest child in the class.

Linda was only one month older than Sandy. However, she knew her letter sounds when school began, and reading came more easily and quickly to her than to Sandy.

*For a list of classroom language materials and the order of their presentation, see Appendix C.

Ed and Emily were the slowest of the class in reading development. Ed represents a child whose natural pace of development was slow but followed a normal pattern. Emily was a child whose development in all areas concerned us. There was a possibility of a learning disability, particularly in the auditory area. However, as the year went on, our observations convinced us that Emily's problem was one of unusually slow development, rather than a specific disability. We considered keeping her in kindergarten because of her slow overall development, her tendency toward dependent behavior, and her young chronological age (she was just five when school began). However, after spring vacation, Emily made a dramatic breakthrough both in her academic and her personality development. On the basis of this sudden spurt of development, we passed her on to the first grade.

September 18   I suggested to Joan that if she gets an opportunity, she should work on the Sandpaper Letters with Emily, Timmy, and Sandy. They are going to need a good deal of work with them. (In the first few days of school, I had gone over the Sandpaper Letters with each child to check his knowledge of letter sounds. Knowledge of a dozen or so sounds including at least one short vowel are necessary before the child is ready to use the next material, the Movable Alphabet. The Sandpaper Letters are letters cut out of sandpaper and mounted on wooden tablets, a blue tablet for each vowel and a pink tablet for each consonant. They are developed by Maria Montessori for use with children still in the sensorial age for touch, approximately two and one half to four. Although a child of five is no longer interested in tracing them spontaneously, they are still useful in developing the child's ability to form letters the correct way and to establish memory of the sound they represent. This is accomplished by tracing them in a one-to-one directed learning situation with the teacher.)

October 11   Sandy kept getting out things that I haven't shown her yet: the Trinomial Cube, then the Phonetic Object Box One. (The Phonetic Objects are a container of four or five fragile miniature objects such as a cat, pig, etc. They can be found in any toy or creative art supply store. The first time I introduce the Objects, I write the label while the child watches me form the letters. He then matches the labels to the Objects. Some Objects are changed each week to sustain interest. After the child has practiced writing letters on a special blue-lined paper, he not only matches the labels but copies them on his own paper when he does the Phonetic Objects.) Sandy told Joan that I had shown the Phonetic Objects to her. She can't possibly do the Objects yet as she isn't certain of some of the sounds that she needs to know first. I want the Objects to be a happy experience for her, so I insisted that she put them back. Then we practiced the Movable Alphabet. (In the past six weeks, Joan or I had done the Sandpaper Letters with Sandy almost every day. She had learned the sounds of eight to ten of them, so I had introduced the Movable Alphabet to her. The Movable Alphabet is a compartmentalized box of cut-out plastic letters, vowels in blue, consonants in pink. I dictate a three-letter phonetic word to the child such as "dog." In the beginning, I give each sound separately after pronouncing the whole word. The child composes the word by finding the letters to represent the sounds. This is not spelling, but mechanical writing. Nor does it involve reading. The child cannot read back the word he has made. He knows what it says only because he has heard the word pronounced before he made it.)

October 12   Today I insisted that Sandy do the Movable Alphabet with me the first time that I asked her. She didn't want to and, because of her young age, perhaps I should not have insisted. However, I said to her, "Sandy, you must because you remember that yesterday you asked to do the Phonetic Objects. We must do this work first, or they will be too hard for you." She seemed quite happy when she was actually doing the work, although the Movable Alphabet is not easy for her.

Sandy's reluctance to do the Movable Alphabet has less to do with its being somewhat hard for her than that it was designed for the interest level of younger children. Montessori children use the Sandpaper Letters at two and a half to three,* the Movable Alphabet at three and a half to four, and the Phonetic Objects starting at four to four and a half. No wonder my children all want to go straight to the Phonetic Objects! I wish that I were clever enough to design materials that would introduce letter sounds and formation as the Sandpaper Letters do, and the beginning construction of words and the development of synthesizing as the Movable Alphabet does—but appeal to the interest level of a five-year-old. As it is, I have no choice but to use the Sandpaper Letters and Movable Alphabet in a remedial way. Fortunately, the children are fascinated by the Phonetic Objects. This motivates those who need to use the Sandpaper Letters and Movable Alphabet first, to work with them.

November 15   Sandy and Emily made world maps together. When they were labeling them, I told Emily to get the control map (a map with the names of the continents and oceans printed on it so that the children can match their labels to it, then paste them on their own map). "I don't need the control map," she said. "Me neither!" Sandy offered. They didn't either! Sandy

---

*The attraction of the Sandpaper Letters for toddlers is remarkable. One two-year-old whom I observed in a Montessori classroom had misplaced one of his letters. He clutched his others to his chest as he went all around the classroom looking for the lost one. "Where is my Sandpaper Letter?" he was saying to himself. His tone was such that he might have been looking for a beloved teddy bear or his favorite truck.

even did the oceans without it. They had done a number of maps, of course, but I still can't imagine how they did this. They are still struggling with most of their letter sounds!

The maps and map labeling has had quite an effect on all the children's beginning reading progress. Since the first of October, I have been writing a simple message on the board which we read all together at line time. At first I wrote only the date. "Today is Monday, October 3, 1978." Later I added, "It is a sunny day," etc. Today I had written, "Can you find the Caribbean Sea on the North American map?" Anna and Linda were trying to read the message earlier in the morning (as they have been doing each day). They are stumped on "Caribbean." Robbie looked up from the map he was making on the floor in front of them, and read it for them. He knew how, of course, because of his almost daily map making and labeling. I was thrilled that he recognized "Caribbean" out of context. All I could think of was "I'm sliding reading in by the back door!"

After class today I got out the Marker Paper. Enough children have progressed from the forming of words with the Movable Alphabet to labeling and writing the Phonetic Objects successfully, that the class seems ready for this next step. The Marker Paper is a special paper three and a half by five inches with a blank space at the top and three blue lines at the bottom. The middle line is a solid blue line a half-inch thick. The top line is for letters with ascenders above the line such as *t*, the middle line for the circle part of letters like *a* and *b*, the bottom line is for letters with descenders such as *g* and *j*. I set out two acrylic trays, each with a sponge and a set of special markers next to the paper. The children will draw a picture of a single object such as a tree or house. They will tell Joan or me what word they want us to write. We will then write it on a separate paper with similar blue lines, and they will copy it onto their own paper. When they make several pages, we will staple them into a book. I am eager to see how the children will respond to this.

November 16   Unfortunately, I had no "readers" in this class when school began, as I have had in other years. However, Lee was *very* close to it, and with just these few months of exposure he is reading phonetic words easily. He has labeled the room for several days now with the Noun Labeling cards (cards with the names of objects in the room written on them—"box," "map," etc.). Today he put "lid" on top of the terrarium lid. Other children are noticing the cards and beginning to take an interest in sounding them out. What a difference it makes to the other children to have just one child with this kind of talent in the room!

The response to the Marker Paper couldn't have been more enthusiastic. Susie, Jesse, Edith, and Anna all made many pages. Jesse made an incredibly accurate freehand miniature map of the world, and wrote "map" under it! It's amazing how the children are grasping the shapes and positions of the continents from their map making. As the children used these papers today, I thought all over again what a good approach to the writing-reading process this is. By dictating the word he wants to us, the child sees the correct formation of each letter; he hears the sound of each letter or phonogram pronounced by Joan or me as we write them; he gains an understanding of the "mysteries" of the English language, the long vowel sounds and silent *e's,* etc., and exceptions to the expected because we mention them as we write them.

November 20   Joan went over the Sandpaper Letters with Sandy today. She is getting them much better. Edith and Susie asked me to show them the Phonetic Objects. (I introduced the phonogram *sh* through the daily board message several days ago. Today I put out a container with objects whose names have *sh* in them—sheep, shell, fish, dish.) The labels have the phonogram written in red, the rest of the word in black. The children use them just as they have the Phonetic Objects, except that they use a red pen for the phonogram, a black one for the rest of the letters. The objects are appealing to them, but the pens attract them, too.

November 27 Sandy keeps wanting to use the Marker Paper, but I asked her to do the Movable Alphabet with Timmy again first. She is much better at composing the words, but is only fair at synthesizing the sounds into words afterward. She did the Phonetic Objects next. (I had introduced the Phonetic Objects to her several weeks ago. She was doing the Movable Alphabet with me almost daily, and had practiced writing letters on the blue-lined paper. She had no difficulty labeling the objects and copying the labels. At this stage, she seemed to be relying heavily on initial consonant sounds for identification, however, instead of awareness of the whole word.) She read the labels that she had copied easily—"egg," "nest," "bed," etc.—so I told her that she could use the Marker Paper now. She had a fine time, making a booklet of five or six pages. Perhaps she is at the right stage of development for this work, but it is so hard to be certain. However, if it isn't right, she will lose interest soon enough. (I was uncertain because she wasn't synthesizing readily with the Movable Alphabet and because she was not aware of the whole word yet in her work with the Phonetic Objects.)

November 29 Sandy and Susie were having a great time with the Marker Paper. Susie made "cat," then came back for "hat." "I'm making a rhyming book," she said. Emily asked again about the Marker Paper. She had even made a "book" of picture pages at home. She only knows a dozen letter sounds. What will she get out of doing this work? Worse, won't she just be tying up materials another child is really ready to benefit from? I realize now that I felt a little testy with her over her desire to do this yesterday and again today. Surely I should be happy that she has such persistence and motivation, not be irritated by it. I'll let her do the Marker Paper tomorrow. If she learns little from it, she will soon give it up. (We had been working almost daily with Emily on the Sandpaper Letters. We had found that not only did she appear not to understand the connection between sound and symbol, she also was having trouble imitating sounds that we made for her, and seemed to have a minimal auditory memory. Emily was so strongly motivated to do what the other children were doing, particularly Sandy, that in spite of her slow language development, I had introduced her to the Movable Alphabet and the Phonetic Objects by this time. When I gave her a word in the Movable Alphabet work, she would ask the other child doing this work to find the letter she needed. She asked another child for help with the Phonetic Objects as well.)

The reading is coming fast now for many children. Sam read his Super Book story to Joan without hesitation today. Linda read several to herself in the library. What a shame that we have only these inane books to give to children. "An apple ran." [The illustration shows an apple with sticks on it.] "It ran and ran. Nan ran. Dan ran," etc. Why not a book about Bach or South America or trees with photographs or good illustrations and phonetically worded text? Something worth reading!

November 30   I let Emily do the Marker Paper. She had a fine time, spending the whole two-hour work period on it. She has some trouble with letters that go above and below the line, and keeping the middle sections of letters within the solid blue line. Otherwise, it went all right. The most helpful thing for her probably is hearing a sound pronounced, then the symbol written while she watches. I'm not certain that she connects sound with symbol in whole words. For now, I'll just have to trust her "inner guide" that this is useful work for her. Her motivation for it is so strong. It must be meeting *some* need!

December 6   I introduced the Verb Game to the children in the room during drama time. It consists of cards with verbs written on them in red ink: "smile," "creep," etc. One child draws a card, then acts out the verb chosen. The other children try to guess what it is. They had fun with it.

December 7   The children are reading a good deal to each other and alone. Susie, Jesse, and Edith all made stories with the new Story Marker Paper that I put in the room yesterday. This paper is similar to the Marker Paper except that it is eight by ten. The top half is blank and the bottom half is filled with the blue lines. The children draw a picture with the marker pens, then dictate a story about it to Joan or me. We write the story on a separate blue-lined paper while the children watch. We can talk about punctuation and capitalization as well as phonograms, puzzle words, etc., as we write. The children then copy the story on their own paper below their picture. They read it back to us when they are finished. At line time, they read the story to all the children.

This is the only time during the year when the children are asked to read orally in front of their peers. Actually, it is a volunteer situation, but I have never had a child not want to share his story in this way. After reading their stories, the children show the pictures to the others, then put the stories in a red folder marked "Our Stories." This folder is kept in the library so that the children can read each others' stories. Each time they write a new story, they exchange it for the one in the folder, and take the older story home.

Writing and reading their own stories has proven an excellent way to introduce the children to reading. I think it is responsible for the high level of reading with comprehension that the children achieve. There are two major factors at work. One, the content of the stories is of personal interest and therefore has meaning for the children. Two, the children are communicating their own thoughts to others. This is a far simpler introduction to reading than reading and assimilating someone else's thoughts.

December 12   What an incredible work day! There was no way that we could break for line at 10:15. Jesse and Timmy were hard at work on North American maps, Ed and Anna on the Story Marker Paper, and Emily and Sandy on the Marker Paper booklets.

The morning had started with Emily and Sandy, still full of yesterday's success making North American maps, asking to make another map. They began a little shakily, getting Canada tilted a bit too far to one side. I helped them to get that straightened out. Then they were off on an independent and successful venture.

It occurred to me as I watched them how important the maps are as an indirect preparation for reading. They develop perception, attention to detail, eye-hand coordination, usually left-to-right progression (the order in which the pieces are traced), and matching of letters on the labels.

December 15   Jesse came in early and I asked him to read the Phonogram booklets with me. I have three out now, one for *sh, th,* and *ee.* These are little books of six to eight pages with a phonogram word on each (the *sh* book has the words "fresh," "dish," "shelf," etc.). The phonogram is printed in red, the rest of the word in black. Jesse was keyed up but thoroughly enjoyed the work. "Sh-e-l-f," he shouted out, then a triumphant flash of recognition crossed his face. "Shelf! like shelf fungus!" At the end of the second booklet, he said, "The last one. Here goes!" He did the *sh* box of Phonetic Objects next. "Plate . . . no, dish," he said to himself as he got the objects out. Next he asked if he could do "the letters like Sam and Ed did yesterday" (practicing writing letters on the blue-lined paper—this is principally for correct letter formation). He made a booklet of thirteen pages. He continued to act keyed up and excited but he worked right through the morning.

December 18   I introduced Ed to the Phonogram Objects because he looked as if he was ready for something new. It was a happy incident because it started a real run on them with many children for the first time this year. Linda, Emily, and Sandy all asked to have them presented. I have introduced them to a few children before, but they didn't seem to inspire the usual response of other years. These are time-tested materials all right. I have to be patient, and occasionally re-present them, but sooner or later the response is there.

December 19   The children were all dressed in their best clothes for the mothers' Christmas party. At one table Jesse was doing the Phonogram Objects, Sandy the Marker Story Paper, and Emily the Collage. This was Sandy's first story. (By the first of December, she had learned all her consonant sounds and three short vowels. She also was synthesizing easily in her Movable Alphabet work.)

January 9   Carmen and Linda finished their stories from yesterday. All read them on the line so well. How does it happen? The content of Linda's story showed so much conceptual thought. "One day I went out to play but I found a lonely tree. I tried to cheer her up, but that did not work. She told me why, and she said, 'Nobody will play with me because they are too busy.' Then I said, 'I will play with you.' Then the tree was happy."

January 18   Sandy, Emily, and Anna all wrote stories. Linda is still reading her "tree" story to herself every day in the library rocking chair! It's been going on for more than a week now.

January 22   We played the Noun and Verb Game during drama time. I showed the children a little tray with a black pyramid made out of cardboard and a small red rubber ball. I explained that we were going to use the pyramid as a symbol for nouns because "it just sits there." Then I bounced the ball, and said that we were going to use it for the symbol for verbs because verbs are action words. I unrolled a red felt rug cut in the shape of a circle and a black felt rug cut in the shape of a triangle. I called the first rug a verb rug and the second a noun rug. I went to each child then, asking if he or she wanted a noun or a verb card. They then drew either from the Noun Labeling basket (which they had used for Room Labeling) or the Verb basket (which they had used for the Verb Game). If they drew a noun, they got the object named and put it on the noun rug. If they chose a verb, they acted it out and we all guessed what it was. At the end of the game the noun rug obviously was full while the verb rug was empty, thus making a visual impression of the function of nouns and verbs. The children responded with the high interest and success I've come to expect when I introduce this game.

January 25   Edith wrote a marvelous story about her dog having a dream. In the dream her bird was getting out of its cage and flying around. The illustration was an outline of a dog's head with a bird inside a cage within his head. "Do you know what I do?" she asked. "On Saturdays at home I make stories like these."

I asked Sam to join Lee and me in a Noun Verb Game. Anna came to join us, too, and finally Robbie. Nick was working with clay right above us at a table, so it was an indirect lesson for him as well. All these children can read the noun and verb cards so well now. Robbie suddenly said, "Why isn't there anything on the verb rug?" "Can't put a smile on a rug!" Sam said. He had just drawn the verb card "smile," and had a smile pasted on his face so that we would guess his card.

January 29   Sandy wanted to do the I Spy cards with me. These are vocabulary cards with matching labels and control cards so that the child can check his own work. Mine are pictures of everyday objects such as kitchen articles (dish cloth, bowl, etc.) or baby things (diapers, bottle, etc.). I change them every few weeks. Sandy's reading is really developing so rapidly and steadily now. She could read back the labels to me when I took them away from the pictures. (During January she had continued to work with the Phonetic and Phonogram Objects, the Marker Papers, and to write stories. We were no longer working with the Sandpaper Letters, and did four-letter words with the Movable Alphabet only occasionally.)

February 6   Sandy not only wrote a story today, but spent the rest of the morning reading books to herself in the library! It is coming along so well for her.

Ed asked, "Don't we have a new phonogram?" I had written the word "directions" on the board with "tions" in pink chalk as part of today's board message (I always write phonograms in pink chalk and punctuation in green chalk to highlight them for the children.) "Yes, Ed," I said. "Well, why isn't it in the basket [of Phonogram cards]?" I wouldn't have been surprised if some of the other children had picked this up, but I had no idea Ed was this alert to the environment.

February 12   Ed read a Super Book to me. I felt that it was a bit of a struggle for him, but afterward he said, "I wonder how I read so fast!"

February 14   Sandy read stories in the "Our Stories" folder in the library with Emily for a long time today.

February 15   Sandy did four-letter words with the Movable Alphabet while Timmy did his three-letter words. We did one with each vowel sound. They both know all five vowels now—long and short. "*A-E-I-O-U* and sometimes *Y*," we chanted together.

When Anna appeared unsettled earlier in the morning, I asked her to do the Noun Labeling Game with Susie, Edith, and me. I have all the labels out. (I had started with only a few and continued to add a few each week.) It takes about twenty minutes to draw the labels, read them, and place them in the room. Edith especially enjoyed it. "I think I'll just play this every day!"

February 21   Lee asked to do the Command Game, which I have just put out. It consists of labels with commands composed of phonetic words: "Dust a box," "Lift a lid," "Get a mop," etc. He and Sam had a grand time with it. Lee's loud voice carried over the room and disturbed the working atmosphere a bit. However, it meant that all the other children had an indirect exposure to this game, too.

Ever since the beginning of February, stories have been a constant part of the scene.

February 27   Jack worked all morning on finishing a seven-page story. "I'm working my bombs away. I'm going to make *this* many pages!" he said to Karen, also writing a story next to him. "This is going to be my longest," she said. "Mine's going to be ten pages," Jack said. It was friendly competition, with both children obviously impressed with their new capabilities. Jack recognized the *or* in "morning" as he dictated his story to me. "Boy, I sure got a lot of phonograms in this story," he said. I'm so pleased with his progress in reading. It has been steady and solid since fall, until now he really does have it. He read his seven-page story on the line with good inflection and without any help from me whatsoever.

One of the things that I like best about this beginning approach to reading is not having to ask all kinds of questions to test comprehension. That must seem strange to children when they are just beginning to read, to be quizzed after each simple story that they finish. In fact, the stories in the readers are so simple by necessity in the beginning stages, that there really isn't an effective way to test comprehension in any depth.

Sandy had quite a morning finishing her North American map, making a calendar, then a booklet of Phonogram and Phonetic Objects. She and Emily were busy with the Marker Pages, then Phonogram Objects. They have settled into a better working team. Sandy is such a consistent, enthusiastic worker that she is exerting a good influence on Emily.

March 1   Linda was reading the board message to herself. I came to see how she was doing with it on her own. Yesterday I had introduced the forming of the planets for the next stage of our universe studies. Today I wrote on the board, "The planets were formed out of the hydrogen from the Big Bang and the other elements cooked up by the stars. There are nine planets." There were three words that she couldn't read immediately: "hydrogen," "other," and "cooked." She only needed the barest of hints with these three, however. Lee, Jesse, Jack, and Robbie all read it during the morning when I was observing, too. They read it as easily as Linda.

I put out all of the Dolch pre-primer level Sight Word Cards yesterday afternoon. At various times during the morning today, I went over them with one, two, or three children at a time: Linda, Anna, Jesse, and Robbie. I was so pleased that there were only a few they didn't know. Both reading the board messages and their own stories must account for their being so familiar with them.

March 2   Robbie began a planet collage. (I have arranged the Collage Tray so that the children can cut out circles representing the planets, place them in proper orbit around the sun, and label them using a control collage that I have made.) Madan wrote a planet story while he waited for the Collage: "I went to Jupiter in my rocket." Carmen had joined our table by now, doing the Phonogram Objects. Anna and I were going over the state cards, which I have just put out. These are cards showing the states of the United States in black outline with their names written below. The states are the same size as the map pieces. They are excellent for learning the states by shape only and for learning to read the states' names.

March 5   Sandy got the Command Cards out on her own, then Emily joined her. Emily has the idea of connecting sound and symbol much better now, but she can't synthesize them into a word. Sandy, on the other hand, could read each command by herself. She carried them out in an unobtrusive way, yet I think she was aware that I was enjoying watching her. It was a perfect example of a child making a connection with the right material at the right moment in her development. She dusted a box, wet a napkin, lifted a lid. She startled Joan, who isn't familiar with this game yet, when she rang the bell. "This is going to be hard, I got to 'Drag a leg,'" she said as she passed me, dragging her leg. Later her head popped up over the next table. "Huff!" she went with a smile over at me. I knew that she must have drawn the "Huff and puff" card.

March 6   Carmen brought in a butterfly, and was busy looking it up in the *Golden Guide* book on butterflies. She found it, too, a painted lady. She wrote the label herself.

March 8   Anna, Karen, and others were dictating stories to me while I was doing the Stamp Game with Robbie. "Is it real?" he asked Anna as he listened. For the past several weeks, all the children have been very much interested in whether a story is true or not. Many stories are now begun, "This is a true story." It has given me a chance to introduce the terminology "fiction" and "nonfiction."

March 13   I put the Noun Article Grammar Box out this morning. It is a small box with compartments for noun words and symbols and article words and symbols. I use it with an Object container and labels like those for the Phonetic Objects. I set this container up and introduce the concept of singular and plural articles, "the" for one noun ("the horse") and "a" when there are more than one ("a pig, a pig"). The children put the appropriate symbol over the word, a large black triangle for the nouns, a small blue triangle for the articles. The symbols are a visual aid to help clarify the concepts of word function.

I was introducing this Grammar Box to Karen when Sam sat down across from her. "I'm just watching," he said. He got the Addition Strip Board then, and began to work next to her. He began to talk to us: "When somebody's doing the thing you don't know how to do . . ." Edith interrupted him, "Then watch." "You watch someone and then you know how to do it!" he finished in a tone that implied how obvious he thought it all was. I wish that I had had the whole sequence on film so that I could show it when I was trying to explain to others why this kind of classroom is so successful.

March 15   Sandy wrote her first really long story. "This is a true story. I went to Hawaii. I went on an airplane. I came home. I went to my grandma's," etc.

April 1   Sam lay down on his back and read *Snip Snap* to himself in the library. I have changed the small readers there, and it was fun to watch the children discovering them. Linda was methodically going through both baskets of books, about ten in all, and reading them from cover to cover.

April 4   Susie and Edith began the Command Card Game. Anna joined them later. Eventually, all three girls and Linda were Room Labeling again. Susie was saying "dish, dish, dish" to herself as she gathered up the dish card and put it back in the basket at the end of the game. "I have to 'rememorize' them. That's what we're playing," she told me.

April 5   Anna and Linda requested the Noun Verb game during drama time. Afterward I introduced the Adjective Labeling cards. They are cards with adjectives that apply to items in the room—such as "little," "blue," "plastic," "light"—written on them in blue ink. The children label the room with them just as they do with the Noun Labeling Game. I also showed the children the symbol for adjectives—a small blue triangle to indicate that adjectives go with nouns, just as articles do. We went over the symbols for noun (a black triangle), verb (a red circle), and article (small blue triangle) again.

April 6   Today I put out a labeled rock collection and a guide book along with a group of unlabeled rocks on the science shelf. Ed, Anna, and Timmy each looked some up in the book. They found and wrote labels for mica, iron, and granite.

Joan and I have begun checking each child for progress in letter formation. We want to be certain that they have gotten the correct writing habits established before going on to first grade.

I love having Lee's adjective labels all over the room. He left them out all morning today: "wet" by a vase of flowers, "short" by a thumbtack, "plastic" on the funnel.

April 9   Sandy was back. (She was a week late in returning from spring vacation.) Both she and Emily stayed outside the door, giggling and peeking in the hallway window at us. It reminded me how much younger Sandy is than the other children. I asked Emily to do the Movable Alphabet with me. She wanted

Sandy to do it too. Sandy did five-letter words while I gave Emily her *at* family words ("cat," "hat," etc.—a remedial approach we are trying with Emily because she still has not begun to synthesize). All morning after that the girls wrote stories next to each other. Joan stayed close by and they gradually calmed down.

April 10   Sandy and Emily are doing the Command Game. I looked over to see Sandy cutting a napkin with the scissors, an intent frown on her face. It is hard to "Cut a napkin!" Emily came up to me saying, "I can wet a glass? Because that says, 'Wet a glass.'" Sandy must have read it for her, yet I sensed some indefinable progress in her language understanding.

I asked Linda to join Madan and me in a Stamp Game. All morning she had been sitting in the rocking chair, looking intently at a very large book of Bible stories. "No, I'd like to look at this *whole* book!" she said. She was still going strong at 10:30 when we stopped for line time—a two-and-a-half-hour stint!

April 11   Sandy started after Emily again as soon as she came in. I told Sandy that I wanted her to do the Noun Article Box with me. "Can Emily do it with me?" "No," I answered firmly. I am concerned that Sandy has been dominating Emily since her return from vacation and just at a time when Emily has blossomed in maturity and sense of self. She obviously enjoyed the work. She had a pleased, proud look on her face the whole time that we worked.

April 16   Anna and Susie did the Noun Room Labeling Game. Susie came up to me and said, "What's this say? D-i-s-h? Dish?" That answers my question if all this practice with labeling was helping her read better. It's slow for her but it *is* coming. Next she wrote a story, about rabbits talking to little girls. Anna wrote a story about kingdoms and dragons.

Linda sat at a table with her hands on her chin for thirty minutes, then she wrote two magnificent long stories. Why the slow start? I have no idea, but I was glad that we didn't have observers today. When they are here, I worry that they might not understand the importance of such situations—letting a five-year-old child sit for thirty minutes, appearing to do nothing.

Anna asked, "Can you do the Super Nova Game for work?" (We had played the game at line time involving a "dramatization" of the development of the elements—hydrogen into helium, etc.) I got out a card for her that had the order of elements on it. "Find a friend to do it with, Anna," I said. "I've already got Robbie," she said. Later I asked her, "Did it work?" (since it involved reading the elements). "Yep, I'm going to do it again!"

April 17   Emily and Sandy started the day in the library together. "Next, let's read our own stories," Emily said. Sandy was getting bossy with Emily again, so I asked each to choose her own work. Sandy spent the whole morning making a map of Europe.

A few minutes after he came in this morning, Jack said, "Mrs. Lillard, did you know my dog died? Got hit by a train. We're going to get a puppy someday. I love puppies." Fortunately, Jack's mother had called last night to tell me that this had happened and that Jack would be upset. When I had finished doing letter formation with him, I asked Jack, "Do you want to write a story about your dog?" "If I do, I'll cry," he said. "But I'll do it, if I know how to make a train," he added. Robbie asked him if he cried when it happened. "I cried about ten times," he said. "Pete was a really nice dog." He began to draw then. "The sun was shining that day," he said, as he drew a sun with the markers. "The engine was bigger than this building and it was going *so* fast. The police buried him in the graveyard. He's already in heaven. Here's one railroad track." Jack drew only the dog's face showing underneath a huge train. The scale was near perfect. "The man in the train is smiling," Jack continued. "They were going so fast they didn't even know it. His arm is going up because he wanted the dog to move. He's blowing his whistle." When he was finished, I said, "Jack, are you sure you want to write a story, too?" "Yes," he answered. He dictated one word at a time to me, "One day my dog ran away. He was hit by a train. His [he choked up for a minute] name was Pete." He then said, "That's all I want to write. Can I take this one home today?" "Of course, Jack," I answered, feeling a little teary myself.

April 19   I asked Ed to do the Sight Words with me. He has forgotten short *i* and *e*. We went back over the vowels with the Sandpaper Letters, and then with the Phonetic Objects Box that has objects representing each short vowel sound. It reminded me of the difficulty that he had learning the Decimal System quantities last fall. He needs much more repetition than I would expect, in order to establish auditory memory necessary for specific skill situations.

April 23   Carmen and Linda were reading the folder of class stories in the library. Carmen took Karen's over to her so she could ask the "author" what one word was. Carmen and Linda wrote stories next to each other for the rest of the morning.

Joan and I stayed late after school to set out new materials and make Phonogram booklets for the children. These are booklets of blue-lined writing paper, on which the children write their own words with phonograms. Each page has an index tab indicating which phonogram words are to go on that page. The children look up words in the National Geographic children's book series and in adult books which I have in the cupboard. The idea is to encourage their awareness of phonograms in the world about them, including in the books that they see their parents reading. When they write the words they find in their own booklet, they use the black and red pens for emphasizing the phonogram. They also use a colored paper book mark to aid their search through the pages of the books.

April 24   I started Anna on one of the new Phonogram booklets that we made yesterday. She spent the entire two hours and fifteen minutes of work time looking up phonogram words in a National Geographic book. When I announced line time, she said, "Can I keep looking?"

I put out new books in the library yesterday: a series called *Breakthrough* and another called *Our Book Corner* published by Addison Wesley. They are the first ones I have put out that are realistic in text (not contrived to use phonetic words only) and illustration. What a success they are! Sandy, Lee, Edith, and Linda just devoured them. Imagine Sandy going from the bottom of the class in beginning reading in the fall to the top of the class now! Linda asked me several words in one book ("easily" and "couldn't"). I was afraid the book was too hard for her, so I asked her to read it to me. "Oh, but I'm doing them all in a line, you know," she said. I thought that it was her way of saying that she'd rather read alone. Instead she brought all five little books on wild animals and read every one to me. "The lion is just like the tiger. It comes out when it's coming dark and time for food," she confided to me, chuckling, after finishing *The Tiger* and *The Lion*. It was a clear indication that her comprehension was good, but I asked her a few questions on each book to doublecheck. She answered them easily. I am thrilled that her reading has developed so! I should have gotten these books out sooner. I didn't realize some children were ready for them. I was asleep at the switch all right.

At juice time Jesse said, "There's a lot of things you put out new. You even put out story paper—new kind!" And so I had: the next level of paper that has a heavy blue line outlining what was the solid blue middle area in the first level of paper. It is a way to lead the children gradually away from dependence on the solid blue line in forming letters.

I had started Ed doing the Noun Room Labeling when he came in. After a few cards, I found that I was really too busy with

Jesse's Chains and the Bank Game boys to keep up with him, too. I asked Joan to take over, and also to keep an eye on Anna and eventually Robbie and Carmen, all of whom were working on Phonogram booklets. (I had told the children to check with us when they found a phonogram word since sometimes there is a confusion as in words like "very" and "could.") After the Room Labeling, Joan said that Ed got the Command Game out. He seemed to enjoy doing it by himself. Then she checked his vowel sounds with the Sandpaper Letters. He seems to have them again now, but we'd best keep up the repetition.

After reading for a half hour or so, Sandy spent the *entire* morning repeating and repeating the Trinomial Cube! (It's a sensorial material that reproduces the trinomial theorem in wooden cubes and rectangular prism shapes. The pieces are fitted together as in a puzzle to form one large cube.) It was a clear indication to me of how ready her mind is to deal with patterns and spatial relationships—both abilities which are required for reading.

April 25   I introduced Grammar Box Two to Jesse today. It adds the adjective to the article and noun of Grammar Box One. I took two pigs from the container of objects. "Jesse, can you give me a pig?" When he handed me the smaller of the two pigs, I said, "That's a pig all right, but it's not the pig that I want. I want the *fat* pig. Can you give me the fat pig?" (If he had given me the fat pig first, I would have said, "No, that's not the pig I want," etc.) "'Fat' told you which pig I wanted. 'Fat' is an adjective. Adjectives are words that tell you what kind of a noun it is," I said. Together we labeled each object with an appropriate article, noun, and adjective label. "A fat pig," "a thin pig," etc.

Sandy wanted to read a book from the *Our Book Corner* series to me. She did so well!

After school today we had a meeting with the reading coordinator for our school. She wanted us to suggest which level of materials she should order for our children for first grade next year. We put Sandy in the top level with Linda, Anna, Sam, and Robbie. Only Lee reads more fluently than they do. We put Emily and Ed in the group for the lowest level of reading materials for next year.

April 26   Emily is back after two weeks at home with strep throat. I gave her a squeeze. "Choose whatever you want to do with me, Emily. I want to work with you." She chose the Article, Noun, Adjective Box and Objects. She seemed tired after she had labeled the Objects so I told her to choose something else. Sandy had chosen to do the Article Noun Box next to her, and continued to work after Emily left.

Linda was doing the Marker Papers and asked me to write "fell" on one. I asked, "Linda, is 'fell' a noun or a verb?" "Verb," she said with conviction, "'cause she *fell*," and she pretended to fall down. I think that most of the children have developed the concepts of noun and verb all right but often they have trouble naming the word for the concept. I don't think Linda could have remembered the word "verb" in this context. She could supply it because I had given the choice "noun or verb" to her. Robbie, Edith, and Carmen were hot into their Phonogram booklets again.

April 30   Linda was sitting in the rocker and Sandy was lying down on the pillows in the library. Each was reading intently from the Addison Wesley books. Sandy read the board with Susie next. She seemed at loose ends afterward. I thought that she might need some room care materials to help settle her, so I suggested that she might like to arrange the daffodils. She shook her head. I didn't think that it was the right moment, but I then suggested a multiplication paper with the Chains. Much to my surprise, her face lit up. She proceeded to spend the rest of the morning on them. She was so quick and confident in counting by ones and then skip counting, and finally in writing her multiplication problems. Joan and I both remarked after school that her pride and confidence in herself are extraordinary these days. It started when her reading and math understanding began to blossom so dramatically.

May 2   Sandy and Emily did the Marker Paper for most of the morning, then the I Spy cards, and finally the Noun Room Labeling.

May 3   Sandy, Linda, Edith, and Lee all wrote stories. Sandy and Emily unrolled the Calendar Roll. Most of the children went to look at it this time. "It's a long thing! Look at that!" Lee said. (It stretches across three-fourths of the room.) "Look at this birthday!" Susie said. "Here's Edith's!"

May 10   Language was everywhere. There are many stories: Nick, Susie, Sam, Madan. *Many* children were on a reading binge with library books: Linda, who read all morning, Sam, Robbie, Lee, Carmen, Anna, Sandy, Edith, and Jesse worked on booklets of the Phonetic and Phonogram Objects. Robbie, Susie, and Anna labeled the room. Karen, Jesse, and Robbie did the Command Game. Lee and Nick labeled the dinosaurs.

May 11   I am so pleased. Sandy's mother came in today. She said that they have decided to send Sandy back to our school for first grade, instead of to the public school as they had planned. She had told me earlier in the year that they simply couldn't afford to keep her in private school next year. They had changed their minds because Sandy had done so well. She particularly mentioned her progress in reading and math. "We've decided that we'll just have to reorder our financial priorities," she said.

It was another busy day of spontaneous language work: stories, the Command Game, Room Labeling, and reading. Emily wanted to read the three-letter Phonetic Cards with me. She can synthesize the first two sounds of a three-letter word now! I think that it will turn out that she is simply slow in developing synthesizing, just as she was slow in talking. (Her parents told me in the fall that she hadn't talked until she was three. They had been concerned that she was retarded.) It doesn't look as if there is an actual block in development. That makes me so happy! Again, she had a calmer day. Was she so tense before because she realized that she wasn't developing in this area as rapidly as the other children?

"Please get me a pencil," she said as she started to do the Phonetic Objects after the Phonetic Cards. I smiled at her. She got up to get it for herself. That, of course, is the other reason why earlier I had considered another year of kindergarten for her. At least part of her enjoys being babied.

May 14   Sandy and Emily had a fine time with the Marker Pages all morning. "I've done twenty-three pages!" Sandy said. Linda and Karen made books with the Marker Papers, too. Sam read to me from the National Geographic book in the children's series. "The skeleton of a dinosaur is a strange and mysterious sight," etc. In five pages of text, he only had to ask for two words: "desert," which he pronounced "de-sert" and realized that it didn't make sense, and "ancestor," whose meaning he didn't know.

May 15   I put out little yellow books for story writing. They were the main attraction of the morning with Susie, Linda, Karen, Edith, and Emily working on them for two and a half hours straight and not wanting to stop then. The children draw a picture with the story markers on the left side of the book and write on the right side. It is their miniature size which makes the books intriguing to the children, I think. They are only three by four inches and have twelve pages. The lines are set like the lined paper that we use, and require much smaller writing. As I watched the children working away all at one table, I thought, "No one would believe it if they didn't see it. Five- and six-year-olds writing a whole small book with writing as small and well formed as second graders'!"

May 16   It was an exciting day. The class was lively and there were some important individual breakthroughs. Emily's was the most thrilling. She was calm and involved all morning—first she wrote a story, then she remembered her U.S. map from several weeks ago. She did an excellent job of finishing the coloring. Afterward she asked to join Ed and Nick, who were doing the Noun Room Labeling with me. I drew out several three-letter phonetic cards for her, "rug, map," etc. She *read* them! She synthesized all three sounds and pronounced the whole word in one breath! She giggled with triumph each time as she went off with the card to label whatever it named. "Emily, you're reading!" I said. She brought the Phonogram booklets to me next. She read all of the *oo* booklet, and three or four words in the *ee* booklet before she began to tire. I *knew* that it had to come, yet there was always that nagging doubt—"What if there's a development problem?" (I had asked Betty, the director of our Learning Disability Program, to observe Emily during the winter. We hadn't reached a definite decision on whether to test her yet.) It wouldn't have been the worst thing in the world if Emily did have a development problem, of course, because we would have caught it so early. We would have given her the special help that she needed before she developed serious feelings of inferiority. Still, I am relieved that she has made this breakthrough!

Sandy was on a reading binge. After she had read all the stories in the story folder to herself in the library, she read all of the Addison Wesley books to Joan. When she was in the library, I could hear her voice above Mozart's music, reading a story by Carmen (the smallest child in the class and within a few weeks of

Sandy in age): "Once I went horseback riding. They put me on a bull. He almost killed me. I was not scared."

May 17   Sandy finished her whole yellow booklet today. She was the first one in the class to do this. It's hard to remember that I was thinking of retaining her in the beginning months of school.

May 21   Language, language, language again! Stories were abounding: Susie, Carmen, Sandy, Linda, Madan, and Ed (who finished his yellow booklet). There was a constant stream of reading, too, a large part of it in the yellow booklets in the library. (Some children have volunteered to leave their finished booklets there for a few days: Susie, Anna, Edith.) Sandy and Anna giggled together over Edith's story about camping and getting "ants" in her "pants."

May 22   Bless Emily. She has developed so this year. She wrote a story today: "One day we went to school. Then we went home. The next morning school was out. We had fun when school was out. Then school was on again. We worked very hard. Then we had fun at school."

May 24   Ed went on a Super Book binge, reading aloud to himself, "Sam's cat is lost. Sam is sad," etc. It pleased me because reading has come more slowly to him than the other children (except for Emily, of course). He was relaxed and contented, lying in the library, his head on the pillows. No wonder he could go on for so long.

This is the kind of child with whom it is particularly important to avoid forced oral group reading. Reading orally to himself is a very different process and experience for Ed than reading orally with his peers. In that process there are many factors at work besides developing the skill to read. How did forced oral group reading ever get to be a standard way of introducing beginning reading? The only thing that I can think of is that it gives the appearance that the teacher is in control of the learning process. In actuality, of course, there is no way for anyone on the outside to have control of the process of learning to read in another person.

The big success of the day was the introduction of Grammar Box Three, which adds the verb to noun, article, and adjective. Jesse said, "That sure is new—article, noun, adjective, verb— that's what it is!" I helped Edith make the sentences "A gray dog sits. A brown dog barks." She placed the dog described next to each one. Then I showed her how to draw and color in the appropriate grammar symbols above each part of speech, red circle for verb, black triangle for noun, etc. "You know what? This is fun!" Edith said. Susie, Karen, Sandy, and Ed all asked to do it. "I got my adjectives and I got my verbs," Sandy said to herself with satisfaction as she gathered the words together to put them in the appropriate slots in the box.

May 25   Sandy went right to her Grammar Box Three and finished symbolizing her sentences from yesterday. Both Robbie and Emily did Grammar Boxes One and Two.

May 29   Carmen and Anna did the Command Game. Linda, Madan, and Sam wrote stories. Sam read all the Addison Wesley books (I have changed them regularly, so there are always new ones out.). Then he read a book called *Harlequin* by Remy Charlip, which I had read to the children on the line yesterday. How can he read so well? I introduced Madan to Grammar Box Three. His writing is *much* better. All the children seem to be catching on to this work and enjoying it.

I wanted to check Ed on reading again just to make certain that he has progressed as well as I think he has. He chose to read Anna's yellow book to me. He did very well with it. I can relax about him now. It's incredible how he has developed this year:

math, language, self-direction, and so much progress in impulse control.

May 30   Ed asked to do Grammar Box Three. This class is so incredibly into language. Emily did six Movable Alphabet words with me, then wrote a story in her yellow booklet: "We went to school and then we went to class and I was in first grade."

I want to close this chapter on language with one of the stories that Sandy wrote in May. It captures for me the essence of her development during this year from a very aggressive, tense little girl to a self-confident, relaxed one who better understands herself and her life. My guess is that she is represented in the story both as herself and one of the friends. "One day I had two friends over. They got into a big fight. They went to my room. They talked about it. I went in my room. I asked them, 'Have you solved the problem?'"

FOUR | # Mathematics

Five years ago when I began using the Montessori math materials in my present classroom,* I was uncertain whether the children would benefit from their use. I was teaching children who
did not have the foundation in the orderly and sequential use of
concrete manipulative materials that Montessori planned for
children two-and-a-half onward. My decision to use the materials was based on the superiority of their design and concept, and
the depth and scope of mathematical understanding which they
represent.

The Montessori math materials are not designed to "teach
math" but to aid the development of the mathematical mind: an
exploring mind that understands order, sequence, and abstraction, and has the ability to put together what is known and arrive
at a new creation. The materials represent quantity and symbol,
the Decimal System, and the four mathematical operations, all
in concrete form. They enable the child to manipulate and repeat the use of materials until he can make his own abstraction
out of his own work.

In introducing any knowledge to the child Montessori pre-

*For a list of the Montessori math materials and the order of their pre-
sentations, see Appendix D.

sented a picture of the whole before breaking it down into its individual parts. In math, for example, as soon as the child understood quantities and symbols one to ten and the concept of zero,
he was presented with the entire Decimal System. Originally,
Montessori designed her Decimal System materials for eight-
year-olds. She discovered, however, that four- and five-year-olds
had the easiest time learning from them and the greatest interest
in them. I will relay the children's response to the math materials primarily through one child, Robbie, but I have included others when it seemed appropriate to do so. I have chosen diary
entries beginning October 17. For the first few weeks of school I
assess the children's knowledge of numerals and quantities one
through ten and the concept of zero. I do this through the use
of the first Montessori materials (usually introduced to three-
and four-year-olds in Montessori schools): Numerical Rods and
Cards, Spindle Boxes, Cards and Counters, Memory Game of
Numbers. The majority of my children grasp this material
quickly (only Emily, Ed, and Sandy were slower with it in this
particular class). By mid-September I begin introducing the
Decimal System Material. Quantities in the Decimal System
Material are represented by tiny glass beads. The Decimal Numeral Cards are color-coded for easier identification: green for
units, blue for tens, red for hundreds, and green again to represent units of thousands.

I have detailed the use of these materials in Appendix E for
readers who are interested in the more technical aspects of the
beginning material. I have begun the diary entries, however,
with the introduction of counting with the bead material and the
Bank Game. The Hundred Chain for counting is a chain of ten
ten-bead bars which the children count from one to one hundred and label by tens with numeral tags. In the Bank Game the
children are introduced to the four operations of the Decimal
System: addition, multiplication, subtraction, and division. At
this point the children know not only the numerals and quanti-

ties of one to ten and the concept of zero, but also, through the bead material, the quantities of one thousand, one hundred, one ten, and one unit and their corresponding numerals. They therefore are ready to learn mathematical operations using numerals up to and including the thousands.

October 17 I was showing Carmen how to count the Hundred Chain. First we folded the chain into a hundred square and matched it to the hundred square on the Decimal Tray One. "Ten squared equals one hundred," I said. Jesse came to stand by us, and I asked if he wanted me. "No, I'm just watching," he answered. We began to count the chain then and lay out the numeral tags at each multiple of ten. He counted with us for a while, and Susie and Robbie joined us, too. That gives three other children a preview of the Hundred Chain. After we got to one hundred, we counted down the chain by tens, (ten, twenty, thirty, etc.), then back up it by tens. We went back and counted the tens, too. "Ten tens. Ten times ten equals one hundred," I said. "Someday I'll show you how to write that."

I have gotten the Bank Game out to start tomorrow, principally with Jack, Robbie, Anna, and Madan in mind. I have delayed doing this so far because it will tie me up for so much with just the four children that I am introducing it to. I must get it out now, however, if we are to get on to the Stamp Game after Christmas and the Dot Game after spring, both of which depend on a solid base of work with the Bank Game.

October 18 Madan asked me to show him the Hundred Chain. Next I introduced the Bank Game to him, Sam, Jack, and Lee. It was particularly successful. The children were well prepared for this first presentation. Everyone knew the quantities and numerals thoroughly. Undoubtedly, it was because they had voluntarily done much more work with the Decimal Tray Two and Decimal Numeral Layout than any group of children that I remember in other years. We even went on to exchanging in our addition problem, ten units for a ten bar, ten ten bars for a hundred square, and they understood it so easily. It was indirect preparation for future material working at its best. To play the Bank Game each child drew a ticket from me with a designated number of thousands, hundreds, ten, and units on it. They then took this ticket to Sam, who was the "banker" at the "bank" rug. He put the appropriate quantities of thousand cubes, hundred squares, ten bars, and unit beads, on the bottom of each child's tray (thousand cubes on left, hundreds next, etc.). Each child then went to his individual small numeral layout which he had set up on a table. Each chose the appropriate numerals to match their quantities, and brought his tray to me. (Numerals were placed at the top of the trays above the correct quantities.) Each child then told me what he had brought ("I brought you two tens," etc.). After each quantity and numeral were presented, I said, "Let's see how much we have all brought together. Jack, you count the units; Robbie, you count the hundreds," etc. Each child who needed to exchange ten of a kind for the next higher category went to Sam at the "bank." The answer was represented by numerals from the Decimal Numeral Layout. When we superimposed the numeral cards, I showed the children how to put each card to the left (so that unit card was in the thousand column), then turn the cards perpendicular and slide the numerals into their appropriate position. It is a "trick" they love, and helps to establish the important of category and zero as a place holder. Afterward, I told the children that they should ask me when they wanted to do the Bank Game. (After they were very confident with all the procedures, I will let them try it on their own.)

Susie has been so happy and busy. It's hard to believe that she is the same child who was so pouty and demanding of attention just a few weeks ago. She wanted me to show her the Hundred Chain, and waited patiently through the entire Bank Game until I was free to do it with her. These children are good counters.

Susie had a little trouble making the transitions 39 to 40 and 49 to 50, etc., in the beginning, but by the seventies she had caught on.

October 24   Robbie, Jack, Linda, and Anna asked to do the Bank Game. They were all business as they went about setting it up. They did it exceptionally well, very carefully laying out the numerals in exactly even lines. They *are* good at the exchanging.

October 25   On the plus side for the morning, the Bank Game went the best yet. Robbie, Anna, and Sam were particularly enthusiastic and wanted to keep repeating it. We did it four times in all. Ed was the exception. He did not remember hundreds and thousands, and, of course, he did not want to do it again. That means out of the whole class only Ed, Sandy, and Emily need more work with the Decimal System at a lower level. That is really quite good!

October 30   Madan asked to do the Bank. Robbie, Jack, and Anna played it with us. This time I let the children choose their own numbers from their numeral setup instead of drawing tickets from me. It's amazing what real interest in numbers per se this chance to choose their own numerals always reveals. Sometimes the children choose the highest numbers they can, sometimes the lowest, sometimes a sequence, but they are intrigued with what they can do with numbers in any case. The children were excellent on exchanging also.

October 31   I showed Robbie and Susie the Twenty-five Chain. (This is a chain of five bars of five blue beads each. The children are familiar with the five bar because of their work with the Bead Stair. After the children know this chain, they can be shown all of the rest, chain of one, chain of four, chain of nine, chain of sixteen, etc.) Susie said, "I love those little things!" We counted by ones, then by fives, then counted the number of fives in the whole chain. We repeated, "Five times five equals twenty-five," then squared the chain and repeated that equation, too.

November 1   I think Robbie is a good example of a left-handed child who will grow out of his problem of reversals and directionality. Today he copied many numbers backward from the wall calendar when he was making his own calendar. There were so many that I suggested that he might want to make another one, rather than erasing so many on the first. When he finished the second one, he brought it to me. "And none of them are the wrong way!" he said with satisfaction.

November 6   I worked on the Hundred Chain with Ed and Sam, both of whom are having trouble going from 39 to 40, 49 to 50, etc. These materials are really helpful. When they got stuck at 29, 39, etc., I said, "Go back and count to see how many tens you have counted." "Three tens—oh, that's thirty," Sam said. When they got to 49, Sam said, "Wait a minute, I can figure it out." He counted his tens, selected the little plastic arrow with 50 on it, and said "Fifty!" The next step for him is to make this counting transition "49, 50" without hesitating. The best part is that he will know *why* he is saying "49, 50."

November 7   Robbie and Jesse asked to do the Bank today. It was perfect because Robbie rounded up Jack and Sam (both of whom I had planned it for today) to do it, too. I have waited some time now for the children to choose the same number spontaneously as they have in other years, so that I can introduce multiplication. They weren't doing it, however, so today I told the children all to choose the same number. They decided on 2999. After they all brought their quantities and numerals to the rug, I said, "How many times do you see 2999?" "Three," they answered. "Right." I took two sets of numerals away, and put a wooden numeral 3 and a wooden multiplication sign by the remaining 2999. "We have 2999 three times. Let's see what three times 2999 is," I said. We added as before, and I told them we had just done multiplication. I shook hands all round. It was obvious that they were impressed with themselves.

November 9   Robbie began the morning practicing writing his numbers. I couldn't have chosen better work for his needs right now.

November 15   Robbie and Jack practice writing numbers every day!

November 16   Emily wanted to do a Strip Board booklet. I felt it was beyond her, but I have learned to be careful of my judgments in situations like this. Too many times the children have amazed me by accomplishing things I never thought they could. She had trouble with the adding of zeros and doubles. Otherwise she managed quite well. Best of all, she had the determination to finish all nine pages. She was so proud of herself.

November 22   I started the morning re-presenting the Decimal Tray One to Ed. When Emily came to shake hands, I asked her to join us. In a minute Sandy joined us of her own accord. These were just the three children that I wanted. It doesn't always work out this way, and that is the negative aspect of structuring the classroom so informally. Sandy has it now, but Emily and Ed still can't remember the one hundred square or the thousand cube in the third period. ("What is this?") This is pure vocabulary and involves no analytical thinking. Why do they have so much trouble? They remember continents, geometric shapes, and geometric solids with far less trouble. It is going to take a lot of repetition.

November 28   Robbie was heading for a map, but I suggested that he finish his Chains from yesterday. (I had started him on counting all the Chains and writing the multiplication equations they represent—10 × 10 = 100, etc.) He really had a great time doing them. I was unsure if I should have steered him away from his original choice of a map, though.

December 4   I re-presented the Tens Board to Robbie and Jack. (I had introduced it first in early November. It consists of two boards with numerals from 10 to 90 written on them. There are slots for sliding in numeral cards as in the Teens Board. This time the child slides the 1 to 9 cards over the zero in units column of ten, for example, making 11 to 19 before going down to 20. He also adds a unit bead each time to the ten bar or bars already set in place. It is excellent to use in presenting the makeup of numbers, "What is thirty-one made of? Three tens and one unit," etc. I was re-presenting it because sometimes both boys were calling 13 "thirty-one," for example.) Jack understood number makeup when using this material, but later he chose to count the Chains and had as much trouble reading the tags correctly as before. He did go to Robbie (who has it now) for help at one point. "Robbie, would you show me something?" he asked. I was pleased about that.

January 8   Lee asked me to show him the Fraction Skittles, which are new. (Conelike wooden shapes with spherical tops, they are five inches in height and finished in a highly polished natural wood. There are four cones: one whole, one split in half with red interiors, one in thirds with orange interiors, and one in fourths with green interiors.) He caught on easily as I showed him how to write the quantities: one-half, one-third, etc., and equations: two halves equal one whole, etc. Robbie asked to use these later, and had the same success with them. They are so beautiful and simply designed. No wonder the children want to work with them.

January 10   Robbie was the biggest success of the morning. I introduced him to the Negative Strip Board. (It is similar to the Addition Strip Board except that plain wooden strips are used to cover the numbers not needed. In the equation $16-9$, for example, a two-space wooden strip covers the 18 and the 17. The blue 9 strip is put next to it then, covering the next numbers to reveal the answer, 7. In a second presentation the child is shown how to use the material to find all the subtraction equations for a certain number, for example, 4, $4-0=4$; $4-1=3$; $4-2=2$; $4-3=1$; $4-4=0$. Again, the purpose of the material is to lead to memorization.) Robbie finished the entire booklet, working for one hour and twenty minutes without stopping. It was a beautiful example of a child making spontaneous discoveries with the materials. I was working with Nick on Robbie's other side and could hear his running commentary to himself. "What goes here?" (a wooden strip). "Uh-huh," and he put it down. "There we go. Now we put the nine here" (a blue 9 strip). "Here we are," he said as he wrote the answer. "Now we're on fourteen" (page with the Tables of Fourteen). "We put the nine rod and that equals five. There. That's a nice five. What do you do now? Hey, that's zero. This is going to equal more than that." All the while there was a quiet excitement and enthusiasm in his voice.

January 11   I did subtraction with the Bank Game with Robbie, Jack, and Edith. They were attentive, but not as enthusiastic as I would have liked. They are really ready to move into the Stamp Game, where less bodily movement and more independent work are involved. The Bank Game was designed for the needs and interests of four-year-olds. I don't think the initial interest of the fall can be recaptured for these children. (The

Stamp Game is used by the children for individual exercises in the Decimal System, after they are familiar with the group exercises of the Bank Game. The material consists of small colored squares: green squares with 1 written on them to represent units, blue squares with "10" written on them to represent tens, red squares with "100" written on them to represent hundreds, green squares marked "1000" to represent thousands. This work is more symbolic than previous work and is used for addition, subtraction, multiplication, and division.)

January 12   I asked Robbie if I could show him "something new," and got out the Stamp Game. I brought Decimal Tray One to show him the connection between the stamps and the beads. Next I told him we were going to do an addition equation. I wrote the first one on the special squared Stamp Game paper. He had fun with the equation, and I was pleased with his ease of transference from the Bank Game. I let him write his own equation for a second problem. He chose his numbers thoughtfully, pausing with each category. "Let's see, I'll have four units," and he wrote a 4 in the space for units, etc. He set up the stamps in neat rows, then put his pencil down horizontally to start his second number with the stamps. He pushed them together then and began to add them. He had chosen six units for his second number, and said, "Hmmm," when he discovered he had zero units after exchanging. He had to exchange again in the tens, but had eight left afterward. "At last! I can keep some," he said. In the hundreds again he said, "I get to keep them."

January 22   Robbie did the Stamp Game today. He is quick. "Oh, that's going to be sixteen," he said. (He was adding 1648 and 2539.) "It's eight plus nine, Robbie," I said. "Oh, yeah. That's going to be seventeen then," he said. He proceeded to count the unit stamps then and exchange for the ten stamp at the right time.

January 25   Momentum from playing the Noun Verb Game seemed to carry Robbie and Lee right into working with the Stamp Game. (I have three sets of Stamp Games in the room because I felt the children would need more opportunity to do this work than one set would provide.) It couldn't have worked out better: My two left-handed, sometimes confused "one-sidedness" boys got those numbers down perfectly, stamps in the right columns, plus sign in the right place, etc. They chose their number together. Both kept looking up at the clock and calendar to see if they were making their numbers go in the right direction. It was Robbie's turn to choose the thousands. "How about eight, eight thousands. Eight goes any way you want!" They counted the stamps and exchanged with ease when appropriate. I wish I could have had it all on videotape, especially their running commentary to each other as they worked.

January 31   Robbie did the Clay for a few minutes, then came to ask if he could do the Thousand Chain, as if he had just that minute remembered it. (He had asked to do it at the end of the morning yesterday, and I said we could do it today.) The Thousand Chain is a chain of 100 ten-bead bars. There are also numeral tags for numbering by tens, 100, 120, etc., ten hundred-bead squares, and one thousand-bead cube. The former are placed along the chain as the child counts each bead, i.e., at the 200th bead the child puts a tag saying 200 and a one hundred square next to it. The thousand cube goes at the end of the chain after it is all counted. The numeral tags for each hundred are in red and the thousand tag is in green.) Madan stayed right with Robbie as he counted the chain, handing him the appropriate tags. Robbie is such a confident counter. There is never the slightest hesitation in going from one category to another. "I'm getting to 260 awfully fast," he said. Madan said to me, "He's so fast!" They finished the entire chain by ten o'clock. Just as Robbie was finishing the last bar of the chain, Nick and Jack sat down to watch. "Was it tiring?" Jack asked at the end. "You bet!" Robbie said. Madan explained, "Well, it's the only work we've done today." It was as if he didn't want them to be *too* impressed.

February 16   The children were quite upset that the Four Chain was suddenly missing during midmorning. There were many spontaneous searches for it, beneath the shelves, in the rugs, etc. It was a clear indication of how the children feel about these materials and their room. Most children couldn't get settled back into their work. They kept going back to look for the missing chain all over again after each unsuccessful search.

February 28   I was doing a Stamp Game with Karen, and Robbie came to join us. "I've done hard work today. Two hard works," Robbie said as he began. (He had just finished "my nine-page story," as he called it afterward.) Karen kept insisting on doing "another one," so we did four problems in all, one for each operation: subtraction, multiplication, addition, and division. (In division, twenty-nine skittles are used to represent each category: nine each of red and blue, ten green, and a large green one for thousands. When dividing by fifteen, for example, one blue skittle to represent one ten and five green skittles to represent five units are used. The child divides by giving the appropriate number of stamps to each skittle.) I stapled the four pages of problems together for a booklet. "It's fun," Karen said. "I'm going to make two booklets!" "Me, too!" Robbie said. "I'm going to do three booklets in one whole day. Now I got the line and two dots" (the sign for division). It was 10:25 by now, however, and one booklet was all we had time for before drama.

March 5   I asked Robbie and Ed to do the Stamp Game with me. For the addition equation they chose numbers in sequence, $4321 + 8765$. "This is fun. I've done this number before," Robbie said. For multiplication, they decided to multiply by one. When they realized that the answer was going to be the same as the number they were multiplying, Robbie said, "This is embarrassing!"

March 8   Robbie and Jack were doing a division problem with the Stamp Game. "Let's divide by one," Robbie said. After it was all set up and they were ready to begin the process, both boys looked puzzled. "How are we going to do this?" said Jack. Sam, who was sitting next to them, said, "Hey, you can't do it at all!" I moved the lone skittle down and gave him all four columns of stamps. The discovery inspired Jack to say, "I want to make a booklet." "Me, too," Robbie answered. We did a subtraction number, then addition. "This is fun. They're such low numbers," Jack said. (They had chosen 2211 for the top number.) I chose 6789 for the second so it would involve changing. While they were counting up these longer columns of stamps, Robbie said, "I tell you, this is fun!" "It's good for our math, too. Right?" Jack asked. By the time we had gotten through multiplication, an hour had gone by. Robbie got the Silver Polish. "I'm going to do this twice," he said, and he did. Then, refreshed, he went on to write a story.

March 13   I asked Jesse to join Robbie and me in a Stamp Game. Jesse has been so negative about working with me lately that I hoped Robbie's enthusiasm would help carry him along. As they were setting up their materials, Robbie said, "I love the Stamp Game. I'm doing two booklets in one day!" "Not me," said Jesse. "I don't like doing the Stamp Game." So much for my brilliant idea. We did a division equation. I kept the numbers low so less counting was involved, hoping that would help keep Jesse from turning off. To my surprise, he enjoyed it. "I'm going to do a book," he said, and went off to get another paper. "All right," he said, and gave a little chuckle to himself as we began a multipli-cation equation. The magic of these materials impressed me all over again in this incident. If only I can keep building the con-nection between the children and the materials, the magic will happen. The materials lure them into a deeper and deeper in-volvement as they feel the stirrings of learning taking place in them. Watching from the outside, it appears almost as if some other power were taking over.

April 24   About 9:30 Madan asked me to show him the Multiplication Board. It consists of one hundred red beads, and a perforated board with one hundred holes in rows of ten. They are numbered across the top from one to ten. There is a small window slot on the left of the board for inserting a card from one to ten. If the child were multiplying by four, for example, he would insert the 4 card in this slot. If he were multiplying four times five, he would put a red disc above the five at the top of the board. He would then lay down four beads in the ones column, four in the twos column, etc., to the five in the "disc" column. He would then count all the beads and find he had twenty. This is a material for aiding memorization of the multiplication tables. I had such a good time watching Madan catch on to this work. When he wrote "9" for three times three, without counting the beads, I said, "Madan, how did you do that?" "Six [the number of beads he had out for three times two] plus three [the number of beads he had just laid out] makes nine. That's how I do that. If you want me to count it for you, I will," he said. When he got to higher answers in the twenties, he counted the beads by two. Finally, by three times nine, he had begun to count as he laid the beads down, starting from the previous answer of twenty-four (three times eight), "twenty-five, twenty-six, twenty-seven. That's twenty-seven," he said. Heady stuff for a five-year-old. He was disappointed when I called for line time at 10:15. "Can I just do the fours?"

April 30   When I checked to see if Emily knew her hundred square and thousand cube, she was still a little shaky about them. She was more secure with the hundreds and thousands numerals, however, so I decided to try the Stamp Game. I want to determine how much understanding she has of the math and language materials at this point. Also it is important to determine how well she can respond to directions when new materials are introduced. She loved the Stamp Game. She counted very carefully and accurately, but needed some help to remember to exchange.

May 1   I am so pleased with Emily. I began the morning reviewing the decimal quantities and numerals with her and Ed together. She knew them. We did addition Stamp Game problems next. She is a very careful counter. "I'm counting it in Spanish, you know," she confided to me with her pixie smile. Best of all, when she saw that she had a great many tens stamps, she said, "When I get to ten, I stop." "And what do you do then, Emily?" I asked. "Get one here," she answered, pointing to the hundreds stamps. She could read the problem when we finished with only a slight hesitation on the thousands each time. Afterward she practiced writing numbers, probably inspired by Sandy, Anna, Edith, and Sam. They were all sitting at one table writing their numerals from one to thirteen on the smaller squared paper.

May 13   I asked several children to do the Cuisinaire Rods* and others came to join us voluntarily: Robbie, Susie, Sam, Nick. We did subtraction this time. I want to make certain that everyone is very confident with the rods as this is their major math requirement for the first grade. Robbie was a little unsure of them, so we'll have to concentrate on them each day for a while.

*See Appendix D.

May 14   I asked Robbie to do the Cuisinaire Rods again. Jesse saw us take a tray. "That's what I was going to do," he said. They both got going on subtraction. They needed me to sit at the table to keep them from getting silly, but they had a tremendous work splurge. They worked steadily for an hour and a half. At the end Robbie said, "I like this. I'm going to do this tomorrow." "For true," Jesse answered, "This week, tomorrow and tomorrow and tomorrow." We'll see. I thought there was a chance that it was momentary exuberance for Jesse.

May 15   Robbie and Jesse did go right back to the Cuisinaire Rods. Nick sat at the table doing them, too. Jesse got Nick off the track several times by acting silly, however. I finally moved Nick to a larger table with other children. All the boys finished a whole booklet.

May 25   The big success of the morning was something new: The Dot Game. It consists of a squared paper with columns headed ten thousand, one thousand, one hundred, ten, and one. The columns are divided into small squares, so that there are ten in each horizontal row. At the foot of each column are two spaces, the upper one for carrying numbers, the lower one for the result. There is a blank column on the side to write the problem in. The aim of this work is to focus the child's attention on the making of tens and the mechanism of carrying. It also allows the child to add very large numbers so that he realizes that it is just as easy to add tens of thousands as units. Linda and Susie both loved doing these. They made up problems with four and five numbers of four columns each. They made dots in the appropriate squares (as the counting mechanism for each category of numeral) with a lead pencil. When they got to ten of any category, they crossed it off and made a dot in the next category with an orange pencil so that they wouldn't confuse it with the uncarried dots for the numeral. Then they wrote the number of crossed-out rows of dots in the "carrying space." They did three papers each, which means they did six problems (as the front and the back of each page are used). They caught on easily and did problems independently right off. I am sorry that I was so lax in not getting this material out sooner. The children have obviously been ready for it.

May 29   I introduced the Multiplication Board to Robbie. He went like gangbusters on it, never a mistake. "Can I finish?" he asked when I called for line time. He got through the sixes before dismissal.

May 30   Robbie warmed up with the Markers, then finished his Multiplication Board booklet. He never makes a mistake in counting. "Every number is going the right way," he reminded me. He has certainly learned how to deal with reversals! And all with no formal drill. Edith, Sam, and Ed asked to do the Dot Game. "This is fun!" Ed said. Their sum of three numbers was 22,489. They were excited about getting into the ten thousands.

May 31   I introduced Robbie to the Dot Game. After showing him how to do one side of the paper, I asked if he would like to choose his own problem for the other side. "I'll choose my own," he said. He wrote:

$$\begin{array}{r} 4321 \\ 5843 \\ 1125 \\ +4781 \end{array}$$

He did it all correctly with no mistakes, and he was obviously fascinated by it. I was disappointed, though, because he didn't respond with his usual outgoing conversation and desire to keep going to more and more problems. "I've got a stomachache," he said, just as he finished his problem. Susie asked to do more Strip Board booklets but without using the Strip Board to find the answers. "I know them," she said. I asked her a few, and she does know them! I was amazed.

FIVE

Special Children

I am fortunate in having both gifted and learning-disabled children in my classes. They thrive along with the other children in the informal, noncompetitive atmosphere of the classroom. Although I have had no direct experience in teaching severely physically handicapped children, my feeling is that they would prosper in the classroom environment, just as the gifted and the learning-disabled do.

The fascination of teaching these children lies in the revelation of the learning process which they represent. The spectrum of this process is spread before the observer. The learning-disabled, no matter what their intelligence level, have blocked passages that create a stop-start, slow-motion learning pattern. The gifted take quantum leaps in creative thought that seem to skip whole steps in the same process.

In this chapter, I have chosen diary entries on Lee, an intellectually gifted child, and Timmy, a learning-disabled child. Lee and Timmy demonstrate that the same classroom environment can serve very different types of children simultaneously. Their lives also deepen understanding of development itself and what aids it.

I did not identify Lee's giftedness until December. Typical of intellectually gifted children, he was careful to hide the unusual way in which his mind worked until he trusted me not to treat him differently from his peers. I was aware quite early, however, that he recognized the difference in quality between his work and that of an adult. His wish to produce beyond his capabilities caused him intense frustration. At first I was uncertain if Lee's problems with directionality and reversals and putting materials away represented a learning disability. Eventually, it became obvious that these tasks caused him no confusion, and that he was simply absentminded about returning materials. By the first of November I noted in the diaries that there was an "unusual" quality about Lee. By Christmas his incredible ability to concentrate, almost losing contact with his surrounding environment, was apparent. Gradually in these weeks, he allowed me to see that he could read, and indeed could read anything. He revealed the unusual connections his mind makes, the constant motion of his mind (running mind games, as I think of them), his heightened emotional responses to others, his humor (sometimes uncontrollable), etc. After the first tentative weeks, he took to the environment like a duck to water. He was captivated by the materials—and by his own work, too, often carrying it about with him all morning after it was completed, referring to it again and again, and sharing it with the other children. The most impressive sign of Lee's giftedness is his self-direction. It is uncanny, even miraculous.

Timmy is an intelligent boy whose learning disability was apparent in the early weeks of school. His major disability is in the area of motor planning and orientation. Typical of learning-disabled children, he cannot respond to the materials in the self-directed manner of the other children. He needs continued assistance with them. In a very real sense, his is a trapped intelligence which is severely dependent on the guidance of the structured environment itself, the other children's activities, and my direction.

TIMMY

September 26   I don't think that I have any children with
the severe learning problems that I had last year. There were
three out of eighteen then, which seemed like a high percentage.
It is too early to tell, though. I need to watch Timmy, Lee, and
Robbie a while longer before I can decide whether to ask Betty
to come in and observe them for possible testing. Both Lee and
Robbie are left-handed and have a good deal of trouble with left-
to-right directionality. Timmy can't write at all and has unusual
difficulty remembering how to use materials.

September 28   I think teaching only five-year-olds is making me much more aware of the importance of teaching three-
and four-year-olds step-by-step procedures in performing physical tasks (as in the Room Care materials). This kind of imitation
of bodily movements of others in completing an activity is the
foundation for the ability to carry out verbal or written directions
later on. Some children do this very naturally with just the exposure that they get in their own homes as they watch parents or
older siblings doing things. But some do not. I am really worried
about Timmy, for example. He is very intelligent, yet he has a
hard time focusing his attention. He could not remember the
procedure for doing the Plant Care this morning. Joan struggled
with him over each step. The sad thing is, it will be the same
thing all over again tomorrow. He is going to have a hard time in
first grade if we can't make a lot of progress in this area this year.

October 2   I feel discouraged about Timmy. We worked on
the Sandpaper Letters. He has to take his other hand to hold his
fingers down to trace over the letter with index fingers. He has

a problem tracing the letters correctly, too, because he doesn't watch me when I show him how. His eyes and attention just wander off into space. My guess is that he is going to need one-to-one teaching in order to get the letters at all. He also will need to make a great many insets to develop his muscle control for writing. On the plus side, there is certainly nothing wrong with his intelligence or intellectual curiosity.

October 4   Timmy's mother came in today. She saw how many maps there were on the wall, and asked where Timmy's was. Oh, dear, she'll worry now. However, it might help set the stage for what I must try to get across to her at conference time: Timmy is an intelligent child who has trouble focusing his attention selectively, has slowly developing muscle control, and has some trouble with body awareness, including verbal control. He has improved so much since the beginning of the year, though. He is much better about raising his hand on the line now instead of speaking out impulsively, and much of the time he remembers to stay next to me and wait when he wants me. On the other side of the coin, he has put his coat on upside down for two days now.

October 5   Timmy came in, looking his usual expectant self, and glanced around in his customary way while shaking hands with me. There is seldom any eye contact at all. "Hey, there's a dead monarch here!" he said, pointing to the science shelf. He certainly has a wide range of general knowledge. I wonder if this is the way creative intelligence works at age five—open to all stimuli and not too selective. He asked to do the map again. We did it sensorially for the third time. "Are we just practicing?" he asked. I decided that he might just as well begin to make one, and asked Joan to help him. She said that it was "painfully slow." However, I thought the finished drawing looked quite successful.

October 6   I am truly worried about Timmy. He cannot connect the sounds that we have worked on—*o, c, g*—with their written symbols. I was coasting along about asking Betty to observe him, but I can't close my eyes to this situation any longer. Better to be safe than sorry. I'm certain tests will show that he has a learning problem. The trouble is that there is always the question in such a situation of how much the child might grow out of the problem on his own, or learn to compensate for it— especially an unusually bright child like Timmy. Also, I dread the agony of having to tell his parents that I suspect a problem with their child. No amount of rationalizing is going to ease that burden for them.

October 10   I have written a report on Timmy requesting Betty to observe him for possible testing. Today I said, "How about finishing your map, Timmy?" "Oh, yeah," he said enthusiastically. Then he looked as if it was supposed to appear magically, all set up and ready to work on. "First, get your rug," I offered. He did, then came back to me. "What next?" he asked. He kept coming to me for programming in a situation that he should have been able to manage quite independently. Then when he did begin to work, he lost interest almost immediately and put the map away. I asked him to do the Sandpaper Letters with me next. I concentrated on just the three letters we have covered so far. His attention was better today. At the end he knew the letters in second period ("Can you find the *o*?") but not in third ("Can you tell me what this sound is?" while I pointed to letter *o*), which indicates mastery. Auditory reinforcement helps him to remember how to form the letters. I said, "Around, up and down," when I traced over *g* on the Sandpaper Letter. He voluntarily repeated this to himself, as he traced it. He is such an eager and cheerful boy with his large brown eyes and long lashes. He is rewarding to work with.

October 16   Jack and Timmy did the Decimal Numeral Layout together. Afterward Timmy really didn't do anything. Joan asked him to get his map out, but again he only worked on it for a few minutes. At 10:00 he got the Clay and seemed to enjoy working with it. He doesn't bother anyone and watches everything that is going on. When I asked him if he wanted to do an inset, he said, "Do I have to?" It is the same dilemma that I face over and over again. What is he getting from the environment? Is it better to leave him alone or try to direct him more? For the moment, I am going to see what he can figure out for himself. Part of my decision is the result of a conversation on the street with Timmy's father yesterday. He said that Timmy had asked his mother for the lid from a jar and a piece of note paper on Friday. He had proceeded to draw a map of the world freehand with all the continents in appropriate places. He colored in the same colors we use at school: yellow for Asia, brown for Australia, etc. He had used the jar lid to make a circle for the hemispheres just as we use a plastic circle at school. The major difference was that he made his map on a miniature scale. Certainly I am not going to force him to finish a map at school if he voluntarily makes one at home all by himself. I have a feeling that what Timmy needs most right now is time.

October 17   Timmy took some real steps forward today. He chose the Wood Polishing, and polished several of the Geometric Solids. It is a brave step for him, choosing work that requires remembering how to go through so many procedures. He did quite well with it, too. Earlier I had shown him how to make addition equations to ten with the Small Numerical Rods and Numerals. He had no trouble with this, and several times he corrected some of his numeral reversals on his own. When I showed him how he could go on and do equations that make nine the next time, he said, "But that's too much for me now." It was, too, of course. He must have to work very hard to manage all this.

October 23   Timmy brought in a wasp's nest this morning. He looked it up all by himself in the *Golden Guide*. At outside time, we went for a walk in the woods by the school. One of those happy accidents happened. There was a bald-faced hornet's nest in a tree. There was a picture of one on the same page of the book as Timmy's wasp's nest. He recognized it immediately!

October 31   At 9:50 today Timmy started his second map. I couldn't have been more surprised. He had a little trouble getting his materials together, but he traced the pieces much more easily than I expected. He switched hands, however, as he was tracing each piece. "There, all done!" he exclaimed when he had finished the tracing. It was 10:15. He can write his name now, too, although he can't remember to form the *t* and the *h* from the top, not the bottom.

November 1   Timmy decided to finish his map. He got the rug, then his map. "What is missing, Timmy?" I asked. There was a long pause. "Crayons," he said, "But what else?" I asked. I had to pick up his map paper before he remembered that he needed a board first. Thirty minutes later he came up to me, aglow with triumph. "All done!" The finished product was just as good as the first map, which had taken him so many days. I am so glad that I hadn't pushed him for completion of the first one. Perhaps knowing that he had completed the first one on his own initiative gave him the drive to work steadily on this second one. I am relieved that I got the phone call to Timmy's parents over with last night. I didn't want to wait and drop a bombshell on them at conference time, so I told them that Timmy had progressed a great deal since the beginning of school, and that he was a joy to teach and to be with. However, we were concerned that he might have a motor visual problem, and we wanted them to consider having him tested by Betty. Mrs. Shore said that she had had that problem and that it wasn't discovered until she was fifteen. She came in first thing this morning to tell me that they want Timmy tested as soon as possible.

November 6   I had had a speaking engagement over the weekend in Georgia and I brought back a horseshoe crab shell and a live chameleon. As soon as Timmy came in, he said, "That isn't a dad one [chameleon]. It doesn't have a red skin on his neck. What is that, a horseshoe crab?" What an amazing child! When I started him on his calendar, he began tracing the numbers down the page instead of across. (I had dotted in the numbers, as I knew that it was too difficult for him to copy them from the wall calendar as most of the other children do.) Later in the day he was doing the Bank Game. He placed his numerals from the bottom up (1 at the bottom up to 9 at the top). Something is so completely mixed up in his mind. His grandmother, who is a teacher, came in to observe today. She said that she was so pleased because he always came home from school calm and contented. If things are as confused in his brain as they appear to be, it is no wonder that he thrives on the quiet, structured environment of the classroom.

November 16   Timmy counted the chains with me. Betty took him out later to begin his testing. I am so glad that they are getting started on this right away!

November 17   Timmy has developed so much. He has gone from a wandering and wondering little boy to one with real grit and determination in finishing hard work. He wanted to make a North American map. Even though I felt that he was far from ready for it, I went ahead and presented it. He worked and worked at it on a sensorial puzzle level. I was busy with other children and couldn't stay with him the whole time. When he began to trace the pieces, he asked me to stay with him. "I can't do it by myself," he said. "I'm sorry, Timmy, I am too busy. Why don't we do it tomorrow?" He stayed with it, however. He retraced several of the Central American countries three or four times. Then he colored it, and took it home today in real triumph.

November 21   I tried the Movable Alphabet with Timmy today. He did a fine job! I only gave him three words. By the last one he was beginning to get distracted, looking about at the science shelf, etc. He was really proud of himself, however. I never thought that he could do this well so soon! He seems to remember the letters that we have covered so far. He can hear and synthesize the sounds well when forming words. Relief!

November 27   Timmy was great on the Movable Alphabet this time. He made eight words with pretty consistent attention to the task. However, he fell over me once because he wasn't aware of where he was going. He spilled juice on his sweater during snack. "There's a little spill, there, just a tiny one," he said. (Actually it was a good-sized one.) He rubbed it into his sweater, a good indication that he is accustomed to such spilling, I think. After snack he forget he was doing the Movable Alphabet with me, and got out the Color Paddles. I called him back to finish the Movable Alphabet, then I asked him to practice writing numbers on the chalkboard. He traced the Sandpaper Numerals first, then wrote on the chalkboard. He switched hands in the middle of a numeral several times, and I asked him to choose just one hand to use. He chose the right, although he has used the left often at other times. He asked me, "Did you take the four?" (the Sandpaper Numeral which he needed to look at while he wrote it). "It's right next to your hand, Timmy," I said. "Oh, I couldn't find it!" What must life be like for him?

November 30   Timmy made a fine inset of the square. He wasn't happy with it, however. I couldn't understand why. How could he not know what an improvement it was over any that he had done before?

The shells are a big hit. Timmy found the crown cone, and Susie the gold ringed cowrie and the cape cowries. The children were impressed that they knew what the book was referring to when I read that cowries are mostly from the Indo-Pacific Oceans and cones from the Caribbean Sea. I also showed them an article in the new *National Geographic* on the "flashlight fish" of the Red Sea.

December 1   We have filled the bird feeder outside our window since the snow has come. I put out a basket with the *Golden Guide* for birds and a small pair of opera glasses for watching the activities there. Timmy was quite excited about this. "I have this book!" he said turning the pages. "There's a kingfisher! I have kingfishers on my vacation!"

December 12   Timmy somewhat reluctantly agreed to do the Movable Alphabet with me, but he went right at it once we were started. He made eight words, forgetting no letters and only reversing two. I meet with Betty tomorrow to go over her report on him. I'm most eager to hear what she has to say.

December 13   Great news on Timmy! He tests very high on I.Q. although he has such a hard time with the actual writing. He does have two problem areas: motor planning and visual orientation. He is two years below his age level in those areas, a truly extreme discrepancy from his other scores. However, these are two areas where development can be aided easily. I am especially pleased that Betty found that his high distractability is not interfering with his absorption of necessary information. She said that he was "up and down and all around the ball park" while she was giving directions to him on each test. In spite of this, he knew exactly what he had to remember on any given task. Apparently, he is so intelligent that he attends to several things at once. Betty will plan a special tutoring program for him and recommend three half-hour sessions each week for this year. It may or may not be necessary for one additional year. In the classroom we can help motor planning in writing by giving more aids such as dots to begin and end a letter. She suggested that he use a marker to help orient himself visually on a page when doing paper work. The Room Care activities and Sensorial Materials will help him with motor planning.

January 8   Timmy wanted to make a Canada map. "What do you need first, Timmy?" I asked. "A board," he said. "No," I answered. "Oh, yeah, the rug!" he said. I gave him a very simple introduction, and he made a fine map all by himself. He was immensely proud.

January 9   Bravo Timmy! He labeled his Canada map today and he is the first child to do so. Quite a change from being the last one (by weeks) to do the same thing with the world map. Afterward I helped him practice numbers on the writing paper for the first time. He needed directional dots for each number, but he is definitely developing in this area, too.

January 10   Timmy made a North American map, completely by himself. "I'm going to leave this one here for Father's Day," he said. He was so proud.

January 12   Timmy practiced numbers with me. Betty has scheduled a meeting with his parents and me next Wednesday. They specifically asked that I be there. I'm afraid that they are hoping that his recent rapid progress means that he doesn't need extra help. He does, though, no question about it. A child of his maturity and intelligence who has tremendous difficulty writing anything at all has a specific developmental problem.

January 17   The conference today with Timmy's parents went very smoothly after all. They were able to understand and agree with the discrepancies in his development, which the testing had made even clearer. They've agreed to have Timmy tutored three half-hours a week after class. Their hurt is deep, however. They kept referring to their own (or relatives') developmental weaknesses in similar areas. However, they are quite aware of Timmy's intelligence, which is probably some comfort to them. His father said that he couldn't believe it when Timmy saw the "flashing fish" from yards away in the Cambridge museum during Christmas vacation. Timmy had run all the way up the steps to them in his excitement. Apparently, he had remembered the article that I had shown the children in the *National Geographic* last fall. Imagine his making the connection from magazine to the actual fish all by himself! I remember now that the first thing Timmy said to me after Christmas vacation was, "I saw the flashing fish!" His eyes were wide, and he was bursting with excitement. I didn't know what he meant. *I* had forgotten the article!

January 18   Sam wrote his name backward on his paper. "What's different about your name, Sam?" I asked. "That's the way I always do it," he answered. "Get your folder out and check it," I suggested. I thought of talking to Timmy's parents yesterday, and trying to explain to them the difference between reversals and directionality problems like Sam's (which are developmental) and Timmy's problems (which represent an actual learning disability). I know that Sam's development lags; his reversals and confusion in directionality will disappear without special aid outside the classroom. Timmy's are going to remain, causing him greater and greater confusion as time goes on. It is both the consistency and the totality of the child's errors, plus his attitude toward them, which help make this distinction clearer. The puzzlement on Timmy's face as he struggles to figure out what is going on is so different from Sam's smile of recognition as he compares his two names. Sam quickly sees his error. Timmy looks ever puzzled.

February 9   Joan worked a long time with Timmy on his writing. He was trying very hard and looked very pleased with himself as he was working. He wandered about after that, however. He doesn't seem to respond to the material in the environment on his own. When I asked him to choose work, he finally decided on a map. "Now, let's see, what do I need first?" he asked. "A rug," I offered. "I have that. What do I need next? The circle thing. No. Paper. No." he said all this to himself. It took a while, but finally he said, "I know! A board!"

February 20   I told Timmy the plants needed watering badly, and that he still had his North American map to label. He watered the first plant. As he returned with it to the shelf, he said, "Next plant!" He watered every single plant, and never once forgot what he was doing or how to do it. When he was finished, I suggested that he practice his writing. "How about labeling North America?" he reminded me. That is the first time that he has been able to remember a sequence of activities. Two labels for his map had gotten lost: Greenland and Panama. He wrote new ones for himself! I really was surprised that he could do it. That means that he is ready to start writing with the Marker Paper. I checked with his mother and discovered that he has started to ask her to help him with writing at home, something that he has always avoided before.

Timmy did three Marker Papers. The words he chose were "war," "capsize," and "explosion." He managed the writing quite well. The whole process tires him, though. "What do I do next?"

he asked as he tried to follow what paper he should pick up, where to draw on it, which paper to bring to me for dictating, etc. He had to ask where to put the tray, sponge, and markers when he was all finished. Emily arranged it all for him, and showed him where to put it.

March 1   I overheard Timmy talking to Edith. "Hey, the Dominican Republic!" he exclaimed. (They were making world maps next to each other.) I was impressed that he could make this association because the scale of the world maps which they were working on is obviously totally different from that of the North American map, where they are accustomed to naming the Dominican Republic. Both children asked me to draw Antarctica on their maps (this piece doesn't remove for tracing). "How do you do that so easily?" Timmy asked. Poor fellow! He appreciates what a complex task copying from a model is.

March 2   I started Timmy on his first Phonetic Objects. He wrote them so well, but writing and learning the procedures for new materials do tire him.

March 7   I asked Timmy to read a Super Book with me. He still has a hard time sounding out the words, but afterward he knows what he has read. Lee, who was next to us, was very sweetly helping him with words. Suddenly, Timmy turned on him. "Stop helping me read!" He's so intelligent. It must be very frustrating to have something his peers can do come less easily for him. At 9:30 Timmy was in the library. I could hear him saying, "Hey, cool! Oh, cool!" to himself. He was looking at the universe book.

March 8   Timmy made a marvelous picture of the "sun, Jupiter with its red spot, moons, *Voyager I*, a solar nursery," and "Earth." He began to count the Hundred Chain next.

March 15   We had talked about Einstein's birthday yesterday. Today I wrote on the board, "Did you know that Einstein had a hard time in school?" We talked about it at some length on the line. I want the children to realize that they may well have a hard time in later grades, but that won't mean that they are "stupid." I was thinking particularly of Lee and Timmy, of course.

April 3   Timmy always takes so long getting his coat off. He wanders and talks to everyone, forgetting about his coat completely. "Oh, yeah," he says when I remind him, but keeps right on with his stimulus-to-stimulus approach to the room. I heard him say to Karen, who was painting. "If you want any brown, you mix red . . ." When I looked at her painting later, I said, "I see you know how to make brown." "Timmy told me," she said. His wanderings sometimes are obviously productive!

April 4   I told the children about Beethoven and his probable "learning disability" on the line today. When I talked about his tendency to daydream so that it was difficult for people to detect when he started to go deaf, Timmy asked in the most touching way, "Did he get better when he got older?" I had described all of Beethoven's symptoms: his constant spilling of his inkwell and general clumsiness, his lack of orientation, his difficulties in school. Timmy had identified with him all right.

This morning I had asked him to do the Phonetic Objects. Unthinkingly, I turned to work with someone else. When I looked over at him a few minutes later, he had spread all the materials all over the table. Everything was there but in total disarray. He never even attempted to set the labels with the appropriate objects. Instead he was trying to write the words from memory, which was a hopeless task for him. He was very unhappy, and I felt terrible.

April 6   Timmy had a fine day. He came up to me after his first "room wander" with the Collage Tray. "Looks like we're on volcanoes now!" (Joan had set up the Collage Tray to make a cut-away view of a volcano erupting. It has labels for side eruption, crater, cone, reservoir, etc. Timmy was able to make one with very little help, even though it required a good deal of organization of materials and procedure. Next he did two very carefully made insets. After these, he did the Command game with Madan. I heard him read, "Pick up a box," to himself, then saw him go to Anna. "Excuse me, can I pick up your box?" he asked. He picked up the box of Sandpaper Letters that she was using to work on letter formation.

April 9   I did a Stamp Game with Timmy. He *cannot* keep his mind on something like this. Following from one procedure to the next is impossible for him without *constant* detailed direction. I'm relieved, however, that he can write his numbers fairly well (as long as he has the Sandpaper Numerals in front of him for tracing and copying).

April 10   Timmy was wandering a good deal. I would have asked him to join Madan and me in a Stamp Game, but I just didn't feel that I had the patience for it today. Instead I asked him to play a game with the Geometric Solids with me. "Bring me the ellipsoid," etc. He can do this perfectly. How can a brain that retains this knowledge so easily have so much trouble following the Stamp Game?

April 12   Joan asked Timmy to get some work to do with her. He chose the Continent booklet. She told me later that he was totally distracted. She had to lead him through the material step by step, although he has done it once before and managed well on his own. Finally, Joan asked him if anything was bothering him. "Yes, my dad's coming home today," he said. When Timmy's father came to pick him up, he told Joan that he had been traveling a good deal lately, something which the family was not accustomed to.

April 16   Timmy brought in a fossil rock and a newspaper article about a volcano erupting in a West Indian island off South America. Both were perfect timing because tomorrow we will begin talking about life beginning, and we've been talking about volcanoes, of course. Timmy wandered and talked with Lee. They discussed Andromeda and the Milky Way on the board display (a replica of each made out of celluloid, like the top of a windmill). "No, no, *this* is where the sun is," Lee said, pointing to a spiral arm of the Milky Way. Then they looked at the rock collection for a long time.

I asked Timmy to write the alphabet for me with the Sandpaper Letters. As usual, going from one thing to the next under direction was hard for him. "What am I looking for again? . . . *c*," he said to himself. He kept pulling the chair up to the table so far that it squeezed his chest unbelievably tight. I pulled it back a couple of inches. "Come on," he said, "it doesn't feel good like that. I like being like this." He pulled his chair back up as tight as he could get it. Each time he found a letter in the box, he pushed it way across the table. This made it awkward for him to get it back within reach each time that he needed another one. Later, at snack time, he spilled milk while he was pouring it. The spout of the pitcher was an inch outside the glass. He just poured right onto the floor. Then he walked right into a table on his way to get the sponge. He simply has no clear judgment on spatial relationships that involve his own body. His nose was running badly and that probably accounts for his being even less together than usual today. Even the slightest pressure of illness or distress makes a clear-cut difference in his ability to function.

April 20   Today I wanted to see what Timmy would do if we left him completely alone all morning long. He simply walked from one child to another; all of the others were hard at work on spontaneously chosen activities. He engaged each in conversation, then went on to the next, like a roving ambassador. I didn't want to risk his upsetting what I felt might be a fragilely held-together atmosphere this particular morning, so, regretfully, I decided I must say something to him. I was careful not to mention choosing work (as I usually do), but simply said, "Timmy, you are interrupting the children's work." Why isn't he sparked by the other children working? He's interested in what they are doing and asks them questions about it, but he so seldom gets similar work for himself. Is it because he knows that he will need help to begin the procedures or is it because he is distracted to the next thought before he can focus on *wanting* to do a particular work?

April 24   I am worried about Timmy. He spent the first twenty minutes of class just waiting until his art time. After he came back at 9:30, he dawdled over his snack until 10:00. He literally did nothing in the room all morning. His tutor told me this morning that she is having a hard time with him, too. He shows no interest in what they are doing anymore, and has lost whatever power of concentration he was developing.

April 25   I asked Timmy if he wanted to do a Bead Stair or the Cleanser. He chose the Bead Stair. He was having a good deal of trouble until Joan sat down with him. He simply needed one-to-one support to keep himself focusing. Next I asked him to do the Movable Alphabet. He managed to get his rug and the Movable Alphabet box, but then he began wandering. He looked as if he knew that he was supposed to be doing something, but what? Finally, our eyes met across the room. There was no real recognition yet, but he did come over to me voluntarily. I said, "Make 'hot', Timmy." "Oh," he smiled, remembering now what he was supposed to be doing. He did make "hot" with the Movable Alphabet, but afterward he had a hard time "wandering" his way back to me for the next word. And so it went.

At 9:10 we went to the gym for rehearsal for the Grandparents' Day program with the whole Lower School. At one point, I saw Joan touch Timmy on the arm to get his attention. He looked for her on the opposite side from the arm touched!

April 30   Timmy was in the library at the beginning of the morning. Joan did the Phonogram Booklets with him. He knows all but *ur* and *ir.* He wandered much less overall today, but still chose no work on his own. I asked him to do an inset at our table at the end of the morning. He did an excellent job of filling in, going carefully from left to right and staying within the lines. He was so proud of it that he took it to show Joan.

May 2   Timmy had a better day. I saw him about nine and asked him what he had done today. "The library, the microscope, and Markers" he reeled off in quick succession. He may have trouble knowing where he is going, but today at least, he knew just where he had been. "What would you like to do now?" I asked. "The Painting," he answered. He went right to it then, and painted quite an intricate picture without any obvious moments of distraction or confusion. When he put the Painting Tray back on the shelf, he called out, "Hey, neato! Red-winged blackbirds!" Sure enough, there were two, right on the little crab apple tree by our window.

May 7   It was Timmy's birthday, so we had cake together on the line. I was somewhat apprehensive about his carrying the lighted candle on the tray, but I needn't have been. It was obvious that he was making enormous effort to keep his coordination and concentration together for those three minutes or so, but he did it. He looked so proud when he finished, which he certainly should.

May 10   Timmy and I were counting the Chains when Karen brought her finished Europe map. "I think this is where

Christopher Columbus is from," Timmy said, pointing to Portugal. He does astound me. I asked him to work on his unfinished Europe map afterward. He began it, but was starting to put it away again almost immediately. Joan sat with him then, and he finished it with obvious enjoyment. He simply needs an adult sitting next to him to help him keep himself focused.

May 14   Timmy watched Robbie, Jesse, and Susie doing equations with the Cuisinaire Rods at the table with me. "I think I'll try that," he said. I was so happy for him! He was able to do all the ten's subtraction equations, $10-1$, $10-2$, etc. "Another good one," he said as he wrote a ten. I showed Timmy's paper to his tutor. She was thrilled. It was a tremendous feat for him.

Earlier Timmy and Lee were doing the Command Game together. "Bend your *own* leg," I heard Lee say, with some irritation. Timmy was trying to take Lee's leg and bend it. (Timmy had drawn the card. "Bend a leg.") "Yeah, but then *I'll* fall down!" Timmy protested. Poor guy, I'm afraid that he was right. This is probably the best material in the room for him right now: carrying through written instructions that require controlled body movement and a completed task.

May 16   I worked with Timmy a long time on Noun Room Labeling. He loves doing it, but it often takes him a long time to find his way back to me. "Timmy, you were playing the Room Labeling Game," I reminded him when he wandered off. "Oh, yeah!" he answered. Several times he read the card to me, then started off to put it by its object. The only problem was that he had forgotten to take the card with him! He didn't come back to the rug for it until after he had gone all the way to the object. His reading is coming well now, and I feel so good about him overall. When I told his tutor yesterday what a great job she had done with him, she said, "But I think that it's you!" The answer has to be that it is Timmy who is doing it. He couldn't do it without the overall structure of environment that I provide and the specific, concentrated work with his tutor, yet it is so clear that it is he himself that is responsible for the dramatic development of these past months. The development, after all, is taking place inside where we can't even see it, much less direct it. That is why the breakthroughs are always so startling. There is no warning that they are coming. In fact, right before they happen, things often appear so much worse on the outside. This was true with Timmy and with Emily this year. It is so hard to keep faith with the child and not get discouraged.

May 18   Timmy spends his time these days reading in the library and looking at the tadpoles and pond life through the bisecting microscope. "Hey, Mrs. Lillard, I think I caught sight of some kind of jellyfish!" he cried this morning. At snack time he set his napkin down at our table. When he came back with his milk, he said, "That's not mine." We said, "Yes, it is." "Oh, I guess it is," he answered. When he came back with his cookie, he walked past us again. How confusing it must all be for him. At the end of the morning he and Madan did the Command Game together. Madan is so gentle with Timmy. "What are you doing over *there*, Timmy?" he asked each time Timmy lost the thread of what he was doing and wandered off.

May 21   Timmy wandered about. Eventually, I looked up to see him doing the Markers. "May I set up snack for you?" he asked. He did it with no lapses in focusing on the task. I was surprised and pleased because on his bad days this would have been a real feat for him. I asked him to do the Noun Room Labeling with me later in the morning. Karen said, "Hold the basket here, Timmy." He was starting off with it tipping over sideways. She showed him how to hold the handles. "And go over *there*," she said, pointing to me at the table. He looked confused for a moment. "Go, go, *go!*" she encouraged him. Satisfied as he finally started off, she went back to her inset. The other children are all so aware of his problems and so helpful with him. I think that it is the noncompetitive atmosphere that encourages their generous attitude toward him. After he had done four labels, I said that it was time to stop work. "Good," he said. "I can put this away now. I'm tired of working all the time." He had only been working for ten minutes.

May 22   Insets everywhere: Jesse, Robbie, Madan, Anna, Karen, Sandy. But most exciting of all—Timmy! I looked over at 8:30 and was surprised to see him starting one. He managed to get all his materials together and get himself organized to begin. He worked very carefully and quite a long time. When he had finished, he brought the inset to me. It was a beautifully done quatrefoil with close lines, none of them over the boundary line. "Congratulations, Timmy!" I said, and shook his hand. "I'm going to make a book of them!" he said enthusiastically. I couldn't believe that he would or could. Yet that is exactly what he did. He worked steadily, all morning, and made a booklet of six pages! I still can't believe that it happened. If only it is the beginning of a real breakthrough for him.

May 23   When he came in this morning, Timmy had a look on his face that (even for him) was unusually absentminded. He wandered all day. I was so disappointed after his concentrated effort with the insets yesterday. At 9:50 I said, "Timmy, let's do the Noun Room Labeling Game." "I'll do it later," he answered. "There won't be time," I said. "It's 'later' now." "Anyways I don't do it *every* day," he continued. "But Timmy, you haven't done any work today," I persisted. "Yes, I have. I did the Binomial Cube," he said, but he looked confused. "No, you didn't Timmy. Why don't you do it now?" I asked. He did then. I am besieged with doubts. Have I done the right thing for him? Should I have tried to direct him more? Yet it would have been cruel to have asked more of him, and a good deal *has* developed: his writing skills, beginning reading, the ability to focus on tasks, good relationships with the other children, interest in his environment—and he is always happy. What is missing is a consistent spontaneous, meaningful connection with the materials.

May 31   Timmy had such a good day. He painted first. It took him a while to remember his paper, to open the paints, and get his brushes. When he finally remembered to get the glass of water, too, he said in triumph, "Okay!" He also did the Clay for quite a while, and at the end of the morning he did the Phonogram booklets with Joan.

June 7   My best memory of this last day of school was Timmy. All the children were washing the windows, tables, and floor after having put all the materials in the cupboards for the summer. They were enjoying themselves immensely with cleanser and water everywhere. In the midst of it all, there was Timmy on the floor, patiently tracing his United States map. For once he was totally focused and oblivious to any outside distraction. It was as if he meant to tell Joan and me that he had come a long, long way, and we were not to be discouraged.

LEE

September 27   Lee volunteered out of the blue today, "My dad *never* pushes in his chair." There isn't much that children miss! He was very cross and easily frustrated today. He almost cried over his first inset. "That's very good," I said to him, and it was. "I don't think it is," he said pathetically. His high-pitched, strained voice gave away the demanding expectations that he was placing on himself. Later in the morning I overheard him having an argument with Sandy. "Well, my nine-year-old brother can beat up your sister," etc. He was just plain cross.

October 2   I started Lee on a map today. I hesitated to do this earlier as he hadn't asked to do one, and I remembered his tears over his inset. However, he and Jesse were the only children beside Timmy who haven't done any maps, so the time had come. He worked hard on it for a long time. I hope that he is pleased with it when he finishes it. He so needs to feel good about himself.

October 11   I introduced the Strip Board to Lee. I have some concern that he might have a learning disability. (How I hate that term. What does it really mean?) It may just be his left-handedness, but he has such trouble with left-to-right orientation, writing his name backward so often, for example. Also his small-muscle control seems undeveloped, or else the connection with visual perception and muscle control may be giving him trouble. He has not done another inset after throwing the first one away in frustration. He is the only child besides Timmy who hasn't finished a first map. I am suspicious that his work requires too much effort for him at this point, although perhaps he simply sets too high standards for himself. I'll know more when I do the Phonetic Objects with him (because of the writing involved).

October 13   After lunch today Joan and I talked about the problem of when to insist on compliance in working with us. She has asked Lee to practice numbers with her several times, she said. He always says, "I don't want to." She feels that he needs the practice if he is going to write well. I told her not to push him. He just isn't happy with the small-muscle work yet. Will the development come without practice? No, of course not, but the question is practice with what. He uses the Binomial Cube and

Trinomial Cube and Cylinders and Bead Stair; they all require small-muscle work. So do the Plant Care and Flower Arranging for that matter. Forcing practice with writing itself isn't the answer with a child like Lee. He is highly motivated, and is constantly working. I think he has to do things *his* way if he is going to be happy and do well. The other consideration is that if he has a learning disability, we will only increase his frustration by insisting on written work at this stage of his development.

October 16   Lee did the Strip Board. He had an especially good day. He was much more relaxed and did a good deal of work. Everything is always organized the wrong way, though: the blue strips on the right of the Strip Board instead of the left, the Bead Stair below and his paper for coloring them above so that he is working from the bottom up, and he walks from left to right around the line when he is carrying the blue tray and vase instead of the other way around. He is one of the few who still leaves a rug or part of his work out when he is finished working, too. However, he *does* see his reversals with numbers and corrects them himself most of the time. That is a good sign that his visual perception and orientation are developing.

October 23   Lee did insets today next to Jesse. This is the first time that he has tried them since he was so unhappy with his first one so many days ago. Best of all, he seemed quite happy with his finished products this time. I didn't think that their quality was much different from the first one that he was so dissatisfied with. Earlier Lee and Madan asked me to do the Bank Game with them. I asked Linda and Timmy to join us. It went quite well, mostly because all the children but Linda knew how to play already, and the other children showed her what to do. They changed in all three categories—units, tens, hundreds—while finding their answer. They had recognized the need for changing immediately. They are a smart group all right!

October 31   I'm still waiting for Lee to finish that first map!

November 1   Lee is so aware and so kind. About 10:00 Timmy was beginning to get a little restless and silly. I asked him to get the Binomial Cube and sit next to me. My voice must have sounded somewhat agitated to Lee. He said to me in a soothing tone, "Okay, he will." Timmy went off to get the Binomial Cube, but he couldn't find his way back to us. Lee got up from our table, and went to him. "Mrs. Lillard said to work here," he said. He guided him gently over to the place next to me.

November 6   Lee is such an unusual child. He wandered so long this morning. Finally he settled down spontaneously and completed all possible addition equations with the Small Numerical Rods and Numerals. Next he got out the Long Rods and Numerals and did the same thing! He really knows how to get the most out of these materials.

November 7   All the Chains for linear counting are out now. They have inspired a good deal of work. Lee went on a regular binge with them. I asked him afterward how many he had counted. "All of them," he said. I asked him to make his calendar earlier as he is the last child to do one. No wonder that he was in no hurry. He really couldn't do it. Numbers were reversed and also the teens placement was backward. 17 was 71, etc. I have dotted one in for him, as I did for Timmy, to do tomorrow. I am wondering again if there is a problem in development there.

November 13   Lee did a whole Strip Board booklet today.

November 16   About 8:15 Lee was working with the Clay next to Jesse. The Bach record was still playing. I overheard Lee say, "Isn't this nice music?" He labeled the whole room with the

Noun Room Labeling Game next. He put the label "lid" on top of the terrarium lid, an unusual choice, I thought. He is so interesting to have in the room.

November 29   Lee makes freehand world maps with the Markers but still doesn't want to finish his "real" map!

November 30   Lee, Anna, and Karen all read the Super Books in the library so easily today. How does this "miracle" happen?

December 1   Lee had asked about the Thousand Chain yesterday. I thought that he might have the drive to stick with it, so we got it out when he came in this morning. It looked quite splendid, spread the whole length of the room on its red felt rug. There were many wide eyes and amazed faces. "I'm going to count all the way down to there," Lee announced to Madan with just the right tone of quiet pride and confidence. Madan said, "You'll never do it in one day, though." Jack said, "This will take the whole morning." Robbie said, "No, the whole day!" Lee looked a bit doubtful then. He looked over at me for reassurance. I smiled, and he smiled back. He started in then.

When Lee was at 400 on his chain, he said, "I'm taking a break." He wanted to start a North American map, not my idea of a break. I told him that he hadn't finished his world map yet. Lo and behold, he got it out and finished it! I was certain that he was going to leave it until June. I sat with him when he went back to counting, just to lend support. "Five hundred and ten," he said. "You know what? I can't believe I've gone so far!" When half the children left for library at 10:30, I let the others keep working: Timmy to finish his map, Sam to label his, Anna and Jesse to finish labeling the room, Lee to count. He finished, too. One of the best things about the whole process was that all the children were aware of it. In a very real sense, it was a group experience. At line time, we counted the last hundred with Lee: 901, 902, etc., all the way to 1000. Then I asked, "How many hundreds in one thousand?" Lee went back past each hundred square placed at the end of each hundred units, and counted them. "Ten" he announced. Then I began, "Ten times . . . ," and the whole class finished with me, "one hundred equals one thousand!"

December 11   Lee did the Phonetic and Phonogram Objects, then at 9:50 he began his second world map! Thank goodness I followed my intuition and didn't push on that first one. I'm convinced that he never would have ventured a second one.

December 12   Lee got his world map out to finish, labeled continents, oceans, and seas, and finished it off with the nativity sticker on Asia. (I had put out labels of the nativity scene for the children to place on Israel to indicate the location of Jesus' birth.)

December 13   Lee worked almost all morning on the Gift Wrapping exercise that I have set up. What a motivated, determined, and independent child he is! Sandy and Emily, who were working next to him, took turns holding down the ribbon while he tied the bow each time. At one point, Lee peeked around Joan with his proud, shy smile, and held up the carefully wrapped present for me to admire.

December 20   Lee was right into the material all morning as usual. It is all so right for him. He has the originality, independence, and motivation to make full use of everything in the room, all on his own direction, too. This time it was the Constructive Triangle Boxes One and Two. He made a rectangle out of four blue triangular pieces, then duplicated it with four colored triangles of the same size. Later he began to paint. At the end of the morning he was lying on his back in the library. His head was propped on the pillows and he was playing with the shelf in front of him with his stocking feet. He was holding up a story from the "Our Stories" folder and reading it aloud to himself. Jeff, head of the Lower School, had come into the room with a candy house that he had made for the children. Everyone crowded about him except for Lee. He continued his reading, oblivious to the excitement and noise going on around him.

By dismissal time, he had come out of his concentration spell. He began to lose control, getting very silly. He was good-natured about it, but he was laughing uncontrollably nonetheless. When he "goes," he always goes completely and all at once.

January 8   Lee asked me to show him the Fraction Skittles which are new.

January 10   Lee got out the new Measuring Exercise. He sat back with a happy smile after he had carefully filled all five beakers. He looked every inch the young scientist in his laboratory. He did the Clock Exercise next, and finally a map of Canada. "My first one!" he said proudly. What a change for him, too, from his attempts in map work in the fall. There is a trail behind him, though: a chair not pushed in, a box from the Clock Exercise left out, some water on the table from the Measuring Exercise.

January 11   Lee had a grand time finishing a whole Addition Strip Board booklet but forgot to put it or his chair away afterward. My reminder brought the usual "Oh."

January 12   I introduced the Stamp Game to Lee, and it went smoothly. The math consultant yesterday had said that he doubted if the children understood much about hundreds and thousands. I thought of Lee counting the Thousand Chain by ones all morning last December, then going back and counting the hundreds. This morning he wanted to know why the thousand stamp and the unit stamp are the same size. (He knew there were one thousand unit beads in the thousand-bead cube. The physical comparison of one unit bead to the thousand-bead cube was obviously dramatic for him. He was seeking to understand this step toward abstraction from beads to stamps.) How much more evidence is needed to demonstrate that understanding is developing?

January 25   I had such a good time watching Lee today. He got out the Noun and Verb Tray. Then he got the box of Grammar Symbols and matched the symbols to their related objects on the tray. I asked him if he would like to play the Noun Verb Game. Robbie joined us.

Lee drew "lid" for his noun word. He got the lid to the Constructive Triangle Box, which is triangular in shape. "See, the same!" he said, as he put it on the black triangular noun rug. Afterward Lee made a very original Big Bang with the Collage Tray. (I have set the Collage Tray up so that each child can make a simulation of the "Big Bang" for our universe beginning display.) He asked if he could make a second one. He kept right on working when I called for line time. He was totally oblivious when all the children got up afterward to go to music. He looked up twenty minutes later when they all came back in, as if nothing unusual had happened!

January 29   Lee wrote two stories today—his first. He does get around to all the materials on his own steam eventually. His stories were very literal and precise.

January 30   It was an active noisy morning. Lee cannot conceive of talking only to the person next to him. I got up twice to ask him to speak quietly to Timmy in the library. Then I gave up. He was just oblivious to the rest of the room. His conversation was fun to listen to, though. They were looking at the National Geographic book *The Amazing Universe*. "Well, *what* do you know!" Lee kept saying in an incredulous voice. He said it at least five times in a row. Finally, Timmy joined in the comments. "No, that's a star there, look." Lee said, "A big red-hot star!" Timmy said, "Hey! That's the red giant!" "Yeah, WOW!" Lee answered. "That is the solar nursery."

February 5   Lee was using the pointer and reading the board message to Carmen and Anna. I had written, "I felt so bad that I was not here on Friday. It is a bad feeling when children don't know what will happen to them next." (The poor sentence structure is a good indication of my mental state today.) "It's really *k-n*," Lee explained after reading "know" in the last sentence, "only you pretend the *k* isn't there." I guess that I must have explained at one time that sometimes you don't pronounce letters, but it startled me that he had known this particular word. He explained it so matter-of-factly, as if it had been part of his knowledge for a long time.

February 8   Lee has been on vacation for three days: He's done nothing. Today he played with the Clock all morning. I had to keep reminding myself how hard he has worked all year. He certainly deserves a break now.

February 9   Lee acted as if he were going to remain on vacation, then delved into a Continent booklet for the morning.

February 12   Lee made a Sun Collage from a setup that we have arranged for the Collage Tray this week. Afterward he was explaining his collage to Sam, who was doing the Markers next to him. "This is my sun. These stickers [four label stickers with "sun spots," "core," "magnetic arches," "solar explosions" written on them] are for these." (He pointed to their various counterparts on the model the children used to guide them.) "You know what this thing here is? This thing here is an explosion coming from the sun!"

February 13 Lee made a very detailed picture of the inside of a harpsichord. We had taken a field trip to see and hear one played by a man who had made the harpsichord himself.

February 22 Lee, always the unusual one, practiced writing the alphabet, first with the chalkboard, then on paper. I showed him how to use the Sandpaper Letters for this in order to help him with his frequent reversals. Next he wrote numbers from one to one hundred on the squared math paper.

February 23 I did the Stamp Game with Lee. We did a four-page booklet of the four operations. It was fun to watch him figure it all out. He knew the sign for division. "How did you know that, Lee?" I asked. "You showed us one day on the line," he answered. That is so typical of Lee. He needs only one exposure.

March 1 A visitor came in while Lee was working with the Geometric Solids and Direction Cards. She asked him what he was doing and he handed her a card which read, "Find the ovoid in the basket of Geometric Solids." "I don't know which is the ovoid," she said. Lee showed her.

March 2 Lee was doing the Phonogram Packets with me. When he came to the *j* packet, he said, "Hey, there's three ways to say *j!*" He showed me the three small booklets on *gi, ge,* and *j.* "I didn't know there were three ways to spell *j*," he continued with a voice full of wonderment. The sense of discovery was still in his tone when he had finished reading them all and said, "Now, we've done the three ways to spell *j!*"

March 6   Lee read his story to me just before line time. When I showed him where he had left out a period, he said, "I don't want one there." He was emphatic, and even began to cry. I felt badly for him. His distress was so deep. I said something about all people agreeing about letters and spelling and punctuation marks so that we could read each other's writing. He wasn't impressed.

March 13   Yesterday I told the children about the form of our earth (crust, mantle, outer liquid core, and inner solid core). I set out a second Collage Tray today with colored papers drawn with comparable circles for each section and identifying labels so they could make a collage of a cross section of the earth. Lee was the first to make one. Afterward he asked Joan where he should write his name. "How about on the mantle?" she suggested. "No," he answered emphatically. "Then how about at the top, on the crust?" she offered. "*My* name in the *crust?*" he asked incredulously. He finally wrote it on the inner solid core section. He carried his collage with him all over this morning, putting it on his table wherever he was working. At one point he was sitting on the floor, leaning against the door in the hallway while Ed was cleaning it with the cleanser. The sun was pouring in on them from the hallway window, and it was a warm, cozy scene. I could hear Lee explaining his collage to Ed: "And we don't live in the mantle, and we don't live in the outer liquid core, and . . ."

April 4   Lee got the Trinomial and Binomial Cubes out this morning. No one has done them for months.

April 5   Lee did the Adjective Labeling Game that I introduced yesterday. How easy he makes it to have a varied alive environment. He never fails to pick up everything I present on his own! He asked me what "narrow" meant. I told him "thin." (I realize now how confusing and incorrect that definition was.) He went to Sam, who was making his calendar. "Do you know anything 'thin'?" They settled on Sam's calendar paper. Timmy got interested, too, and left his North American map (his third this week) to help for a while. "Here's something light here," Timmy said. "Hey, lightest!" Lee said, holding up the floor cloth. "Light as a feather!" Timmy said, holding up one of the little red paper flags from the Plant Care and letting it float to the floor. "Yeah, that's a great idea!" Lee said.

April 11   Lee did the Phonogram packets, then I introduced the Noun Article box to him. His writing is much better now. He still presses much too hard with the pencil, but at least he no longer gets frustrated with the results. He helped Madan on the Thousand Chain for a few minutes, but I think he prefers to be independent in his work. He got the Hundred Chain, and began to count it by himself instead. He counted from the bottom up. There's that slight twist that he always shows on directionality and general orientation. I showed him how to square the Hundred Chain and then write ten squared equals one hundred in equation form. "You can do that with all the chains," I said. "Okay, I'll do that!" he said, looking pleased. And he did, working right through line time. I wouldn't have thought of interfering with him.

April 16   Lee brought me his story. "Would you put a *p* here?" he asked. He had made a picture of a man in a fire, and written "leh" on it. "Lee, it goes the other way—h-e-l-p," I said. "Oh," he said. How can he read so quickly and easily with such inconsistent directionality? Somehow his mind works with superior quality in either direction. He wrote another long story under his picture after that. I'm pleased that he's getting so deeply involved with writing lately. It was a long time coming.

April 20   Lee did the Trinomial Cube. The box slid open as he turned it over afterward. "Oh, I have to do it all over again," he cried, fighting back tears of frustration. "Stupid thing!" he cried. Jack, who was across the table from him, must have laughed. "It's not funny!" Lee fumed at him. Later he was doing the Bank Game. "Hey, I just noticed something!" he said, as he laid out his math numerals. "Nine—ten!" and he pointed to the nine at the bottom of the units column and up to the ten at the top of the tens column. When the equation was all done $(2695+8942=11{,}637)$, he said, "This is neat. This is this [pointing to the numerals] and this is this and they equal this. Isn't it a lot!"

April 24   Lee read the Addison Wesley books in the library for a long time. Afterward he continued his writing binge.

April 26   Lee came up to me. "Where's that water book?" he asked. He was referring to a book on water which I had read to the children at dismissal time two days ago and had left in the library for one day. "It's back in the cupboard, Lee, do you want it?" I asked. He got it out and pored over it for thirty minutes. I asked him if he would read it with me. He said, "I'll read one page." He did it perfectly, much to my surprise because the text is at least third-grade reading level. Afterward he said, "I don't like reading out loud." It's easy to understand why. Reading out loud is for others. Lee obviously reads for himself. He also reads so rapidly that he can barely get the words pronounced before he has gone on to the next sentence. He is visibly irritated at having to go more slowly to accommodate pronunciation.

I introduced the Snake Game to Lee after the assembly. He

really enjoyed it. After one game, he said, "Can I do this all over again? Got another even one!" he said as his colored bead bars made an even ten to exchange for a golden bead bar. He had inadvertently made his snake out of the combinations of colored bead bars that he had set up to check his previous snake (7+3=10, etc.). He was therefore getting all even exchanges.

May 1   Lee worked on his Multiplication Board booklet. He's on the tables of nine now. He didn't want to stop for music, so I let him keep working.

May 2   Lee got his Multiplication Board booklet out. He finished the nines. When he was working on the tens, he cried, "Hey, all the tens are twenty, thirty, forty, fifty!"

May 3   What a funny mood Lee was in all morning. He was practicing sneezing in the bathroom. "Ker-choo! Ker-choo!" The whole room was assaulted with the noise. When he finally came out, he was totally oblivious to the fact that he had startled us all. Afterward he went to the library. As he read, he began to make a strange, high whinny. Again he was totally oblivious to the rest of us. Both he and Timmy have running mind games going on in their heads, I think. How I wish I could have a tape of them for just one morning!

May 9   Lee came in announcing proudly that he had ridden his bike to school. I asked if he would like me to introduce the Noun Adjective Box to him. He looked at it for a moment. "I don't *really* feel like it *now*," he said. Edith came in then. When I asked her the same question, she enthusiastically said, "Okay!" Lee did the Markers, then read a book in the library. By 8:15 he was back to me. "I'm ready to do that," he said. "All right, Lee, as soon as I've shown it to Edith," I answered. Edith enjoyed the work, but her reaction is not as extreme as Lee's to any of the materials. She is more cautious and methodical, and catches on slowly. Lee gets a shy smile on his face while the materials are being introduced. When he begins to use them himself, his eyes positively light up with discovery. Today he carried his finished booklet around with him and looked at it all morning, as he so often does with work that he has finished.

May 10   Lee made a booklet of all the Phonetic and Phonogram Objects, then labeled the dinosaurs.

May 16   Lee had his usual special morning. He saw me introducing the Asia map to Ed and got out North America for himself. He made and labeled an excellent map. He got the Small Numerical Rods and Numerals out next. He was making up equations. His work looked disorganized, so I went over to see what he was doing. I thought he had made a mistake, making $8+1=8$. "I'm making subtraction next," he said. I looked more closely then and saw that it wasn't a plus sign that I had seen. It was a times sign. Of course, he was correct. He made equations using the three different operations of addition, subtraction, and multiplication for the rest of the morning.

May 17   Lee made and labeled a map of the world. He got very frustrated because he had colored over South America. Joan helped him to begin again. When he had trouble a second time, she said, "Come walk with me to the lunch room to get some cups. That will help you to relax." When he came back, he handled the situation much better—even when he colored over Antarctica. "You won't believe what I just did!" he said. I'm glad I didn't assign maps to him weeks ago. I did have them marked down for him in my notes since he wasn't doing them. It is obvious now that he was avoiding them because he wasn't ready to deal with the frustrations this work would cause him. He waited until he felt he could be successful with it. I could never have pinpointed accurate timing like that from the outside.

May 18   After Lee's usual room check, he said, "I want to do a map but I don't know which one to do." We looked at them together. "I've done the world and North America and Canada. I haven't done Europe or Asia," he said, pointing to each map. "Let's do Europe," I said. I asked Joan to help him because of his frustrations yesterday with the much easier world map. He worked for two and a half hours on it, and surprisingly had no trouble with the coloring. Next he labeled the mammals from the science display shelf. He *never* misses a new material in the room.

May 21   Lee asked to do the Asia map. True to form, he spent the entire morning making a magnificent map. He is so consistent!

May 22   Lee continued his "map explosion." He made another one of Asia, this time totally without help. We are learning the countries together, as I do not know them all. He corrected me on Burma and Cambodia, neither of which I remembered, but he did!

May 23   Today Lee finished off his map binge. He did the United States perfectly and all by himself.

May 24   Lee's map binge is over. He did the I Spy cards, then wrote his first yellow booklet.

May 29   Lee asked me to show him the Dot Game. I was surprised that he only wanted to do one side of the paper. It will be interesting to see if he goes back to it. He asked me to show him the Grammar Box Three next. He seemed to enjoy this more, again carrying his paper around with him all morning.

May 30   Lee did more sentences with the Grammar Box Three. Afterward he did come back to the Dot Game paper. He made up a problem with 16,461 for one of the numbers to add. He wasn't supposed to go over 9000 but he got it all right and all by himself anyway!

May 31   Lee got the Thousand Chain out, but he just couldn't get going on it. He made several attempts but never got past one hundred. Is he ready for school to be out?

June 4   Lee did a new box of objects and labels for sentences that I have set out for Grammar Box Three. He loves the construction of sentences all right. He carried his paper around all morning again. He then read *all* twelve of the Addison Wesley *second*-shelf books. Afterward I showed him how to make all the numbers to the right except 6 and 9, hoping that it might help him with reversals next year. He was so fascinated with the idea that he stayed back from drama to practice writing them.

June 7   This was the last day. Lee did the Snake Game, then the Seguin Boards, and finally the Grammar Box Three. It was a marathon of concentrated work. How I will miss having him in the class next year.

SIX | Personal Development

To try something new in one's teaching is to place a burden on one's own life. There is more self-doubt and anxiety to deal with, experiences which are already prevalent in a profession where there can never be perfect solutions. There is danger of pride when successful and defensiveness when failing. There is a need for more energy to deal with others who wish to understand what you are attempting. There are administrators to convince and colleagues to reassure. There are parents who need explanation and attention which in other circumstances they might not have required. There are visitors who want to observe and discuss the classroom.

On the other side of the coin, there is the exhilaration of the wholly new. Pioneering presents the opportunity to learn something new each day about what children are like and what will best aid their development. And though it often hurts at the time, there is the pleasurable outcome of ever deepening self-knowledge.

September 3 Two full days of faculty meetings. It always seems so overwhelming; the schedules, new rules, discussions of procedures, boring trivia that has little to do with children and how to teach them. All the teachers feel it. It is an agonizing way to begin the year.

Just before I left school, I looked into my classroom: my bright, bare, beautiful classroom. I quickly walked out, not quite ready to face the task of beginning all over again. I will go early tomorrow morning before our first meeting at 10:30. I need to be fresh, to begin before the details of the day at home and at school rush in and overwhelm. Have there always been so many demands and pressures in our society? If my parents and teachers felt a similar way, I was certainly unaware of it. Today everyone I know feels this frustration and pressure. It helps, knowing that it is not just me. It seems strange to come back from a two-and-a-half-month vacation and not feel ready to begin again. Jeff, our head of Lower School, calls it the reentry syndrome. That's a good way of putting it. Just naming it helps me to accept it for what it is: a normal reaction which every teacher feels in one way or another, especially those of us with large families who wonder how we had time to teach at all.

Fourth Day   I forgot four children should go to art for the first time today. I felt bad because I hadn't prepared them ahead of time by showing them how to open the door and come back into the room without disturbing the other children. When they came back, they accidentally slammed the door and startled all the children who were working with deep concentration. Later at line time I gave a presentation of opening and closing a door quietly. The children were fascinated watching the lock go in and out when the knob was turned. Our door does shut with a bang, even when it is closed in an ordinary way, so it is necessary to take extra care with it. Every adult who goes out of the room leaves us with a loud "bang," for example.

At times like these I have a nagging feeling that people are wondering, "What is that queer woman doing in there, teaching children to close doors with such care, push in chairs, sweep up their crumbs, etc.?" Perhaps I *am* a little odd! If so, I am grateful to the children for their tolerance. They are invariably responsive and interested in these details of daily living.

On the playground I was thinking that this was the most interesting group of children that I had taught. I smiled at myself then because I remembered that I had thought the same thing last year and the year before that.

Fifth Day   I stopped work time at ten o'clock, although the children didn't seem ready to. I have a fear that there are really not that many materials out yet and that they will get bored with what is there before I can provide more academic work. Perhaps it is a cultural prejudice on my part, believing that academic work is more interesting than other kinds of work. Five-year-olds are interested in polishing tables and scrubbing floors, as well as learning how to read and do equations.

I was glad that I had shown the children how to use the hangers the first day. It rained today and many children came with raincoats. This time I had managed to do what I promised them that I would try to do the first day of school—prepare them ahead of time for coping with new situations.

I had bad news tonight. My seventeen-year-old daughter, Angel, must have an operation. It is not expected to be a serious problem, but it is major surgery nonetheless. I am wondering how I am going to cope with all this and my teaching, too.

September 15   Susie came in looking pouty—a tentative pout as if she couldn't decide whether to follow through with this approach or not. After a while she simply sat on the line with her hand on her chin. She has done this before and worked herself out of it, so I didn't pay much attention. Later in the morning, I caught her starting out the door. "I don't like this school. I'm going home," she said. I spoke firmly to her, "You can't do that, Susie." "I know the way," she said. It gave me heart failure to think that she might have really slipped out on us, and perhaps gotten hurt or lost. Her wanting to leave shook my confidence in what I have done so far with the children, too. Have I expected too much too soon? Will this group of children find the pleasure in my class that children have in past years?

In spite of all going well with the class as a whole, I do feel low. I think that it is the enormous way there is to go, and wondering how I will ever accomplish it. The learning all happens so gradually and without a great deal of direct group instruction. I keep forgetting that. Today, for example, I showed Lee how to discover odd and even numbers with the counters. All four of the other children at the table looked up from their work to watch. It is this indirect learning that makes possible the tremendous development of the children during the year. I believe this, yet planned group instruction is the customary way of teaching. Perhaps that is what is making me uneasy: that I am not teaching in the customary way.

After all of these down thoughts, I have to mention that before class this morning, I saw both first-grade teachers in the lounge, and they volunteered out of the blue how well the children had been prepared for first grade this year. That has to make me feel better about all this hard work of the present. I must just be tired.

September 18   I thought today that the routines have been so readily adopted by the children. Yet Joan and I have worked and worked to get them established, and it has taken a good deal of energy from us. I think I say "so readily" because the children's cooperation in these early weeks always amazes me so. It is as if it was in their nature to accept the routines necessary for the culture that they are exposed to, whatever they might be, provided they are presented with conviction and consistency, and in an organized manner.

September 19   Perhaps I am expecting too much. I need to relax and have more faith in the children. That is the key to being patient with them at this point—knowing that the development will come, sooner or later.

September 20   I told the children that I wouldn't be in school when they first came tomorrow because my daughter was going to have an operation. I hoped to come after they had been there for a little while, however. They were so open in their worry and concern. It made me feel very close to them.

September 21   I left the hospital as soon as they took Angel to the operating room. I wanted to be back with the children because I never think about the outside world when I am with them. It is as if it didn't exist for me. Perhaps that is one reason why I like teaching so much. It is a totally absorbing experience for me.

It is hard to describe what I felt walking into the classroom at 9:30. Perhaps it was the contrast from the hospital atmosphere, but the peacefulness and other-worldly quality of the room were startling. I did feel as if I was entering a sanctuary: a sanctuary of child life. The room was alive with the serious, gentle quality of children as they work. The room isn't always like this, of course, but at that particular moment, and partly because I was feeling deep emotions myself, the spiritual atmosphere of the room was distinct for me.

September 23   I had asked a friend who is particularly interested and knowledgeable in education to come in and observe my class last Tuesday. We met today so that he could give me his reactions. He had visited the class last spring, and I had wanted him to come back this fall to observe and comment on the differences that he saw. He said he saw two differences: one qualitative and one quantitative. The children this year were choosing their own work, using it, and putting it away with minimum supervision. But there was more of this last spring. The children now were slower to choose and their behavior often looked tentative, as if they weren't quite sure of themselves. "As if they didn't have a road map yet" was the way he put it.

The qualitative difference was that the children were not as cooperative with each other. There was a definite competition among them—a "significant rivalry" he called it. "Not many children were helping each other. In fact, I didn't see any," he said. "They didn't seem to be taking much pleasure in each other's accomplishments as the children did last spring. One child [Karen] was acting very devious, disturbing another child [Emily] and looking over each time to see if you were watching. [I missed this completely.] She was obviously getting her kicks from swimming upstream."

As for my teaching, he felt that I was pretty much the same in both situations. He remarked on the quiet atmosphere in the room—"the tranquility of your scene," as he put it. He said that I seemed to be making constant decisions, when to intervene and when not to, when to insist and when not to. He gave as an example my showing one child how to carry the map pieces, holding them by the knob in their center, from the puzzle to the paper to trace, taking care not to twist them even slightly. We had to repeat this a good many times to get the process just right. He was surprised that the child didn't get frustrated. I remembered that I had insisted on this repetition and hadn't gotten discouraged, because this is the only way that children can use this material successfully. I also know that it is within their developmental range to do so. "That resonates," he said. "They *know* that you know."

He talked about our using the "awe of the wholly new" at the beginning of the year when the children are so "unfrozen" and old habits are not operating as much. Out of this new situation a new culture is created. When one child tests the situation, the others see it and learn from it. Eventually, they begin to take care of the "testers themselves because they don't want anyone messing it up for them." The payoff is "enormous: the sense of fulfillment they experience as they develop."

I'm confident the quantitative differences in the classes will take care of themselves. I am more concerned about the qualitative differences. Perhaps last year's class was just an unusual one. I feel each year that it will be a significant feat to develop a cooperative culture in the classroom. Our culture simply doesn't place a premium on cooperation, whether between man and nature or between man and man.

September 25   My nine-year-old daughter, Poppy, awakened me with screaming at four o'clock this morning. She said that she had something in her eye, but I couldn't see anything. Suddenly, she was asleep again, and I left her with her father this morning, so I didn't now what was wrong when I went off to school. I stopped by the hospital first to see Angel, and she is still in so much pain.

I was too tired to feel much enthusiasm at school, yet the children were having a real run on the maps, and in retrospect I think that it was a good morning.

I had to stay after school to get materials out for Parents' Night tonight. I had no enthusiasm for a sales pitch at that point. I wondered if I would even make it through the evening. I stopped at the hospital for an hour to be with Angel. I don't know of anything that is harder for a parent than watching a child suffer. I went home to find Poppy's eye still bothering her, so off we went to the doctor's. He couldn't find anything seriously wrong. It was obviously just one of those days. I gathered my thoughts together, and felt better by the time I got back to school at eight.

I think it was getting out the work the children did last spring to show to the parents that helped me. It is always an inspiration to me to see what the children can do.

September 26   I'm afraid this was pretty much of a lost day for me. Poppy started crying hard with the pain in her eye at 9:30 last night. I kept thinking that she would surely drop off to sleep, but she didn't. Finally, I called the doctor, and I took my first nighttime trip to the emergency room of the hospital in my twenty-five years of mothering five children. They found that she had scratched the cornea of her eye quite badly. She will have to stay home for a few days, but the pain seems better. Thank heavens John is home and not on a business trip! Angel is the good news, though. She was feeling much better when I stopped to see her on my way to school, and is coming home tomorrow.

October 3   Already I am beginning to go to school with a lighter, happier feeling, knowing that I won't just feel like a policeman all morning, as I sometimes do at the very beginning of the year. I have a feel at least, for each child's level of development, special talents, and difficulties. I have a program planned for the day in terms of what work I will try to do or get started at some point with each child. And there is something for me to learn each day, too. Yesterday it was about salamanders, and today it was more about Pompeii. (There is an exhibit about Pompeii at the Art Institute.) Karen and Ed both brought books in about it.

October 6   I got quite irritated with Anna and Karen today. I worked with both of them early in the morning, hoping to get them involved so they wouldn't continue to bother others as they had tended to do the last few days. Actually, it is only Emily that Karen is "after." Anna goes up to everyone, trying to get them to choose something to do with her. She has been very aggressive on the playground, and I think she is trying to establish something of a leadership role in the class. I suggested that she make an inset booklet. She sat next to Ed, who was practicing writing "my *d*'s," as he calls them. (He had gotten into the habit of forming them the wrong way through writing his name.) Soon they were acting silly together, and Ed was putting his paper on his head. I had to leave my work on the Teen Boards with Karen and Timmy to ask Anna to move to a small table where she could work alone. This was about the third episode with her this morning, and we were both annoyed. She scribbled her insets with a hard-pressed pencil, which clearly showed anger, and definitely wasn't up to her usual quality of work.

October 10   I took extra care shaking hands with Anna this morning to see if she seemed to be thinking of Friday's struggle. I could sense no trace of it, but I was careful to make an opportunity to work with her during the morning. We made equations to ten with the Small Numerical Rods, and I showed her how to write them. Earlier she had done the Tables of Twos with the Strip Board, then the Binomial Cube, and at snack time I noticed her sweeping her crumbs off the table so carefully with the yellow crumber and broom. She had decided to cooperate at least for today. I feel some relief about her now. I didn't like the feel of our relationship on Friday.

At juice time, a cheerful Bach record was playing, there were children sitting in small groups at the tables, singing grace to each other, and Karen was walking on the line in time to the music, balancing a hand-painted blue glass vase on a blue tray, and a beanbag on her head. All I could think of was that anyone coming in on such a scene of five-year-olds would think we were all a little crazy. It isn't the usual kindergarten, that is for certain. Thank heavens for a tolerant administration. I must worry that I do things so differently from the expected kindergarten way. Last night I had a dream that I had gone into a kindergarten class. It was full of easels, and newspapers covered the floor for the day's project. "We really have fun in here!" the teacher said to me enthusiastically. I went back into my own room. It all looked so orderly and I particularly noticed the children's maps on the board. I had a terrible feeling that I wasn't doing the right things. Then I started to think about how much the children had learned just since the beginning of the year, and it had turned into a good dream by the time I woke up. However, it's obvious the anxiety is there. Perhaps it always is when you diverge from the customary way.

Carmen had a tough time getting going today. She kept going up to Joan, saying, "There's nothing to do in this room!" Interesting that she goes to Joan and not to me. She must sense that she can't manipulate me easily. She is accustomed to worried concern from her parents, and perhaps is not comfortable yet with having so little fuss or bother made about her here. Work was the answer finally. She decided to make a map. I asked her if she would like to label it when she brought it to me all completed. I showed her how to practice first with the two outline maps of the continents—one labeled and one not—and the box of matching labels. She was able to label the unlabeled map using the demonstration map as a guide, so I got the dittoed map labels Joan had made for the children to paste on their own maps. Carmen did an excellent job of pasting on the labels on her own map, and was so proud of her work when she was finished. She seemed to go home quite happy, but I have marked down in my notes for tomorrow that she is a top priority for material introductions.

October 11   Things finally have calmed down at home, and I got to school at 7:30 this morning, as I like to do each day. It makes such a difference in how I feel as I greet the children if I have had a few minutes of peace before they start coming. It takes twenty minutes at least to get the classroom ready for them: sponges wet, paints out, glue in the plastic coasters, flags changed in the plants, record ready to turn on, the toad's terrarium wiped out so that we can see him, flowers ready to be arranged if I have brought any in, new exhibits arranged for the science shelf, etc.

Edith's parents requested that Betty test her for a learning disability even before school began. I certainly haven't seen any evidence of a problem in class yet. Later this morning Betty told me that she hasn't found anything much in her testing so far either. I feel exasperated with all this careful searching for possible problems. Surely we overdo it, yet there is always the worry in any particular situation; how can I be sure? I'm feeling little confidence in my judgment today in any case. Betty told me today that Ali, who was in my class last year and whom I had strongly recommended for retention, was doing just fine in first grade! I had been so convinced that he would have trouble. He was the youngest child in the class, was in the learning-disability program, and came from a different linguistic and cultural background. His parents, however, insisted that he go on to first grade.

Since he had covered the minimal curriculum requirements for promotion, I reluctantly passed him on. His parents had continued his tutoring all summer (which the administration insisted on), and that undoubtedly helped. Still I was way off in my predictions on his adjustment to first grade. The year before I had been certain another child, Rita, should repeat kindergarten, principally because of her young chronological age in the class and a slower pace of development than the other children. Her parents, too, insisted that she go on. Consequently, she spent a terrible year and ended up repeating first grade. I was so certain the same thing would happen to Ali, who had had even more difficulties in kindergarten than Rita. This is a good lesson in humility for me. I won't even try to be so sure next time. There is just no way to predict what is going to happen with children.

Certainly I am not going to waste so much emotion trying to convince parents of my point of view again.

Betty and I talked about Timmy briefly, and I felt terrible. It is perhaps an irrational way to have felt, but it made me feel as if we were gossiping about him. I guess it's the uncertainty in any situation of this kind that bothers me so.

October 13   Jack's mother brought his grandmother to class after dismissal to show her the room. She must have told her all about the class, because after Jack's grandmother had looked at the children's maps and math papers on the board and commented on the orderly way that the children kept the room, she said, "And they get to do whatever they want to!" My inner reaction was "Good heavens no!" but I simply said, "Well, not exactly." I hoped my tone would indicate how far from the truth I considered such a comment. I thought of the exacting demands that I had been making on the children's behavior in the past weeks. It is the fact that they are allowed some choice in their morning's work that confuses adults, I suppose. Some see it as spoiling children for the real world, whereas I see it as developing the initiative and enthusiasm the children will *have* to deal with the world successfully.

After lunch Joan told me that Anna had had a "funny day." I had only seen her doing a map, and later painting. It all seemed to be going well to me. Apparently, I missed completely that she had been slouching way down in her chair and doing her work in a perfunctory way, and at the end of her painting, she had been quite aggressively and sloppily brushing the paint, so that the tray became a mess and there were flecks of paint on the table. Joan had had to supervise her to see that the cleaning up afterward was done properly. My intuition wasn't that far off last Friday after all. She had simply sent her hostility underground. We still have a problem then.

October 17   Anna was back today, and I was relieved that she came in looking happy and eager. The note she brought in from her mother said that she had had strep throat and that "she missed school very much." The illness explains a lot, and I feel guilty that I was not more perceptive in my intuitions about her. It has brought home to me again how generous children can be with adults—another humbling experience for me.

At lunchtime another teacher told me that Bobby, a child we had both had in class in the past, was having a great deal of difficulty this year. I felt terrible about it. We had worked so hard for this child, and he had responded by using every bit of his talent in whatever we asked him to do. He had a great many learning difficulties, but he had excellent motivation and a strong self-image. Now he was losing both motivation and self-confidence. I am full of doubts about my teaching and feel somehow that I have let this child down. I want to reach out to him and to his parents, who were so supportive and apprecia-tive of all our extra efforts for him. I'm worried that they may be feeling that we were not truthful with them when we told them what progress Bobby was making in our classes, now that his whole school world has collapsed on him. We had been, though. It was remarkable what Bobby achieved. There is no way of telling whether such progress is going to plateau and fall off in future years for a child who is dealing with the diffi-culties that Bobby has. I keep telling myself that I can't let my energy be drained in worry and concern over this situation. My time for this child is over. I no longer have a place in his life. That is the way the system is set up in this country. It makes no sense to me: nine months of building a depth of under-standing and caring and trust, each for the other, teacher and child, and parent and teacher, so that learning *can* happen, and then—nothing more. It is all over a few months later, and must be carefully developed from scratch all over again, another teacher, another child, another relationship the following September.

October 18   Anna's mother came to school today for a mothers' coffee for both kindergarten classes. She told me that Anna talks about me a good deal at home. "Your eyes are blue," she said, "and I know what color skirt you are wearing every day!" I was certainly far off in Anna's feelings about me! It helped my confidence to hear all the mothers talking about their children's responses to school. They particularly mentioned the maps, and that their children were picking out the continents on their globes at home. One mother said her son had shown them where Pompeii was in Europe and where Renoir was from. He was begging them to take him to the Art Institute. "The whole class has been," he insisted.

The lull after the storm of Angel's operation and Poppy's eye trouble is definitely over. This is only Wednesday and so far this week: the dogs have hookworm and must go to the vet for treatment; my car is in the garage getting repaired; Monday night I was in the barn until nine o'clock at night with the plumber trying to figure out what needs repair on the automatic watering units; the icemaker in the refrigerator is frozen shut; the electric garage door opener is broken and the repairman never came to fix it as promised. The TV repairman is coming tomorrow to fix the TV set. John is away on a business trip all week.

No wonder it was hard to get back to teaching this fall. Life was already full. The trouble is, of course, that it was full of trivia for the most part. And so I teach, and hope the trivia will take care of itself.

October 20   I have made a big mistake these last three days when I was introducing the Bank Game. It had gone so well the first day with Jack and others that I got carried away and continued to introduce stages three and four instead of stopping with one or two. As a consequence, the children haven't shown the usual enthusiasm for it, and therefore I didn't enjoy it as much either. It was a lesson to me in going slowly and not trying to rush through steps. These materials end up being little better than other kinds of learning tools if they aren't used in the step-by-step way for which they are designed. When they are used properly, they are promoting the child's development, not merely implanting knowledge in him. I can feel the difference when I get off the track like this, and it always makes me feel cross and discontented. I've cheated the children and myself.

November 1   I awakened from a very unpleasant dream this morning. I was teaching a class of children. I waited for them to choose their work, but in fact they didn't. They were still milling around an hour later. I finally admitted defeat, and called them together for a discussion time. This has never happened to me in reality. The children as a group have always chosen their work soon after they have come into the classroom. It's amazing that after all this experience, I still have these anxieties. It shows how deep the prejudices are that I have grown up with, I think. I want to believe that children can function independently, and my experience has shown me that they can. Yet I was brought up (even the phrase "brought up" is revealing) at a time when children were expected to be well-behaved and obedient, not self-confident and self-directing, particularly if they were female. Hence the dream, I suppose.

November 7   I had a low blow after class today. My room mother called to give me the conference times that she had set up with the parents for next week for me. She told me that Carmen's mother said Carmen was very unhappy at school. She felt it was because they should be playing, not working in class. It makes me feel terrible. I had made such an effort on Parent's Night to convince parents that I was available at any time to talk with them about their children or the program. Other years I have made a special point of early conferences with parents who have anxious personalities like Carmen's mother. This year I was just pressured enough at home that I didn't make that extra effort. Now it will take more time and energy to deal with, and it has shaken my confidence, too.

November 9   I was feeling upset about Carmen and wondering if I was allowing the children to work too much. I've felt this way before in other years. Then it seems we always have a day like today to cheer me. The children worked happily all morning, then at snack time I asked several children how they felt about working in school. Timmy looked up from the Continent booklet that he was doing and said with pride in his voice, "Speaking of hard work, this is hard work, too!"

I called Carmen's mother tonight to tell her what a good day Carmen had today. I am certain that she will be all right now. She was so grateful. I do feel guilty that I hadn't followed through on this situation earlier. As I look back, there were plenty of signs that I should have taken more seriously. Carmen's mother hung around the door so often this fall. She looked tense and anxious. I knew that I should have made myself more available to her, but I didn't.

November 22   All the children handled the school assembly well. Now off for vacation and a much needed and deserved break for all of us.

November 27   I was so immersed in my "other life," with all five of my daughters home for Thanksgiving, that my teaching seemed like a dream to me all during vacation. Only after I was actually in the classroom again this morning did it seem a natural part of my life. Before she went up to her own classroom, Poppy said, "I love your room, Mom. It's so peaceful in here." Was it a little hectic for her, too, to have all those big sisters come home? At any rate, it was nice to be back!

November 28   My daughter Lynn, herself a teacher, visited my class last week and remarked on the careless way the children were doing the insets. "They're to develop hand control, Mom. They're not getting a thing out of doing them that way," she said. She was right, of course, and I hadn't even noticed. Great teacher! I re-presented them to Jesse, Robbie, and Ed today. After I began my inset, I let them start theirs. I told them that if they went faster than I did, it would mean that they weren't doing their best work. More important, it would mean that they weren't helping the muscles of their hands develop. I took twenty-five minutes to finish my inset. I was amazed at the enjoyment that they obviously felt in this very slow, demanding work. Robbie said, "This is hard work." Jesse answered, "I know it is. I keep saying that!" I told Jesse that two such carefully made insets were enough for one morning, but he insisted on doing one more. "My muscles feel like doing it!" he said.

December 3   I had an unsettling dream last night. It was June, and the children were no further along in their reading than they are now. I couldn't imagine where the months had gone. There was a feeling not of panic, but of bewilderment, as if over an inexplicable happening, something fate had slipped in on me. The dream must have been brought on by a teachers' meeting yesterday in which the headmaster discussed a new teacher evaluation program that they hoped to get started for next year. It reminded me of the anxieties we teachers live with these days as a matter of course. Just last night John gave me an article from *The Atlantic* magazine entitled "Testing the Teachers: A City Gets Tough with Its Schools." I also thought of the fragility of the human self-image. The best thing about an evaluation program might be in reminding us how the children feel in our classrooms when they are evaluated by us!

December 8   I am continually grateful that I didn't have this class the first year that I was setting up this program. Certainly I would have thought that the program had something to do with the children's ability to get along with each other. Can my approach help these particular children develop harmony among themselves? It is supposed to, of course. The hypothesis is: Meet children's needs for self-fulfillment and they will spontaneously develop a generous spirit toward each other and a responsible concern for their environment. It worked for my other classes. Isn't it going to this time?

I don't know how it's going to turn out, but I do know one thing. This class is teaching me humility about the effectiveness of my teaching and the program that I am evolving. What's happened now to my self-satisfied smile last fall on the playground as I thought, "Every year I think that I have the best class that I've ever taught!"

December 20   It was a good day, with the children starting off so quietly, industriously, and confidently. I was quite impressed since it is the day vacation begins.

Now for my other life, with three daughters coming home again. I wonder if I'll need to come back to school again for a "vacation" as I did after Thanksgiving.

January 7   It was wild all right. Why were we so unaware when we had all those darling babies that they were going to grow up into great big adults with adult-sized problems? The hardest part this time was getting all that food in the house, meals on the table, garbage emptied, getting used to the logistics of running a house with so many people in it again. Having no time to myself was next, waking up each morning and running down the list of daughters, remembering what it was I wanted to do for or with each one. Now it's over. Lisa has packed up her wedding presents and our spare furniture to be vanned to her apartment in California; Lynn has finished her interviews for a teaching job here next September and has returned to Washington; Pam has gone back to finish college in Maryland; Angel has made her plans to join the School Year Abroad program in France that was interrupted by her operation this fall. Poppy and I will go back to school tomorrow. I'm relieved to go back to five-year-olds and five-year-olds' problems.

And yet . . . And yet . . . I will have a letdown after so much companionship, and this changed way of life with its own rewards. It's all in the adjustment. No sooner do I feel comfortable with the mother role again, and they are off, into their own lives and worlds. It's like a whirlwind rushing in and out, and it leaves me feeling a little buffeted. Thank heavens for Poppy and my teaching.

January 11   We have had a math consultant here visiting our classes for the last several days. We had a primary teachers' meeting with him this afternoon. He said that it was "all right" to introduce the children to hundreds and thousands since he felt that we were doing it in a "low-key way." He did say, however, that children of five couldn't understand one thousand as a quantity concept. He had watched Robbie and Anna using the Stamp Game with complete understanding today. How could he not see that it is possible? I wanted to say that I felt children in my class like Lee and others who had counted the Thousand Chain by ones, tens, and hundreds had a better concept of one thousand than I, who have never done that. I sat quietly and listened instead. He said that we should add "grubby" materials to the "beautiful Montessori materials." His examples were bottle caps and milk bottle tops. Why is it that adults think any old thing will do for children? No wonder children learn to be careless with their school environment.

Next he told us that "you people are always looking for more" and a certain manufacturer "has just come out with an excellent new kit of materials that you should look at." There it is again—the curse of our culture—"more is better." Assuming the parents were able to pay for the latest equipment that manufacturers come up with each year, where in the world would I put it? My cupboards and shelves are full now. One reason for purchasing the Montessori materials is their permanence and lasting value. I can hardly throw them away to make room for material which will need replacement in a few years because it wasn't made to last and because the manufacturers continually change their educational approach. It gets back to the philosophical concept behind the Montessori materials: They are keys to knowledge, not knowledge itself. The concept of a sphere is presented to children by a single wooden sphere. It is left to the children to discover spheres in their own environment (and they do). Children do not need many different spheres of different sizes, colors, etc., in the classroom to be able to do this. We rob children of their opportunity for independent thinking by second-guessing them every step of the way, and getting there first with knowledge they would have enjoyed discovering on their own.

Ah, well, I am digressing and using up my energy in rhetoric. It is the Timmys and the Lindas of this world that I want to spend my time thinking about, not consultants and manufacturers.

January 12   The math consultant has left me feeling a little depressed. Joan says that it is my dedication which causes me to think through situations like this so thoroughly. Maybe, or maybe it is my lack of emotional discipline and inability to keep my mind on the larger picture. Whatever the cause, the results have a negative effect on my energy level.

January 18   What an incredible winter. I feel like crying. The oil man called to say that they must deliver oil tomorrow if we are not to run out. The oil pipes he must use are buried under mounds of dumped snow by the walk. Angel and I tried to dig them out and couldn't. John called from Texas to see if we were all right. I was so frustrated and upset that I didn't respond to his concern as I should have, and felt only a little guilty about it. Next I talked to our builder, who said we had better shovel the snow off of our roof if we are to be safe from roof collapse. It was six o'clock and I went out in bad weather to get gas for the tractor. The man came to repair it today, as if it will do any good for plowing. Five different snow plows got stuck over the last four days, trying to dig us out from the last blizzard. It took a front loader to clear it finally, digging up the snow and dumping it over the banks on the side. When I got back I put on my cross-country skis to get to the barn to feed the animals, something I have had to do for days now. Tonight I'll have to get up several times to empty overflowing buckets of water filling up from roof leaks about the house. I feel old.

February 3   I've had three really tough days. I had to go out of town to help with a family crisis and have missed several days of school. I am totally exhausted, but feel I was helpful and that things are back on the track. It is amazing and frightening how much chance seems to operate in emergency situations. It is a humbling experience to realize just how fragile and vulnerable the human situation is.

February 9   Jesse was working away on one more favorite car a day for his book. Today it was a tow truck. At one point I called him back to his work because I thought he was bothering Jack, who was setting up juice. Joan then called him back to help. "Oh, I'm sorry," I said to Jesse. "Mrs. Lillard had a mistake!" Jesse confided to Jack. At line time Madan said it was

Friday for the date. I said, "No, it's Thursday." (It *was* Friday.) "You're having another mistake," Jesse said. "Oh, my," I said. In truth, I am still shaky from last week's family crisis, and I'm not quite back on even keel. I hope by Monday I will have calmed down.

February 27   There were two more family crises in the past weeks. Both involved serious operations and one was an emergency which involved near death and possible life paralysis. My presence wasn't required because neither my own children nor my own parents were involved in either situation, but they were draining experiences nonetheless. John and I got away for a long weekend for some much needed rest. When I came back this morning, I had that feeling of entering another world again. Being so involved with the class day to day, I lose the perspective of the overall scene. What struck me so totally today was the energy and eagerness of those little people, and the definiteness of their decisions in their choice of work.

March 8   We had a visitor a good part of the morning. It annoyed me because we were told that we would not be asked to have visitors this week because of conferences and Father's Day. I must be feeling the strain of reports, testing of new applicants for next year, and conferences, all in the past two weeks, and a steady stream of visitors for the last six. The other teachers say they feel "put upon," too. The weather is gray and foggy with a blanket of melting snow covering the ground. That doesn't do much for the spirits either.

March 12   Back to school for Madan's conference tonight. Then it will be smooth sailing all week with no more out-of-class duties until after vacation. Whew! This time it will be a real vacation: six days in Hawaii alone with John—a twenty-fifth anniversary trip.

April 1 I did feel so rested coming back. All the rush of reports, testing, visitors, etc., seemed like a dream. I came in yesterday for four hours to go over the room and organize some of the curriculum for spring: an introduction of Beethoven in music and Picasso in art, setting up the volcanic rock and books on volcanos that I had brought back from my trip, etc.

April 3 A great day with the children, but we tested new applicants all afternoon and I didn't get home until past five. We have thirty applicants for eighteen new places now, so the pressure of selection is a reality for the first time in years. We test again Thursday, then Charlotte (teacher of the other kindergarten class) and I meet on Monday to determine final recommendations to pass on to Bill, the head of school admissions. We had three teacher visitors today, so I spent the twenty minutes of the children's music period talking to them about our program. They were enthusiastic and interested, but it all made for a very full day. There are teacher visits planned for tomorrow and Friday as well.

April 5 I felt extremely tense as the morning began. I found myself getting the morning started instead of letting the children do it on their own. I was aware that I was doing it, and puzzled because there was no reason to feel this way. In the middle of the morning my notes say, "I feel *so* irritable!"—something I have written only several times each of the years of my note taking in class. Those were always times that I was sick, but I don't feel sick now.

I had snack with Emily. I asked her how to say milk in Spanish, then water and flower. (Emily's mother is Spanish and always speaks to her in Spanish. Emily had refused to speak Spanish in class, however, until after spring vacation.) Emily answered each with a crinkly-eyed smile. I had called her mother yesterday to report on Betty's observation and to tell her that I would ask

Emily to do five minutes of the Movable Alphabet each day. I was concerned that Emily might begin balking at coming to school again. Her mother told me that they wanted to have Emily tested and that she was leaning toward her spending another year in kindergarten. I saw Ali's teacher yesterday. He is in the *top* reading group in his class and third in his class in math! I certainly was wrong on that one! Am I wrong on Emily, too, in thinking that she should repeat kindergarten?

April 6   There was an incredible storm beginning late yesterday afternoon and lasting throughout the night. The winds got up to hurricane force of seventy miles per hour. There was ten million dollars' worth of damage, several people were killed, and a number injured. I was worried that my nervousness yesterday was old age creeping up on me. I could think of no other explanation for hovering over the children and feeling so irritable. It's a relief to know that it must have been prestorm tension. I have always been so aware of it in the children that I have never noticed it in myself before. I guess if the storm is going to be big enough, I am aware of it in myself, too.

April 9   Charlotte and I were dreading this day. We made a list of our recommendations on our thirty applicants for next year. It's horrible to have to make a judgment on a four-year-old child, yet the reality was there. The administration would need our input to help them with their final decisions. They made it easier for us by asking us to put the children in four categories: strongly recommended, recommended, acceptable, and waiting list—without regard to the number of places we suspected would be available in the classes.

I am so grateful that I have had a number of years of teaching a class of children who were not preselected by the school. It was much more meaningful to discover that the program I was developing could work with all types of children. Of course, we will still have all types of children. We accepted Andy, who socked the headmaster in the stomach when he met him, and several others who appear to have learning disabilities. However, it will not be the same as taking a chance with blind fate as we have done in the past. I will miss that.

April 16   I am proud of the children and enjoy having others see what they can accomplish, but I'm sick to death of visitors. It's been almost a nonstop production since the first of February, both prospective parents and other teachers. The children don't ever seem to notice them, but I wonder if they feel the same way at this point.

April 23   Timmy was wandering, looking at the snails, etc. I asked him if he would like to do the Polish or the Pouring. He chose Pouring. He tried hard to remember how to do it. He needs me very much right now, yet I feel irritated with him. I think that I'm upset that the year is nearly over and I'm concerned that I may not have helped him that much. I'll have to watch this reaction with some of the others, too.

April 24   I am thrilled that Linda's reading has developed so! I should have gotten these more advanced books out sooner. I didn't realize that some children were ready for them. I have been asleep at the switch.

May 3   I had a nightmare about Jack last night. I had gotten so angry that I spanked him in front of the whole class. As I was doing it, I was thinking to myself, "This won't do any good at all!" It was a clear indication to me of my frustration with him yesterday.

May 10   After class the morning's visitor asked me, "Why Mr. Bach?" I had never thought about it. Now I realize that I had fallen into the adult trap of seeing children as "cute." It sounds on the "precious" side to hear a five-year-old talking about *Mr.* Bach. It is not helping him to enter the adult world where the accepted reference would be simply "Bach." In this area I have been treating the children with the same negative approach as our culture does generally, as an entertainment, not to be taken too seriously just yet. It means that there are vestiges of negative influences and cultural hangovers in me still. Will I never be rid of them! The one thing I am absolutely determined to do is to treat children with respect.

May 24   Joan and I loaded all the children into one large van at the end of school for Anna's birthday party. We both felt the pain of separation as they drove off. It was a warning to me that the end of the year is here. It is the hardest thing that happens to us all year—forcing ourselves to let these children go. I don't want to do it, not yet.

June 5   This was the worst day. I had asked a teacher friend to visit and give me advice on my classroom and my teaching. I knew it was a poor time to see the class, but she couldn't come earlier. The children have simply stopped working. I went through many children's folders to encourage them to finish work already started. Perhaps I didn't have enough materials in the shelves to bring out for this last week. Everything is out now. There should always be something left in reserve for that child who is ready to go one step further.

June 6   I went over the notes from my meeting last Tuesday with my teacher friend whom I had invited to visit and comment on my class. She had some excellent suggestions which I am eager to try next year. In the area of social development she suggested having the children help each other a good deal more. I had done that in nonacademic areas—for example, by always asking the children to tie each other's shoes. I hadn't emphasized it in academic areas for fear of stirring their competitive feelings. My friend said, "But they should learn to accept help from each other in all areas. That is the natural way." She said, for example, that I could try showing several different Geometric Solids to different children, then ask them to teach the ones they know to each other. This could be done with maps, letters in the beginning of the year, phonograms, etc. Since the children consider themselves to be the same age (because they are in the same class), it would be important to switch the teaching role often between individual children. This is not a problem in classes where there are children of different ages. There it is natural for older children to teach the younger. She said, however, that she thought it could be done with children in the same class, and I am anxious to try.

As far as academics are concerned, she felt that I needed a good deal more material in language extension. She explained to me a way in which I could make The Farm material, for example. The Farm is an expensive Montessori material. It consists of a barn, fences, trees, pond, animals, and human figures of dollhouse proportions. It is used to teach the function of words and is presented before the Grammar Boxes. "Where is the lost cow?" (to emphasize the adjective "lost"). "It is under the tree" (to emphasize the preposition "under"). It is not hard to imagine the appeal and interest this miniature, dollhouselike material has for five-year-olds. My friend also suggested that I get the Division Board (similar to the Multiplication Board, which the children had used with such success this year) and the Finger Charts, which aid the memorization of the basic mathematical facts. She said that it wasn't at all unusual for children of this age to learn the addition facts (as Susie had done) when being exposed to this material.

June 7   Our last day. Toward the middle of the morning the children helped to put all the materials back in the cupboards. Amazingly, the whole transformation—from sophisticated learning environment, nine months in the creating, to bare room—took less than an hour and a half. Finally, we took the terrarium out in the yard to let Fred go. We sat in a circle watching his first tentative leaps to freedom. We sang grace and had cookies and juice. It was very much of a spiritual experience for me and, I sensed, for the children, too. We were late getting back into the classroom. There was a part of me that simply did not want to let the children go. The mothers had come into the room to wait. They told me that they were shocked by the stark contrast of the room today from other days. Our good-byes were hurried since we were late, and that made it easier, but several mothers mentioned how sad they had felt when they saw the room.

Another year is over. How glad I am to have my daughters coming home and a full family life to ease my sense of loss over these children. I'll be too busy to think about them very much this summer, but next fall a current of feeling will pass between us every time I see them in the halls. It will subside gradually as intimate relationships develop with my new children. That is what teaching is all about—human relationships, the gift of oneself that each gives to the other, teacher, parent, and child.

Appendix A

Classroom Schedule

8:10 to 9:35   Lee, Jesse, Ed, Sam, Susie, Karen, Emily, Anna

10:00 to 11:30   Timmy, Jack, Robbie, Edith, Sandy, Carmen, Linda, Madan

8:10 to 8:20 or 10:00 to 10:10

1. Spacing—walk in and out on line, how to sit, raise hand to speak, ask to be excused
2. Greeting—shake hands, waiting for acknowledgment, how to use hanger

8:20 to 8:30 or 10:10 to 10:20

3. Calendar
4. "Hello, hello, this is a game to tell your name," etc. (song game)
5. Explain how will call to attention. ("Excuse me, please"—statue game)

8:30 to 8:45 or 10:20 to 10:35

6. "Whose room is this?" "Yours," etc.
   Children stand by: Folder box (explain papers and name on folder)

Bathroom (explain sign—green go in,
    red in use)
Wash hands (special towels)
Talk about empty shelves and bringing
    out materials gradually
Explain not to take materials unless
    shown first
Library—explain two at a time
Tissues
Drink of water
Wastepaper baskets
Towel hamper

8:45 to 8:50 or 10:35 to 10:40

  7. Present rugs, how to roll and unroll, how to walk around
     and not disturb persons working on them.

8:50 to 9:05 or 10:40 to 11:05

  8. Toy Box—give children choice of two, explain to return
     to box when finished. Give choice of rug or table to
     work on.

9:05 to 9:10 or 11:05 to 11:10

  9. Line walking and listening games, body movement

9:15 and 11:20

  Juice, dismissal, story.
  Introduction to playground if time. Show each structure.
    Explain use of slide, pole, rope, swing. No chasing rule.

SECOND DAY

    Introduce: Room Care utensils, broom, etc.
              Button Frame
              Clay and Markers
              Carrying a chair, how to push it in, etc.

Sandpaper Letters (beginning of children's
names)

THIRD DAY
Introduce: Closing a door quietly
Walking in the hall
Standing and waiting for recognition
Chalkboard
Cutting and Pasting Exercises
Color Paddles
Sandpaper Letters (children's names)

Each successive day more and more materials are brought out
and introduced to the group as a whole, until all the Room Care
and Art materials are in the room. Time is given to reiterate any
ground rules which the children need help with. Gradually, the
choice is given between the Toy Box and a material from the
shelf during the short work time. This individual work time is
gradually extended as the children show that they are ready for
it. Eventually it fills the entire morning, and the beginning introductory time in group presentation at 8:30 is omitted. The Toy
Box is also removed when the children no longer choose from it,
but show their preference for the materials on the shelves.

Occasionally a group of children will need to go back to a
tighter schedule and more collective times during the morning
for a few days. Freedom is given only as the children demonstrate that they are ready for it.

In establishing freedom in the classroom, it is important to remember that freedom is based on choice, and choice is dependent on knowledge. The child must be prepared with knowledge
of his environment, how to function there, and what use he can
make of the materials there.

Appendix B

**Classroom Materials: Room Care,
Art, Geography, Science, Cultural,
Personal,* Sensorial**

ROOM CARE MATERIALS

The purpose of the room care materials is to continue the
process the child has already started in his home of developing
control over his environment. The child unconsciously absorbs
the life of his home and the people within it even before he himself walks. When he begins to move, it is important that he begin
to do things for himself and to contribute to the life of the home.
This activity is continued in school through the room care materials.

A second purpose of these materials is the development of coordinated controlled movement: the union of intelligence and
will with outer organs used for execution of action. Sequential, orderly action to achieve a task is established by laying out
and using the materials for each activity in left-to-right, top-to-
bottom progression. In the process of doing these activities the
child develops independence, security, pride, and responsibility
for his environment.

1. Floor Cloth
   Dust Pan and Brush
   Broom

*Language and math materials are dealt with in Appendixes C and D.

Dust Mop
Wet Mop and Bucket
2. Cleanser Tray
Mirror Polish
Wood Polish
Silver Polish
Flower Arranging
Plant Care

All of group 2 are carefully arranged in baskets or on trays, with great attention given to the details of the activity. Necessary sponges, cloths, etc., are color-coded, and all materials are beautiful and well maintained.

THE ART MATERIALS

Many people associate creativity primarily with art materials. In reality, a creation is an outward expression of interior development. There can also be interior development without an outward creation. This is often the case in human development, for the child's creation of himself is not always outwardly visible. We see only the periphery, not the creative center from which individuality emanates. Because the child uses all the materials in the environment to help him create himself, all classroom materials are associated with creativity.

Creativity is what is known and understood by the child as a new idea or a new form. A new connection to the child is not necessarily new to us; he re-creates the discoveries of others. This is why in the use of the materials in the environment, all variations are not presented to the child, but are left instead for him to discover for himself.

Because all of the materials in the environment lead to creative use and expression of self, it is not necessary to have a large number of "art materials" in the classroom. The ones that are chosen, however, represent the various senses and are open-ended in their usage.

The Clay (in a wooden bowl with a wooden cutting board to work on and with a palette knife)

The Markers (watercolor marker pens)

Color Paddles (plastic paddles of the primary colors for exploring color mix)

Painting Tray (primary colors in small plastic coasters with palette paper for mixing colors)

Collage Tray (Materials are changed every few weeks.)

Pasting Tray

Like the room care materials, the art materials are arranged with attention to detail—special sponges, trays, boards, etc. All are in good condition and carefully maintained.

As I have mentioned in the text, my children also have a period for art each week with a special art teacher and in a special art environment.

THE GEOGRAPHY MATERIALS

The geography materials are presented not in isolation but as they relate to history and science. In my classroom I use *National Geographic* magazine and books to show where events are taking place. We also relate all current events and happenings to their geographical locations.

Sandpaper Globe (Land is in sandpaper so child can feel what is land, how much of earth is water.)

Painted Globe (Land parts are painted in different colors by continent.)

Puzzle Maps: The World (Continents are painted as on globe.)

> North America
> Australia
> Asia
> Europe

United States

Canada

(In the presenting of maps, the breakdown goes from whole to parts: first the world, then the child's continent, then the other continents, and finally the child's country.)

Control Maps (outline maps of cardboard)

Labels for Control Maps

Labels for Pasting on Children's Maps

Continent Cards and State Cards

I would like to list an additional material which I have added to my class for the next year, but which was not used in the year of the diary entries presented. These are the Folder Packets for each continent. The folders are marked on the outside with the shape of a continent. They contain pictures of continents collected from magazines. They are selected around fifteen points of exploration: geographical region; climate; invasions and movements of population; languages of past and present; physical and political positions of cities; names of cities and their meanings; capitals of the world, old and new; divisions of continents into countries and countries into states or provinces; oldest roads in the world; houses; food, costumes; customs and crafts; fauna of various regions; flora of various regions; work, industry, and products. Facts can be printed on the backs of the pictures, and the pictures can be changed every so often.

THE SCIENCE MATERIALS

The purpose of the scientific materials is to develop an awareness in the child of all the forms of life that surround him. At age five he is particularly fascinated by facts. Therefore, it is important to give him exact vocabulary and specific names of plants and animals, etc. The goal is to present keys to as wide an environment as possible.

As the five-year-old turns six, he enters a developmental stage in which he is absorbed with the creation of the world and his place in it. Therefore he should be presented with a total picture of life on earth and of man's responsibility to the environment.

> Science Table (consisting of items brought in by the children or me from the environment)
> Science Baskets (baskets with *Golden Guide* booklets for looking up items from science table)
> Magnifying Glass
> Binoculars
> Microscope
> Prism
> Terrarium and Toad
> Plants
> Outdoor environment and field trips
> Presentation of the Universe: a panoramic sweep from the Big Bang to the evolution of man (created by the children through a model shelf display, described in chapter 2).

It takes many years to develop a fully representative classroom environment. Two areas in science were very much lacking in my environment: scientific experiments and language extension cards. The latter are cards with the names of animals, flower parts, etc. In preparing experiments for the classroom, the following principles are followed: attractive appearance, careful preparation, and detailed organization. The materials are child-sized, designed for independent use, and offer the possibility for further experimentation and creative discovery. The experiments are brief and specific, and isolate one fact that is perceivable through the senses. Ideally, a new Experiment Tray is prepared every two weeks.)

THE CULTURAL MATERIALS

The purpose of these materials is to awaken the child's interest in the quality of life. It is necessary to present only a sample from the artistic and religious achievements of man. I have chosen the fields of art and music, and the religions represented by the children in the class in any particular year. The key to the success of these materials is the depth of feeling which the teacher has for them. Therefore, I ask the parents of a child representing a religion different from my own to present their religion to us. Religious holidays and ceremonies provide a natural way to do this.

Art

A Print Displayed in the Library (changed as we study various artists)

Basket of Post Card Prints (also changed)

Basket of Artists' Portraits

Books of Artists' Lives and Works

Print Displays in the School Halls

School Learning Center Materials

Field Trip to Art Institute to see works of artists studied (Artists studied this particular year were Rembrandt, Renoir, and Picasso.)

Music

Records (played daily at the beginning of school and again at individual juice time)

Basket of Composer's Portraits

Books about Composers (Composers studied were Bach, Mozart, and Beethoven)

Field Trip to musician's home to see his harpsichord

Classroom Concert by a father who plays the cello.

Religion

Christian Celebrations of Christmas and Easter

Jewish Celebrations of Hanukkah and Passover
Hindu Celebration of Diwali
Islamic Celebrations of Ramadan and the 'Id
School Learning Center Materials
Books about the various religions
Display of the Bible, Torah, Koran, religious costumes and
   foods

PERSONAL MATERIALS AND EXERCISES

This is not a separate category of materials with its own section in the room. Rather these materials belong with the Room Care section because they have a similar function and purpose. (The exception is the Cutting Exercise, which is next to the art materials, and aids the development of cutting skills.)

Mirror, Brush, and Comb
Dressing Frames: Zipper Frame
                  Bow Frame
                  Button Frame
                  Snap Frame
                  Safety Pin Frame
Gift Wrapping Exercise (at Christmastime)
Food Preparation (carrots, nuts, cheese, etc.)
Pouring Exercise (practice in pouring from one small
   pitcher to another)
Measuring Exercise (pouring practice using metric containers)
Cutting Exercise (practice cutting papers along black lines
   of graded difficulty—straight, curving, etc.)
Clock Exercise (wooden clock face with manipulative
   hands and removable numbers for learning to tell
   time)
Exercises for Manners and Courtesy (done as a group)
   Opening and closing a door

Saying "Excuse me" when passing in front of others, accidentally bumping them, etc.

How to carry a chair

How to push a chair into a table quietly

Carrying a table

Waiting instead of interrupting

Shaking hands

Being a host or hostess

Hanging up someone's coat

Serving others and passing food

Clearing the table

How to cough and use tissues

These exercises are intended not to produce a "model" child with artificial behavior, but to give the child an opportunity to be part of social life. The five-year-old (and the younger child) is eager to take part in the social customs he observes about him. There is no other time in his life when he will learn these customs with such ease and lack of self-consciousness. Adults inadvertently put children in situations where they are not prepared ahead of time for accepted social behavior. Children therefore suffer social embarrassment, developing self-consciousness instead of social ease. Again, no one follows the child around correcting his social behavior. The lessons are presented and rehearsed in isolation of the actual event. The child then has a choice in his reaction to any given situation. The fact that the children universally choose to follow accepted manners in the classroom leads me to believe that children under five are in a sensitive period for developing awareness and thoughtfulness of others.

THE SENSORIAL MATERIALS

These materials were designed primarily for use by children under age five who are still at the peak stage for classifying their sensorial impressions. I do, however, find several materials useful in my classroom as extensions of the mathematical materials and as materials for the children to use in a relaxing, creative manner. It is interesting to observe how often the children turn to these materials when they are keyed up or feeling below par physically or emotionally, as if they wished to regress temporarily to a lower level of development.

Geometric Solids

Painted wooden solid geometrical forms: sphere, ovoid, ellipsoid, cube, rectangular prism, cone, triangular prism, cylinder, square-based pyramid, and a set of wooden tablets which have the same base as the rectilinear solids or the same shape as a vertical cross section of the curvilinear solids. Purpose: to establish awareness of the solid geometrical shapes in the environment and to prepare indirectly for geometry.

Constructive Triangles

Several boxes—rectangular, triangular, and hexagonal—filled with colored triangles. They enable the child to see what type of figures are made when two or more triangles are joined together in different ways. They permit a subconscious accumulation of geometrical facts through experience and repetition. Purpose: to give experience in the construction of rectangles, triangles, and hexagons and to prepare indirectly for geometry.

Binomial Cube and Trinomial Cube

Wooden cubes and rectangular prisms, painted in various colors according to the formulas $(a + b)^3$ and $(a + b + c)^3$. Red sides of cubes represent a^2, blue represents b^2, and yellow represents c^2. The colors aid the child in constructing the cubes, which he views as puzzles. Purpose: building of the cubes and introduction of algebra and proof of the formulas $(a + b)^3$ and $(a + b + c)^3$, and as a formula for finding cube root.

Metal Insets

Insets of various geometric shapes, quatrefoil, trapezoid, etc. Purpose: familiarity with geometric shapes. (Also used for older children as a material for developing hand control in preparation for writing.)

Solid Cylinders

Four blocks of wood containing ten cylinders with knobs of different dimensions, each fitting into its own hole. Purpose: visual discrimination of dimension and preparation of the fingers for holding a pencil.

Knobless Cylinders

Four boxes, each containing a set of ten cylinders with the same dimensions of the Solid Cylinders. Each box corresponds to one block and is colored red, blue, green, or yellow, depending on which block it relates to. Purpose: comparing different series of dimensions.

Appendix C

The Language Materials

The purpose of the language materials is to allow the child to explore communication. Communication is a function of organized thought. In order to write clearly, the child must think clearly. Therefore, he needs experiences which will help him develop ordered sequential thought. The structure of the classroom environment, the math materials, and the room care materials (because they involve organized activities with step-by-step procedures) help provide these experiences.

Work with the language materials in the classroom is a continuation of development the child has already started. All of the child's experiences with written language have his spoken language as their base.

Language in its spoken form tends to be debased. Therefore, it is important to impart to the child a sense of the power and mystery of language when presenting it in its written form.

The teacher who cannot buy additional materials for her classroom can make all of the language materials herself. It is even possible to make the tiny Phonetic Objects for the Phonetic Object Game in a ceramics workshop. No expensive workbooks or textbooks are used. Yearly expenses are minimal, involving only the consumables: marker pens, paper, pencils. If the language materials are well made (by laminating cards, for example) they last indefinitely with only occasional minor repairs.

PREPARATION FOR WRITING
Sandpaper Letters
Movable Alphabet
Metal Insets

When these materials are mastered, the child begins to write on his own initiative. (It is necessary, however, that the child see other children or the teacher writing in the classroom.)

PRACTICE OF WRITING
Chalkboard
Blue-Lined Paper

INTRODUCTION TO TOTAL READING
The phrase "total reading" refers to reading which incorporates comprehension of thought expressed, an understanding of style, and an awareness of the sentiment intended.

1. Keys to Decoding Words
    Phonetic Objects
    Phonetic Word Cards
    Phonogram Objects
    Phonogram Cards
    Phonogram Booklets
    Phonogram Books
    Puzzle or Sight Word Cards
2. Function of Word Exercises*
    Noun

*See reference to The Farm, page 221.

Noun Room Labeling Game
Article and Noun: Grammar Box One
Article, Noun, Adjective: Grammar Box Two
Adjective Room Labeling Game
Grammar Symbols Introduction (symbols are designed so
    that pattern and structure of grammar can be shown
    sensorially)
Verb Game
Noun and Verb Game
Sentence Analysis: Grammar Box Three
Command Game

CONTINUATION OF WRITING AND READING
Marker Paper
Story Marker Paper
Yellow Booklets

Language enrichment activities throughout the year include
daily reading of literature to the children by the teacher, the
board message, Vocabulary Cards, and the library corner. Language extension materials are used in other areas: labeling associated with maps, science and art activities, geography cards,
cultural activities, etc.

Because beginning reading books of quality are difficult to
find, I have included the following partial list of those used in my
classroom library. I suggest that it be supplemented by teacher-
made booklets on subjects covered in class such as Bach, Picasso,
and universe. Large index cards glued together for firmer support make excellent pages. Colored pictures from magazines
which match the text can be mounted on the top of each card
and the text printed below with black felt pen. These cards can
be laminated or covered with contact paper for protection, and
held together by binder rings.

Our Book Corner series. Addison Wesley Publishing Co.,
Inc., Reading, MA 10867.

Books for Young Explorers series. The National Geographic
Society, P.O. Box 2643, Washington, DC 20013.

Little Owl Books. Henry Holt & Co., Inc., 115 W. 18 St.,
New York, NY 10011.

MacDonald Starter Series. Children's Bookcenter, 140
Kensington Church Street, London W8 4BN, England.

Appendix D

The Math Materials (in Order of Number Work Progression)

To establish the numbers to ten:

Numerical Rods
Small Numerical Rods
Numerical Cards
Spindle Boxes
Cards and Counters
Memory Game of Numbers

To give a picture of the Decimal System as a whole and an impression of how the system functions and of the four basic mathematical functions:

Decimal Tray One
Decimal Tray Two
Decimal Numeral Layout
Bank Game—Addition, Multiplication, Subtraction, Division
Stamp Game
Dot Game

To introduce Teens and Tens, and develop the ability to recognize and count any number:

> Introduction with Beads 11 to 19 (Bead Stair and Tens Bars)
> Introduction with Cards
> Association of Quantities with Symbols 11 to 19 (Teen Boards and Beads)
> Tens Board with Beads 11 to 99
> Linear Counting—Hundred Chain, Thousand Chain
> Skip Counting—all Chains
>
> Memory Work to establish abstract terms:
> Addition
>> Snake Game
> Addition Strip Board
> Subtraction
>> Negative Snake Game
>> Negative or Subtraction Strip Board
> Multiplication
>> Bead Bars
>> Multiplication Board
> Division Board (not used in my class)

I did not use math materials leading to abstraction in my classroom, but I will list them here in order to show that the passage to abstraction is provided for in the Montessori materials:

> Small Bead Frame
> Wooden Hierarchical
> Short Division with Racks and Tubes
> Long Division with Racks and Tubes

A set of Montessori materials also introduces fractions. I used only the Fraction Skittles.

Work with the Decimal System, counting with the Teens and Tens, and Memory Work are all done simultaneously by the child. All of the above materials were developed by Maria Montessori.

CUISINAIRE RODS

Designed by a Belgian mathematician as manipulative learning materials in mathematics, these are sets of ten rods ranging in length from a centimeter to a decimeter and color-coded for quick recognition. Children in my class used them for addition and subtraction equations. I varnished them to add to their attractiveness, and arranged them in four small wooden trays, two sets in each tray with ten centimeter cubes for discovering the size of the other rods. I also made an outline card for each tray so that the children could determine rod quantity by matching with the card.

Appendix E

Key Introductory Montessori Math Materials

NUMERICAL RODS

Ten wooden rods, the longest being a meter and the shortest a decimeter. The rods are marked in alternating colors of blue and red for each decimeter of length. This enables the child to place his hand on each decimeter as he counts. Rods are placed in order of length in stair formation and used to form addition and subtraction equations by matching the length of the rods. (Put the ten rod down. Put the nine and one rods below it, the eight and two, etc.) Purpose: to learn the names of numbers, to

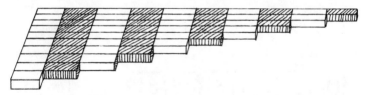

NUMERICAL RODS

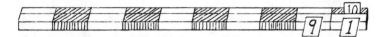

BUILDING OF TENS

understand that each number is a separate entity, to memorize the sequence of numbers one to ten, to make the association between the spoken number and a quantity.

SMALL NUMERICAL RODS
Similar to the Numerical Rods except that they are on a much smaller scale.

NUMERICAL CARDS
A set of cards with numerals 1 to 10 printed on them. After it is established that the child knows the numerals, they are used with the Numerical Rods. Purpose: to associate the written symbol and the quantity.

The pattern followed in presenting all Math materials is to establish (1) the quantity, (2) the symbol separately, and (3) the relationship between quantity and symbol. Again, the Three-Period Lesson of Seguin is used in all naming processes. (See Appendix F.)

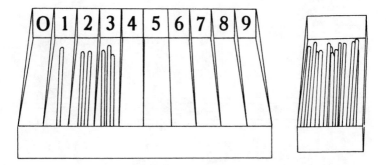

SPINDLE BOXES

SPINDLES

Two boxes divided into five compartments each. The compartments are numbered at the back with numerals 0 to 9 in sequence. There are forty-five wooden spindles and eight rubber bands or ties. The child counts the appropriate number of spindles for each compartment, then ties the spindles together to form the full quantity, and places them in the compartment. Purpose: to introduce the concept of zero as demonstrated by the first empty compartment, to clarify the concept that symbols represent not only an entity (as the rods do) but a collected quantity of separate objects, to reinforce the natural sequence of numbers and that there are no numerical symbols other than 0 to 9.

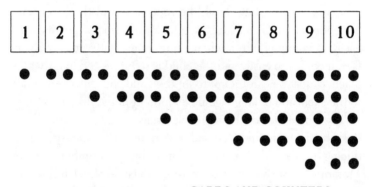

CARDS AND COUNTERS

CARDS AND COUNTERS

Number cards from 1 to 10 and fifty-five red plastic discs. The child arranges the numerals in order, then counts out the appropriate number of discs by pairs, thus establishing a visual memory of the odd and even pattern of numbers. Purpose: recognition of the figures 1 to 10 in their correct sequence, and a visual representation of odd and even numbers.

MEMORY GAME OF NUMBERS

Eleven folded slips of paper, each with a number on it from 0 to 10, all in a basket. Played with a group of children, preferably eleven. The child draws a slip, leaves the slip on the rug while going to get the number of items from the environment represented on the slip (five pencils, for example), brings the items to the rug, counts them while the others watch, then returns his slip to the basket. (The teacher checks the slip. All the children get their items at the same time, but the counting is done individually for maximum reinforcement.) Purpose: to train the memory by keeping a fixed mental image over time.

These materials complete the work done to establish the numbers to ten. They should be repeated until these concepts are understood. Usually this is not a long period, as math comes easily to young children when using manipulative materials. In fact, it comes so easily and the child is so interested in it that the teacher must be careful not to let the child concentrate on math to the exclusion of language development in the first months.

The remainder of the math materials are all used simultaneously by the child: the Decimal System material, materials introducing Teens and Tens and counting by any number, and the Memory Work, which is done to establish abstract terms (see Appendix D). I will describe here those materials which are not discussed in the chapter on mathematics.

DECIMAL TRAY ONE

A wooden tray with one unit bead on a square of green felt, one bar of ten unit beads wired together on a square of blue felt, one hundred square made of ten-bead bars wired together on a square of red felt, and one thousand cube made of ten hundred-bead squares wired together on a square of green felt. They are arranged in the order in which they would be written—thousands on the left, etc. Each category is named and counted to see that there are ten of the previous category, the exception being the units. Purpose: to familiarize the child with the names of the categories and to give him an impression of the comparative size of each through handling as well as counting.

DECIMAL TRAY TWO

A wooden tray with ten each of units, tens, and hundreds, and one thousand cube. The beads are laid out by categories vertically on a rug. Purpose: to give a visual presentation of the decimal system in quantity form.

Further work is done with bead quantities by asking the child to give the teacher six tens, six units, etc. Purpose: to give the child an impression of the difference in bulk between six units and six hundreds, for example. (More thousand cubes are used at this point. Because they are expensive and heavy to handle, wooden cubes and wooden squares are substituted for the bead cube and bead square. The wooden cubes and squares have black circles on them to approximate the beads they are representing.)

DECIMAL NUMERAL LAYOUT

Four sets of cards: one set from 1 to 9 in green symbols, one set from 10 to 90 in blue symbols, one set from 100 to 900 in red symbols, one set from 1000 to 9000 in green symbols. The one thousand, one hundred, one ten, and one unit cards are named for the child and the zeros counted in each. When the child knows these, the rest of the cards are presented. The teacher then puts each category of cards in a pile at the top of the rug. She begins by placing the unit cards down the right-hand side of the rug, from one to nine, and in an exact straight line with even spacing. Other children can then place the tens, hundreds, and thousands, but care must be taken that they are placed with exact spacing and in straight horizontal and vertical lines. (Contrary to what adults might suppose, children do not find this exact placing tedious, but seem to enjoy it. It is important, of course, in order to establish the exactness and precision required in all math work.) The teacher then asks the children to point to five tens, eight hundreds, etc. I use a small collapsible metal pointer kept on a special tray for indicating the numerals. The children enjoy using it, and it adds a special point of interest to

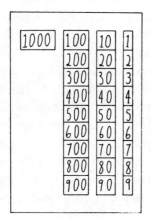

DECIMAL CARD LAYOUT

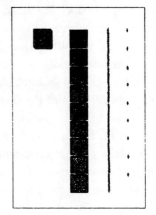

GOLDEN BEAD LAYOUT

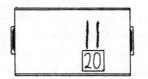

SINGLE CATEGORY: CARDS
AND BEADS ON TRAY

this work for them. Purpose: to acquaint the child with the written symbols for the new quantities he has learned, and to establish that the addition of zeros changes a category.

When the child is familiar with both quantity and symbol of the Decimal System, the two are combined. The teacher gives the child a slip asking for a certain quantity. The child then takes a tray with a small bowl and goes to get that quantity and then the numeral card that represents it. (This can be done by giving the numeral cards first, then later using separate slips.) When the child shows that he can do this successfully with all categories, the teacher combines several of them at one time. She shows the child how to slide the cards together (superimposing them) so that they form the numeral 194, for example, instead of three separate cards with the zeros showing on each. Children love this sliding "trick" and it reinforces their concept of zero as a place holder.

THE BANK GAME

Played with three or four children. The Decimal Numeral Layout is set on one rug. The "bank," consisting of thousand cubes, hundred cubes, hundred squares, ten bars, and a bowl of units, is set on another rug by categories. Each player also places a small set of numeral cards on a table. (The thousand cards in these sets only go to 3,000 in order to keep the number of thousand cubes involved to a practical quantity.) Each player also has a wooden tray with a small bowl for units. The child draws a slip with a designated number on it from a basket (six tens, etc). He goes to the bead "bank" and gets the quantities represented by the number, then goes to his numeral setup and places the appropriate numeral at the top of his tray above the categories. All three children bring their trays to the rug and put their quantities on it. A child is selected to classify each category and count the quantity. The numerals are put together with the sliding "trick" and placed below each other. The teacher says, "Let's see how many we have all together." After counting each category, the numeral is selected from the Decimal Numeral Layout on the rug for the answer. This is the introduction to addition with the Bank Game. Similar procedures are followed for subtraction (in which the quantities are placed on the rug, then removed by each child with his numeral), multiplication (in which each child chooses the same numeral and brings that quantity to the rug to count), and division (again the quantities are on the rug, this time divided evenly among the children). This use of the body in presenting the four operations is an extremely successful approach, ensuring fuller understanding and capturing interest.

BEAD STAIR

Nine bead bars, with one bead each for each quantity. Each bar is a different color for easier identification. The child forms them in a triangle shape, the one unit bead on the bottom, the nine bar on the top. The child counts the beads and learns the value of the bars. Next he combines them with the ten bars to make eleven, twelve, etc. Purpose: to distinguish each number to ten as a separate entity, by putting together the ten and the colored bead stair the child can construct the numbers eleven to nineteen and can see the respective relationship of each separate unit to the ten.

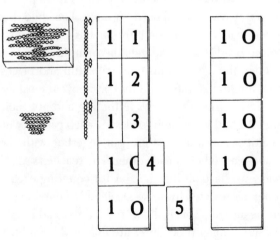

TEEN BOARDS AND BEADS

TEEN BOARDS

Two boards with nine tens in perpendicular sequence. Each space is compartmentalized and slotted so that loose wooden tablets with the numerals 1 to 9 printed on them can slide into place over the zero space of the 10. The number tablets are placed in sequence in a pile. The child then slides them in place and names the number (eleven, twelve, etc.). After the numbers are well established in the child's mind, the ten bead bars and Bead Stair are used with the Teens Board to form the proper quantity for each number. Purpose: to associate the quantity name and written symbol.

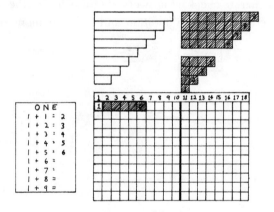

ADDITION STRIP BOARD

ADDITION STRIP BOARD

A board divided into eighteen squares across from left to right and eleven squares from top to bottom. The topmost squares are numbered from 1 to 18. There are two sets of numbered wooden strips: one set in blue with a symbol from 1 to 9 at the end of each strip, the other set in red, subdivided into squares by blue lines, with symbols from 1 to 9 at the end of each strip. There are a set of prepared papers with the addition tables to be completed, a page with 1 + 1, 1 + 2, etc., a page of twos, threes, etc.

The numbers to the left of the equation are represented by the blue strips. The child places the appropriate one from the setup he has made of the blue strips to the left of his board. The numbers on the right of the equation are represented by the red strips, which the child has set up to the right of his board. The child places the appropriate strips for an equation on the board, then looks to the top of the board to see the answer, and writes it on his paper. This material aids the memorization of the addition equations. There are many variations in its use so that the child is constantly challenged and discovers more and more about possible combinations of numbers in the process of addition. He also uses a control chart to check his answers. Purpose: to give the child all possible combinations in addition and aid their memorization.

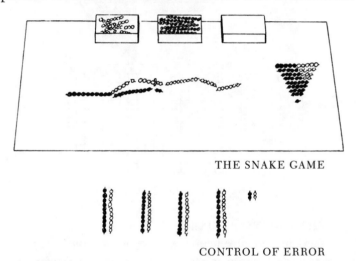

THE SNAKE GAME

CONTROL OF ERROR

THE SNAKE GAME

Ten each of colored bead bars in a box. Twenty-five golden ten-bead bars in a box. A set of the black-and-white bead stair in a black-and-white box (bead bars from one to nine, with beads up to five in black and each succeeding one in white to facilitate quick counting, e.g., "five, six" for the six bar, "five, six, seven" for the seven bar, etc.). A felt mat. A small notched card for a place holder. A box or tray to hold the bars of the colored stair that are removed from the snake after they have been counted (the black-and-white bead stair box may be used for this purpose).

The black-and-white bead stair is set up on the mat. Colored bead bars are chosen to arrange in a zigzag pattern across the mat. The "snake" should be at least a foot and a half long (choose even tens for the introduction, so pairs will be even at the end when combinations are checked, $5 + 5 = 10, 6 + 4 = 10$, etc.). Explain to the child that the colored snake is going to be re-placed with a golden snake (of ten bars). Begin to count each bead in the colored bars starting from left to right. Each time ten is reached, place the white notched card over the point, place a ten bar above the colored bar, and place the appropriate bar from the black-and-white bead stair next to it to mark where the beads that have not yet been counted begin. Remove the colored bead bars now counted and begin counting again, this time be-ginning with the beads marked by the black-and-white bead bar. Continue in this manner until the entire snake is replaced by golden ten-bead bars. When the snake is completed, take the colored bead bars back out of the box and line them up in com-binations of ten next to each bead bar. Repeat each combination: "$9 + 1 = 10, 8 + 2 = 10$," etc.

LINEAR COUNTING, THE CHAINS

A Hundred Chain of ten ten-bead bars with numeral tags for each ten, i.e., 10, 20, 30, etc., in blue, and the hundred tag in red. A Thousand Chain of a hundred ten-bead bars with numeral tags for each ten, i.e., tags like those for the Hundred Chain plus 110, 120, etc., with even hundreds in red and the thousand tag in green. One hundred-bead square (see Decimal Tray One) is placed at each hundred beads counted. For the Thousand Chain, a thousand-bead cube is placed at the end of the chain when the counting is finished.

The child folds the chain into hundred squares and compares with the bead squares. He then pulls it out over the length of a felt rug. He sorts the labels into colors in three columns (i.e., one red, one blue, one green). He counts the beads as he goes. After the chain is counted and labeled, the child walks up it repeating 10, 20, 30, etc., and then walks backward down it again repeating 100, 90, 80, etc.

These chains consolidate the child's knowledge of counting. Until now he has worked with hundreds in the decimal system, but with this exercise, he becomes familiar with the sequence of numbers with each individual bead in the long chain that makes

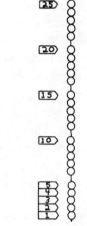

SKIP COUNTING:
TWENTY-FIVE
BEAD CHAIN

one hundred and then one thousand. It is an indirect preparation for squaring and cubing as well.

The Colored Chains are chains of the bead bars 1, 2, 3, 4, 5, 6, 7, 8, 9: They represent the squares of each number. For example, the chain of twenty-five is five five-bead bars, the chain of thirty-six is six six-bead bars, etc. There are tags for each bar, e.g., 5, 10, 15, 20, 25 for the Twenty-Five Chain, and each chain is color coded, e.g., blue for the Twenty-Five Chain, yellow for the Sixteen Chain, etc.

THE STAMP GAME

For individual exercise in the decimal system, to follow the group exercises done with the golden bead material of the Bank Game. Small colored squares of wood (i.e., "stamps"), green squares with the numeral 1 written on each to represent a unit, blue with "10" written on each to represent ten, red with "100" written on each to represent a hundred, and green again, marked "1000" to represent a thousand. There are twenty-nine skittles: one large green, nine each of red and blue, and ten green to

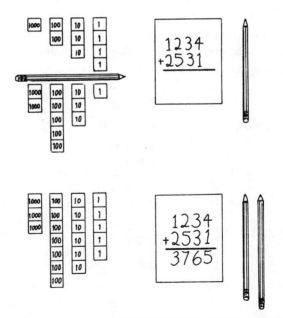

STAMP GAME: STATIC ADDITION

represent numerical categories. There are colored circles—green, red, and blue—to represent decimal system categories.

After the child has worked with the Bank Game for a number of months, the Stamp Game is introduced. The child should be working with at least addition and multiplication. Individual presentation and work are more symbolic than previous collective work with the golden bead material. The Stamp Game is used for addition, subtraction, multiplication, and division.

The child is shown the relationship between the stamps and the golden bead categories in Decimal Tray One. The teacher writes a number such as 1234 and then adds a second number such as 2534. She writes a plus sign with a purple pencil and draws a line with it under the equation. She then lines up stamps for the numbers, lining them up in columns from top to bottom. She pushes them together and counts. The answer is written with a lead pencil. Dynamic addition is introduced next. Stamps are traded for the next higher category as necessary. Continue until all four operations have been introduced. In division, stamps are piled instead of being placed in columns. Skittles are used for the sharing out of stamps.

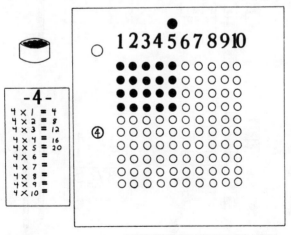

MULTIPLICATION BOARD

THE MULTIPLICATION BOARD

A perforated board with a hundred holes in ten rows of ten, numbered one through ten at the top of the board. In an indentation on the left side of the board there is a little window with a slot where a card can be inserted. There are a set of cards numbered from one to ten, a hundred red beads, multiplication-table forms in a prepared packet, and a red counter.

This material will help the child memorize the multiplication tables. Select a card and slide it into the window slot, e.g., the card marked with the numeral 4. The red counter is placed above row one, four beads are counted out for the perforated holes, and the number four is written in the answer column on the form. The counter is then placed above the second row, four beads are counted out for the holes, and the number eight is written in the answer column on the form. Continue until the tenth row is reached and forty beads have been counted. Beads are always placed and counted vertically. Counting is begun from the previous answer—e.g., after 4×4=16 is counted, the next beads counted are 17, 18, and 19, to the final answer 20 (for 4×5=20). The child eventually makes a collection of all the tables. He then goes through them to cross off duplication equations.

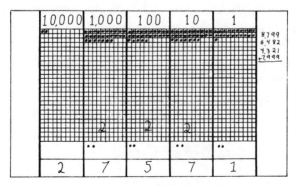

THE DOT GAME

THE DOT GAME

This material will help the child focus on the mechanisms of carrying figures. The child will add several large numbers (the numbers should be large in every category to create a sufficient amount of carrying). The Dot Game paper is made up of columns that are divided into small squares, ten squares in each horizontal row. The column heads are for units, tens, hundreds, thousands, and ten thousands (the child can be shown ten thousand cubes of the golden bead material to give him a visual representation of ten thousand). At the foot of each column there are two spaces, the upper one for carrying figures, the lower one for the result. There is a blank column on the right side where the problem to be done is written.

The teacher writes the problem in the right-hand blank column using four or five addends and eliciting some of the numbers from the child. She puts dots in columns for each of the addends, starting with units and moving from left to right within each column. One addend is done at a time—e.g., all dots for 8799 (see the illustration) are filled in, before going on to the second addend, 6482. When dots for all the numbers are filled in, start counting the units. Each time ten is reached, cross off the row and add a dot with a colored pencil to the next highest category. Also mark the number of dots carried in the upper of the two rectangles at the foot of the column. Next count the dots left in that category and write the number in the rectangle beneath the category counted. When finished, the answer is written in these bottom rectangles, and should be transferred up to the problem. After much practice, the child can put dots in for all the units in the addends before going on to all the tens, etc. After dots have been marked for all the addends, the dots are counted as before, rows of ten crossed off, dots added with a colored pencil to the next category, etc.

Appendix F

The Three-Period Lesson of Seguin

I present all materials in my classroom that involve learning new vocabulary in a three-period lesson. Developed by the pioneering French doctor E. Seguin in the nineteenth century, this approach to learning simplifies the process for both teacher and child. In the first period, the name of the object is given: "This is an ovoid." In the second period, the child is asked to find the object after it is named for him: "Can you find the ovoid?" In the third period, the child is asked to name the object pointed to: "What is this?" (as the teacher points to the ovoid). A great deal of repetition is often necessary in periods one and two before going on to period three. Usually three new objects are presented to the child in one lesson. This is enough variation to keep the child's interest without confusing him. Contrasting objects are chosen when possible. For example, in presenting new letters to the child, *l, m,* and *s* are presented, not *o, a,* and *c.*

Index

THE MONTESSORI METHOD
Maria Montessori
Maria Montessori's own classic introduction to her
groundbreaking method of education.
0-8052-0922-0

Available at your local bookstore
or call toll-free:
1-800-733-3000 (credit cards only).